DISASTERS 2.0

The Application of Social Media Systems
for Modern Emergency Management

DISASTERS 2.0

The Application of Social Media Systems
for Modern Emergency Management

ADAM CROWE

Foreword by Dennis Mileti

CRC Press
Taylor & Francis Group
Boca Raton London New York

CRC Press is an imprint of the
Taylor & Francis Group, an **informa** business

CRC Press
Taylor & Francis Group
6000 Broken Sound Parkway NW, Suite 300
Boca Raton, FL 33487-2742

International Standard Book Number: 978-1-4398-7442-4 (Hardback)

Library of Congress Cataloging-in-Publication Data

Crowe, Adam.
    Disasters 2.0 : the application of social media systems for modern emergency management / Adam Crowe.
        p. cm.
    Includes bibliographical references and index.
    ISBN 978-1-4398-7442-4 (hardcover : alk. paper) 1. Emergency management. 2. Social media. I. Title.

HV551.2.C76 2012
363.34'802856754--dc23   2012005949

Visit the Taylor & Francis Web site at
http://www.taylorandfrancis.com

and the CRC Press Web site at
http://www.crcpress.com

Contents

SECTION II SOCIAL MEDIA POLICY, PROCEDURE, INTEGRATION, AND ANALYSIS

SECTION III SOCIAL MEDIA TOOLS AND THE POWER OF VIRTUAL COMMUNITY

Foreword

Even a casual consideration of human history leads to the conclusion that the human condition changes slowly or evolves because people constantly endeavor to refine and improve their circumstances and to "get things right." But slow evolutionary change, on rare occasions, is abruptly interrupted by revolutionary or transformational changes. Historical transformational moments have occurred rapidly, created a wealth of new possibilities for the human future that simply were not possible prior to the transformational moment, and have had a permanent revolutionary impact on society. Nothing is ever the same again. Major human transformation moments are revered and typically given special names. Chapters in high school history textbooks are written about them so that they can be taught to and remembered by subsequent generations.

What have been the most significant transformational moments in human history? One early transformation moment happened in prehistory and is now referred to as the "Stone Age." It is the period of human history that occurred after someone chipped a rock and created the first hard, sharp-edged tool. Human society was permanently changed because people were then able to use those stone tools to create things that were simply not possible without them. This was not an evolutionary change that happened slowly over time; it happened in a single transformational moment. I suppose that people then spent centuries, perhaps millennia, refining those stone tools, improving on them, and trying to get them just right. That is, until the next transformational moment happened that we refer to as the "Agricultural Revolution." This transformation enabled people to live in much larger groups and to live in a single location since intense amounts of food could be grown right where people wanted to live. Urban centers and cities then appeared, and human society has never been the same. And, then of course, there was the "Industrial Revolution," characterized by the manufacture of steel that enabled skyscrapers to be built, cities like New York and Tokyo became possible, and systems and infrastructure began to evolve such as railroads and highways to distribute what industry produced. In large part, the Industrial Revolution enabled something new in human society, the rise of the middle class and a quality of life that had never before been seen on planet Earth. But this may be enough about history.

You may have thought that the book you are about to read is about social media and emergency management. It is, but I encourage readers to consider that this book is about something much broader. It is first and foremost about social media, which is destined to be soon cast as another major revolution or transformational moment in human history by those who classify history with colorful names. Social media is as transformational to the human condition as have been stones, agriculture, and industrialization. Social media is here. It came into existence quickly. And nothing will ever be the same since. The human condition has, once again, been transformed. Here are some examples why. Web 2.0 is rendering top-down news distribution obsolete (people get their news from each other and not from evening TV news broadcasts and newspapers); community participation is no longer limited by how many people can attend an evening meeting in an assembly hall to talk with each other (everyone who has a laptop or a modern telephone can participate by being there electronically); social movements no longer need time to transcend large distances via word of mouth to recruit members (distance and time no longer matter, and demonstrations and even revolutions now occur in just days and almost begin across entire nations rather than start in one place and then spread); and much more. What we once referred to when we said "top down" meant from those in authority down to the people and "bottom up" meant from the people up to those in authority, but these have quickly transformed into what we might call "bottom down," which suggests that Web 2.0 has flipped power out of the hands of those in hierarchal positions of power above the people and into the hands of everyone else. The result may well be that positions of power and authority may now be located below the people with no authority and not above them.

What might this recent human transformation mean to the field of emergency management? Emergency management has long been firmly rooted in a traditional top-down model: The Stafford Act takes a top-down approach, the Incident Command System is top down, the distribution of emergency supplies to disaster survivors is certainly a top-down activity, public warnings are distributed using a top-down model, and risk assessment is organized using a top-down approach—as is almost everything else in emergency management. Indeed, the word "management" in emergency management implies a top-down model. Herein lies the significance of this book: Readers are given the opportunity to consider the diverse field of emergency management and its practices from the transformative viewpoint of social media, from the bottom-down point of view that social media has thrust upon us. Not much in emergency management will be left untouched, and not much may ever be the same.

I recommend to readers that there are two ways this book can be read. One way is by hanging on dearly to our pretransformational, pre–social media views. As must have been the case for our human ancestors who may have viewed, for example, the emergence of agriculture while longing for a weeklong hunting and gathering expedition to hunt and gather food as they might have always done with a dozen of their closest clansmen, you could read this book from the historically appropriate top-down and/or bottom-up viewpoint. The book's author observes that some emergency managers hold this view by suspecting that social media is a fad, and that pretransformation days will soon return.

Alternatively, you could read this book with your imagination turned loose and as a journey into emergency management's and human civilization's bottom-down future. The truth is likely that none of us can yet imagine all the changes and new applications that social media will bring to our diverse emergency management field. The book you are about to read is well crafted and researched. It likely is one of the best, if not the best, compendia of social media and emergency management issues assembled to date. If only a few readers of this book are sparked to invent an innovative social media application for emergency management (to chip a stone for the first time in some new way, so to speak), this book will have accomplished its mission. As the author suggests, social media demands that we now all get involved in creating a new and optimized vision for emergency management.

Dennis S. Mileti, PhD
Professor Emeritus
University of Colorado

Acknowledgments

Although there is exponential growth in the number of social media practitioners in emergency management, the forerunners are few and far between. Their clear vision and risky behavior helped crack open a box of revolutionary communication tools to an industry renowned for slow adoption. The practitioners profiled in this book highlight a few of the true leaders in the emergency management community who openly engage in social media and web 2.0 systems to improve the overall readiness of their communities for emergencies and disasters. Additionally, special thanks must be given to Dennis Mileti, Dan Robeson, Tom Erickson, and Hal Grieb for their willingness to review this book and provide frank and honest feedback.

Author's Note

This book was written for emergency managers in any public safety or preparedness sector interested in how social media is changing the form and function of how their type of emergency management is applied. Every attempt was made to address the implementation challenges that exist from as many angles as possible. The referenced disasters and the social media systems highlighted in this book are as accurate and timely as editorial and publishing timelines allow. Please excuse any references to social media systems that are no longer utilized, have changed names, or been absorbed by other systems, as that happens frequently but does not impact the conceptual issues discussed throughout each chapter. Each chapter within this book ends with a practitioner's profile that highlights one of the leaders in the application of social media. With the exception of Chapter 9, these profiles are based on personal interviews conducted by the author between February and June of 2011.

SOCIAL MEDIA, ORGANIZATIONAL ENGAGEMENT, AND THE IMPACT OF CITIZENS

I

Why join the Navy when you can be a pirate?

—**Steve Jobs, co-founder of Apple, Inc.**

Chapter 1

Introduction to the Application of Social Media in Modern Emergency Management

---

> Hopefully at the end of the day [social media] can prove to the naysayers that these technologies can be miraculous. They can be life savers.
>
> **—Leigh Fazzina, injured Connecticut triathlon biker who was saved by Twitter[12]**

Chapter Objectives

- To comprehend the current level of the impact of social media on emergencies and disasters
- To define modern emergency management
- To consider the impact of centralized and decentralized organizations
- To understand the demographics of social media users
- To comprehend the historic development of the internet and social media

DISASTER FOCUS—STRANDED CONNECTICUT BIKER

In August 2010, Leigh Fazzina, a 36-year-old media consultant, was participating in the Farmington (Connecticut) Triathlon that ran through a 300-acre portion of Connecticut forest (Figure 1.1). After completing the first leg (swimming) of the triathlon, Ms. Fazzina took to her bike to complete the second portion. Focusing intently on her speed, she quickly realized that she was no longer riding on the marked trail for the event. She was lost and alone in the Connecticut woods. Because of this realization, she decided to increase her speed in an attempt to find her way back to the official course path; however, her bike hit a tree root, which caused her to sail over the handlebars of her bicycle. Ms. Fazzina screamed out for help but was not heard by anyone. Over the next ten minutes, no other bikes ventured near the area of the forest where she had accidentally ridden. She attempted to call her cousin on her cell phone, who she knew was at home, but had difficulty maintaining a voice phone signal long enough to speak with the cousin or to leave a message. Although she was unable to maintain a voice phone call, she ascertained that a simple message through social media would work. Consequently, she utilized a Twitter application on her smartphone to post a message to her more than 1,000 Twitter followers that said: "I've had a serious injury and NEED Help! Can someone please call Winding Trails in Farmington, CT tell them I'm stuck bike crash in woods." Within minutes her Twitter followers from all over the world—including Pennsylvania, New Jersey, Washington, Chicago, Canada, Italy, and Oman—responded to contact the Farmington Fire Department and police service on her behalf. Emergency crews quickly found Ms. Fazzina and took her to a local hospital where she fully recovered. According to the Cellular Telecommunications and Internet Association (CTIA), it is not that uncommon for hikers and bicyclists to get stranded and be unable to make calls, but they are able to use Twitter to notify someone of their location.[13] Unfortunately, some people—including those within the traditional media—criticized Ms. Fazzina for utilizing social media during a crisis. On the other hand, others stressed that she utilized a tool that was available to her that was more robust than the primary and trusted sources.

Modern Emergency Management

As the title suggests, this book is intended to present the application of social media in the context of modern emergency management principles and practices. Although the title is simple and straightforward, the complexity is great. To begin, emergency management in the strictest sense includes activities that incorporate preparedness, response, recovery, and mitigation—the four phases of emergency

Figure 1.1 Bicycle racing as part of triathlon. (From U.S. Air Force Airman Nathan Doza.)

management. These activities can be performed by various first-responder disciplines, including law enforcement, public safety, homeland security, fire, emergency medical service, public works, public health, and hospitals. Additional emergency management activities are also performed by researchers and practitioners within academia as well as business continuity professionals.

The concept of emergency management was clarified in 2007 by a collection of professional emergency managers who established a set of eight core principles. These professionals were led by Wayne Blanchard of the Federal Emergency Management Agency's (FEMA) Emergency Management Higher Education Project and included professionals from throughout the United States at all levels of government. The project was driven by a lack of continuity in emergency management research to find a clear and concise definition of the profession.[1]

Additionally these principles are applicable to emergency managers who serve a diverse spectrum of communities, including those defined by population, demographics, ethnicity, functional needs, socioeconomic levels, business types, and organizational missions. Or put another way, emergency managers are present in all communities regardless of urban, suburban, or rural environments and for all communities regardless of languages, income, or activities conducted in that community. Each of these parameters is paramount in understanding the potential impacts of hazards that may affect a given community as well as the best mechanisms to conduct preparedness, response, mitigation, and recovery activities.

Emergency management is conducted at local, state, and federal levels of government as well as some regional areas and for many businesses as they identify ways to ensure the continuity of their operations and economic stability. These levels often have slightly modified functions and/or priorities, but at the most fundamental level the emergency management concepts are the same. For example,

EIGHT CORE PRINCIPLES OF EMERGENCY MANAGEMENT

1. Comprehensive—Emergency managers consider and take into account all hazards, all phases, all stakeholders, and all impacts relevant to disasters.
2. Progressive—Emergency managers anticipate future disasters and take preventive and preparatory measures to build disaster-resistant and disaster-resilient communities.
3. Risk-Driven—Emergency managers use sound risk management principles (hazard identification, risk analysis, and impact analysis) in assigning priorities and resources.
4. Integrated—Emergency managers ensure unity of effort among all levels of government and all elements of a community.
5. Collaborative—Emergency managers create and sustain broad and sincere relationships among individuals and organizations to encourage trust, advocate a team atmosphere, build consensus, and facilitate communication.
6. Coordinated—Emergency managers synchronize the activities of all relevant stakeholders to achieve a common purpose.
7. Flexible—Emergency managers use creative and innovative approaches in solving disaster challenges.
8. Professional—Emergency managers value a science- and knowledge-based approach centered on education, training, experience, ethical practice, public stewardship, and continuous improvement.[1]

the U.S. Department of Homeland Security (DHS) has modified this perspective of emergency management slightly by adding protection to the four phases of emergency management, strengthening its mission. This concept includes DHS functions such as counterterrorism, border protection, immigration, and cybersecurity. Although not fully included in the model established through the eight principles of emergency management, these functions are considered to be critical to the future of modern emergency management and therefore are important to consider when evaluating how social media can be utilized to meet the spectrum of needs.

As a result of Homeland Security Presidential Directive 5 (HSPD-5) established by President George W. Bush in 2003, a national model of emergency management and response was mandated. This model ultimately became the National Incident Management System (NIMS), which incorporated the longstanding best practices established through the Incident Command System with broader concepts including preparedness, resource management, and specific management structures. It helped establish basic principles for emergency management and response activities, including span of control, unity of command, flexibility, resource typing, and technological integration. Training and compliance to this system quickly became mandatory for emergency managers across the spectrum as part of compliance to federal funding and support requirements.

In addition to the principles established above and the systems and protocols required through national models, modern emergency managers must also bring multifaceted knowledge, skills, and abilities to the profession. Specifically, they must understand these principles in the context of their operational settings. These settings or specified job functions may include redundancy, interoperable communications, technological application, planning, operational accountability, cost-effectiveness, continuity of operations, media management, and crisis communications. This inherent necessity to be an emergency management generalist drives the field and defines how the modern emergency manager approaches new challenges such as the implementation of social media into operational, planning, communication, and public information challenges.

For instance, the management and support of public information is one of the most critical facets of emergency management in the twenty-first century. Having the ability to monitor what traditional media is saying and having the ability to analyze its impact on local citizens is invaluable. This real-time situational analysis is critical to mold operational decisions regarding the given emergency or disaster and to handle the information that is to be disseminated to the general public. Until recently, this process was performed utilizing standard monitoring tools and processes, including watching televisions, monitoring print and web publications, releasing media advisories, and conducting press conferences. However, these processes were both time consuming and resource intensive and have been significantly undermined by the rise of social media.

The Rise of Social Media

In March 1989, British engineer and computer scientist Sir Tim Berners-Lee proposed a new system called the World Wide Web that was intended to link the numerous computers throughout the world. His new system created a device to better utilize the network of computers known as the internet, which had been created during the 1960s when both private and U.S. military researchers created robust and distributed computer networks.[2] This technology interface quickly became the foundation for drastic changes to the modern communications framework and ultimately the rise of the internet and social media.

Traditionally, scholars and historians have identified that the exponential growth of the internet and the beginnings of the virtual age were linked to the invention of the Mosaic web browser in 1993. This browser was quickly followed up by the Netscape browser and eventually Microsoft Internet Explorer. This quickly contributed to the exponential growth of the internet and the "dot com" boom that marked the rise of technology businesses utilizing the tools and the nearly ubiquitous acceptance of the capability of the internet. This browser-based internet access was designed and continues to primarily be utilized to push information to the general public. Since the initial rise of Netscape and Microsoft Internet Explorer, many browsers have been developed that are available for free. These additional browsers include Google Chrome, Mozilla Firefox, Apple Safari, and Opera.

Emergency managers have traditionally utilized access to the internet to provide static public information regarding current policies, educational components, warnings, and other risk information.[3] Emergency management website content is often written in technical terminology and jargon that is difficult for an average public citizen to read, interpret, and/or understand, which ultimately leads to an erosion of effectiveness of an emergency management website. Unfortunately, many emergency management offices are staffed by a limited number of paid and unpaid workers who are not always well qualified to present public information and education in forms and formats suitable for all audiences—particularly in light of the growing need to address issues related to special, functional, and accessible needs.

The field of emergency management faces additional challenges related to the timeliness and relevancy of the content of its websites. Information related to emergency management is often time sensitive, subject to constant change, and critical to the preparedness of communities to respond to emergencies and disasters. Unfortunately, as social media and non-browser-based access to the internet (e.g., mobile phone devices) has grown in popularity and relevance, this dependency on websites has created a significant challenge to the ability of emergency managers to disseminate and distribute time-sensitive, relevant data. For instance, when it was announced by President Barack Obama that Osama Bin Laden was killed on May 2, 2011, there were more than 5,000 Twitter posts per second![16] (See Figure 1.2.) Clearly, this level of information exchange would be impossible to maintain or engage in for nearly all emergency management offices.

Figure 1.2 President Obama prepares speech to announce Bin Laden's death. (From Pete Souza, Executive Office of the President of the United States.)

FUNDAMENTAL RULES OF SOCIAL MEDIA

1. Facilitate conversation
2. Transparent intentions
3. Cost effective
4. Nearly instantaneous

This type of internet access is contrasted to the rise of social media and Web 2.0 technologies that have arisen over the past decade. Social media and Web 2.0 technologies are both umbrella terms to cover the creation of online systems that allow that facilitation of nearly instantaneous communications through shared networks and technological systems. One source estimated that nearly 4,000 different social media systems currently exist, with some of those networks containing thousands of additional subnetworks.[4] Some of the most common social media systems include Facebook, Twitter, and YouTube; however, many more are available to emergency managers and some of those are discussed throughout this book.

Although the above consideration may seem complex for something as prevalent and pervasive as social media, defining social media and Web 2.0 technologies can be difficult due to the wide spectrum of available systems and constant developments within this arena. However, regardless of the type of system under discussion or its pervasive use, there are some fundamental concepts related to nearly all social media and Web 2.0 technologies. These concepts help frame the conceptual approach to how citizens and responders can engage in social media systems. These basic rules are that social media must instantaneously facilitate transparent conversations at no cost (or nearly free).

Traditional media, including conventional emergency management websites, push information to citizens to be received and processed but do not allow for feedback (i.e., conversation). Social media inherently allows for a push and pull of information from citizens. Or perhaps more importantly, survivors, responders, and community partners can give and receive information during emergency preparedness and response and recovery. It is this defining quality of social media that makes it an invaluable tool that may be viewed through the prism of history as a mass communication development on par with the inventions of the printing press, radio, and television.

If social media is the structured system, Web 2.0 technologies are often the tools to implement these concepts. Web 2.0 technologies are often so intertwined with social media systems that they are difficult to distinguish other than in their comparison to traditional internet websites and technology systems. These Web 2.0 systems provide interaction and capabilities based on the foundation of conversation and not on directed information. Sharing and collaboration become the formats of persuasion, communication, and emergency notification rather than the statements and directives that typically mark most emergency management and emergency public information activities. As these technologies have continued to develop, there has been some discussion about referring to technologies as "3.0" or "4.0"; however, this is unnecessary considering the terminology is strictly referring to how these technologies and media systems compare to traditional outreach strategies. The term "3.0" is slowly beginning to be utilized to describe the capability of social media and Web 2.0 systems to predict the actions and interests of the users; however, this capability and the supporting technologies are so poorly defined and developed that they will be avoided in this book.

Social Media Users

Understanding who utilizes social media and Web 2.0 technologies is critical in reviewing the application of these systems for modern emergency management. According to a 2010 Pew Internet and American Life Project survey, 79% of Americans use the internet.[6] Of those surveyed, the demographics were broken down by race, income, age, and education. For instance, approximately the same number of white and Hispanic respondents utilized the internet, while there was a small decrease for African American users. For age, there was an inverse relationship between age and usage. Specifically, the younger the respondent, the more likely he or she was to actively use the internet; those respondents between the ages of 18 and 29 were at 95% utilization.[6] The reverse was true for income. In particular, internet use went up incrementally as income went up.

Although a good basis toward understanding citizens and stakeholders of emergency management, it is critical to consider what types of individuals are utilizing social media. According to a separate Pew Internet study in May 2010, 38% of those surveyed used social networking sites such as Facebook.[7] Interestingly, unlike the generic internet usage, the generational cohort from age 50 to 64 is the fastest growing demographic for social media utilization.[8] Clearly, the perception that social media and Web 2.0 technologies are limited to young digital natives is wrong. To counteract this misperception, emergency managers should consider it in the same vein as other disaster mythologies, especially to ensure that the utilization of social media during emergency preparedness, response, and recovery activities is not stymied.

Major social media systems such as Facebook and Twitter have over 600 million[9] and 200 million[10] users, respectively. Of those users, there are approximately 150 million Facebook users in the United States and, although the breakdown for Twitter users is not readily available, it is safe to assume this figure is approximately the same percentage as Facebook. The number of accounts is not as important as the amount of activity on these systems, however. For example, 50% of Facebook users log on at least once per day and an average user generates 90 pieces of posted information per month.[9] Twitter also generates thousands of tweets per second for major events like the Super Bowl, Women's World Cup, and the aforementioned announcement of Bin Laden's death. These system utilizations as well as the various other social media and Web 2.0 systems are further discussed in Chapter 2.

Centralized versus Decentralized Organizational Structure

Several years ago Ori Brafman and Rod A. Beckstrom released a book called *The Starfish and the Spider: The Unstoppable Power of Leaderless Organizations* that established eight principles about how organizational structure is impacted by the engagement of social media and Web 2.0 technologies. The title itself is intended to create two paradigms of organizational structure—the starfish and the spider. The spider model described centralized organizations as controlled by hierarchal management with an ultimate head of the organization. Governmental operations and most major businesses—especially emergency management—are clearly defined by this spider model. Conversely, the starfish model described decentralized organizations that were structured around models of mutual independence but a shared and common cause or purpose (e.g., Alcoholics Anonymous). In the case of a spider (and thus the spider model), if the head is cut off or removed, the organization is significantly impacted if not permanently damaged. On the other hand, in the case of a starfish (and thus the starfish model), if an arm is removed or damaged, the entity divides and creates multiple new versions that are identical to the original.

Consequently, for governmental or organizational emergency managers to adopt social media, they must consider significant systematic changes in how their organization is structured and supported. For instance, the third principle established by Brafman and Beckstrom is that decentralized systems do not have centralized intelligence because it is spread throughout the shared system.[5] This is inherent in social media due to the nature of the transparent and conversational tone that is the foundation of these systems. At any one time, the collective knowledge of all followers of a given system (e.g., Facebook or Twitter) will have superior knowledge and situational awareness to any one person (such as a professional emergency manager). That is why it is critical for emergency managers to continue to find and adopt social media and Web 2.0 concepts fully within all phases of emergency management but particularly with regard to disaster response.[5]

Another "starfish and spider" principle that has direct application to modern emergency management is the concept that people involved in decentralized systems automatically want to contribute to the shared networks and/or communities in which they are engaged. All social media systems (Facebook, Twitter, YouTube, etc.) are built on shared and accepted networks of like-minded individuals. This like-mindedness can be multifaceted in nature or fringe in its application, but the individual members nonetheless are engaged and possess a virtual citizenry within that community. For emergency management, this involvement in virtual community is critical to ensure effective mitigation, preparedness, response, and recovery.

For instance, local schools engaged in social networking may learn of best practices for safe rooms to reduce the risk of severe weather in a given community and/or to better prepare for the next disaster. Likewise, during an actual emergency or disaster, the ability to call on local citizens or stakeholders to volunteer and/or donate needed goods is critical to streamline those response and recovery components. These concepts of collecting ideas from a broad community and the utilization of social media to improve donations management and volunteerism are further discussed in Chapters 9 and 11, respectively.

The final and perhaps most effective "starfish and spider" principle that can be applied to the application of social media in modern emergency management is that centralized organizations tend to become even more centralized when challenged by systems or circumstances that are not initially controllable within standard hierarchal systems.[5] Many emergency managers across all disciplines have questioned the need and applicability of social media and Web 2.0 technology.[11] In many cases, these organizations have challenged the implementation of new systems for a variety of reasons, including policy realization, resource allocations, personnel availability, and purposefulness for organizational emergency management implementation. Often these objections are presented definitively without the option to consider or incrementally implement social media in the future. It is this type of centralization that is potentially very harmful to the emergency management field.

The challenge for emergency managers is that there is currently no industry norm for the consideration and adaptation of social media. Additionally, systems like the National Incident Management System (NIMS) and the Incident Command System (ICS) create inconsistencies in how, when, and where social media should be used for emergency preparedness, response, and recovery due to their centralized structure. Although NIMS and ICS stress the importance of flexibility and adaptation to new technological systems, they are still built around the framework of a review and approval hierarchy that runs contrary to the transparent and conversational tone necessary during the utilization of social media. The challenge of utilizing social media during emergency management activities that include emergency preparedness and response coordinated through NIMS and ICS is further discussed in Chapter 10. (See Figure 1.3.)

Additionally, there are no standards for policy implementation for social media utilization by local governments, much less enough practitioners in the various emergency management disciplines to provide clear and consistent guidance. As discussed in Chapter 2 to a greater extent, social media systems are a combination of owner-controlled and user-controlled content. This balance is part of the equation that ensures transparent dialogue but also creates the potential for many challenges, including time-sensitive monitoring, censorship of public opinion, and a perception of implied endorsement. Without industry-wide standards, these issues may create the appearance that the use of social media by emergency management has more potential risk than reward. Unfortunately, this interpretation—even with the limited policy guidance currently available—is short-sighted considering that

Figure 1.3 Command personnel in Emergency Operations Center (EOC). (From FEMA, Brian Glaviano.)

citizens and stakeholders alike share the same tools as local emergency managers. Consequently, conversations about mitigation, preparedness, response, and recovery activities are occurring with or without emergency management engagement in the various social media systems. These issues about policy implementation challenges are further discussed in Chapter 4.

Systems Fade, Concepts Remain

Emergency management practitioners must be careful to embrace the concepts and philosophy first and foremost rather than any particular system that currently exists. With its more than 800 million worldwide users, Facebook is currently the top social media outlet both globally and within the United States. For instance, Facebook constitutes more than 25% of all U.S. internet page views and 10% of all global internet page views.[14] This level of utilization surpasses all other internet sites, including search engines like Google. Unfortunately for Facebook, technology systems tend to eventually fail and be replaced by something else.

For example, by 1998, Microsoft had grown into the industry leader for personal computers, software, browsers, and many of components utilized by an average user. They became so powerful that an antitrust lawsuit was brought against Microsoft by the U.S. Department of Justice (DOJ) on behalf of 20 states pursuant to the Sherman Antitrust Act that forbids the monopolization of industry. Although the case ultimately was settled between the DOJ and Microsoft outside of the courtroom, it represents the apex of Microsoft's status as the "king of the hill." Since that time, other companies have made significant jumps in the utilization and acceptance of their software and systems. For instance, there are alternative office productive products like Google Documents and Open Office as well as secondary browsers like those already mentioned.

Likewise, by 2000 AOL and Time Warner merged, resulting in a near monopoly in the provision of internet services to local providers, and by 2007 Google had risen to the top utilization of websites used for internet searching. In both cases, the singular power and influence wielded at these pinnacles has passed and the competition and availability of alternative sources quickly rose. Consequently, it is not unreasonable to think that Facebook, Twitter, YouTube, or any number of other growing social media and Web 2.0 technology systems may falter or eventually fail no matter how powerful and influential they become.

On the other hand, it is not safe or appropriate for emergency managers to expect the demise of social media before they engage these systems. Unfortunately, there are groups of emergency management practitioners who have yet to institute the use of social media for any emergency management purpose and who hope that systems like Facebook and Twitter are merely fads. Clearly this is a faulty premise. With millions of users, integration with traditional media outlets, and nearly complete pervasiveness throughout modern society, it is clear that social media and Web 2.0 concepts are not a fad. In fact, they are relevant and practical for nearly all governmental or business entities seeking feedback and acknowledgment from stakeholders and/or customers. Consequently, it is critical for emergency management practitioners to apply these concepts and philosophies given whatever systems exist at a given time that best optimize the mission and vision of modern emergency management.

Overview of Chapters

The design of this book is to divide the application of social media for modern emergency management and response into three major sections—(1) Social Media, Organizational Engagement, and the Impact of Citizens; (2) Social Media Policy, Procedure, Integration, and Analysis; and (3) Social Media Tools and the Power of Virtual Community. These sections are broken down into a total of fourteen chapters, including this one. They include major topics such as citizen journalism, policy implementation, aggregation and validation of social media information, and crowdsourcing, as well as current and future tools that may be utilized by emergency managers.

Each chapter presents a specific topic that addresses one of the many challenges to successful implementation of social media within emergency management. The structure of each chapter includes a mixture of real events, practitioner profiles, key concepts, and a broad discussion of these issues. The intention of this structure is multifaceted. Emergency management, regardless of the specific discipline or focus, must first accept that the utilization of social media during emergencies and disasters is real and timely. Because social media is extremely common among the general public, common practices must be discussed to ensure the implementation and adaption is done efficiently and effectively with little risk to the organizations involved. Lastly, emergency managers must look to the future and consider how these tools may be applied as well as ways to utilize these tools in support and augmentation of current tools and systems utilized for emergency preparedness, response, and recovery.

Practitioner Profile: Jeannette Sutton, PhD, Disaster Sociologist

Jeannette Sutton is a leading disaster sociologist who specializes in research on the uses of social media during emergencies and disasters (Figure 1.4). Her research is helping transform the way that emergency managers understand public communication during disasters and engage their citizens and stakeholders in times of crisis. When asked to define social media and Web 2.0, Dr. Sutton stated that "Web 1.0 was the read web [and] Web 2.0 was the read-write web [while] social media is about sharing and dynamic interaction in a networked format." Moreover, when initially asked about how well emergency managers understand the impact of social media, Dr. Sutton stated that "There is a misunderstanding of the power and functionality of social media…[because] many emergency managers…are complete skeptics until they see supportive research about the uses of social media." Interestingly, Dr.

Figure 1.4 Dr. Jeanette Sutton.

Sutton's first observations of social media being used during a disaster were during the 2004 East Asia tsunami, while the first use of social media by emergency managers was the Los Angeles Fire Department's (LAFD) use of Twitter in 2006 in response to Hurricane Katrina.[15] According to Dr. Sutton, "In the wake of the 2004 East Asia tsunami…people posted pictures of missing loved ones on Flickr and the Sahana Foundation rolled out its missing persons finder (similar to what Google does now)." She went on to explain that this shift from paper-based photos to web-posted photos was a "sea change" and was vastly different from the manually posted pictures around the City of New York after the September 11 tragedies just three years earlier. In closing, when Dr. Sutton was asked if social media implementation would continue to be a challenge to emergency management, she stated, "Emergency management professionals are concerned about trustworthy information, validity, and availability of personnel and resources for social media response efforts in a disaster." Clearly, Dr. Sutton's research in many ways has initiated the conversation about how social media is and will continue to be implemented in disaster response.

Chapter Terms

Modern emergency management: Multidisciplinary approach to emergency management that is comprehensive, progressive, risk-driven, integrated, collaborative, coordinated, flexible, and professional.

National Incident Management System (NIMS): Emergency management model that incorporates long-standing, best practices established through the Incident Command System (ICS).

Social media: Type of utilization of internet access, communication systems, and social networks that instantaneously facilitates conversation through transparent intentions and is cost effective for use and application.

Web 2.0 technologies: Internet-based or mobile utilization of social media systems to provide communication and operational tools that reinforce and support the connections between people and organizations often robustly and for free.

Chapter Questions

General Questions

1. True/False: A decentralized organization is more likely than a centralized agency to adopt social media for use.
2. True/False: Demographics indicate that social media is a fad for diverse populations and older citizens.

3. Which of the following is not a fundamental concept of social media?
   a. Facilitates conversation
   b. Cost effective
   c. Short messaging
   d. Nearly instantaneous

Essay Questions

1. Describe the differences between centralized and decentralized organizations when considering the application of social media in emergency management.
2. Explain why emergency managers must consider social media concepts rather than the particular systems that currently exist.
3. Explain why social media and Web 2.0 technologies must be embraced by modern emergency managers.

Works Cited

1. "Principles of Emergency Management Supplement." *International Association of Emergency Managers* (IAEM), September 11, 2007. http://www.iaem.com/publications/documents/PrinciplesofEmergencyManagement.pdf (accessed December 30, 2010).
2. Ward, Mark. (2009) "Celebrating 40 Years of the Internet." BBC News. http://news.bbc.co.uk/2/hi/technology/8331253.stm (accessed October 27, 2011).
3. Crowe, Adam. "Emergency Management Websites." *Crisis Response Journal* 4, no. 4 (accessed December 30, 2010).
4. "How Many Social Networks Are There?" *TM.biz*, August 5, 2010, http://networks.tm.biz/business/how-many-social-networks-are-there/ (accessed December 30, 2010).
5. Brafman, Ori, and Rod A. Beckstrom. *The Starfish and the Spider: The Unstoppable Power of Leaderless Organizations*. New York: Penguin, 2006.
6. "Who's Online?" *Pew Internet and American Life Project*, May 2010. http://www.pewinternet.org/Static-Pages/Trend-Data/Whos-Online.aspx (accessed December 31, 2010).
7. "Trend Data." *Pew Internet and American Life Project*, May 2010. http://www.pewinternet.org/Trend-Data/Online-Activities-Daily.aspx (accessed December 30, 2010).
8. "Senior Surge on Social Media." *USA Today Online*, December 15, 2010. http://www.usatoday.com/yourlife/parenting-family/2010–12–15-graytech15_ST_N.htm (accessed January 3, 2011).
9. "Facebook Statistics." *Facebook*. http://www.facebook.com/press/info.php?statistics (accessed January 3, 2011).
10. Schonfeld, Erick. *TechCrunch*, June 8, 2010. http://techcrunch.com/2010/06/08/twitter-190-million-users/June 2010 (accessed January 3, 2011).
11. Baron, Gerald. "Social Media May Be the Biggest Change in Emergency Response since the Radio." *Emergency Management Magazine Blog*, December 20, 2010. http://www.emergencymgmt.com/emergency-blogs/crisis-comm/Social-Media-may-be-122010.html (accessed January 3, 2011).

12. Scott, Tess. "Injured Biker Saved by Her Twitter Followers." *ABC News*, August 5, 2010. http://blogs.abcnews.com/theworldnewser/2010/08/injured-biker-saved-by-her-twitter-followers.html (accessed January 3, 2011).

13. Toor, Amar. "Unable to Call, Stranded Biker Uses Twitter to Call for Ambulance." *USA Today Online*, August 3, 2010. http://www.switched.com/2010/08/03/unable-to-walk-or-get-phone-signal-stranded-biker-uses-twitter/ (accessed January 3, 2011).

14. O'Dell, Jolie. "Facebook Accounts for 25% of All U.S. Pageviews." *Mashable*, November 19, 2010. http://mashable.com/2010/11/19/facebook-traffic-stats/ (accessed January 5, 2011).

15. Havenstein, Heather. "LA Fire Department All 'aTwitter' over Web 2.0." *PC World*, August 3, 2007. http://www.pcworld.com/article/135518/la_fire_department_all_atwitter_over_web_20.html (accessed January 5, 2011).

16. Parr, Ben. "Bin Laden's Death Sparks Record 12.4 Million Tweets per Hour." *Mashable*, May 2, 2011. http://mashable.com/2011/05/02/bin-laden-death-twitter/ (accessed January 5, 2011).

Chapter 2

Social Media Systems: Overview and Purpose

> At its foundation, social media is a set of technologies and channels targeted at forming and enabling a potentially massive community of participants to productively collaborate.
>
> **—Anthony J. Bradley,** *Gartner Blog*[1]

Chapter Objectives

- To understand the basic foundations of social media and Web 2.0 applications
- To identify the basic characteristics of social networks, microblogs, and blogs
- To identify the utilization of photo- and video-sharing sites
- To understand the application of tags, keywords, and other categorical devices
- To review the emergency management systematic applications of social media

Foundations of Social Media

As described in Chapter 1, social media and Web 2.0 technologies are based on a wide-ranging spectrum of historic events, processes, concepts, and theories of utilization. Perhaps the most significant of these was the development of the World Wide Web in 1991. This established a common process for individual citizens and

DISASTER FOCUS: H1N1 PANDEMIC INFLUENZA

By mid-March 2009 the Mexican government first reported influenza-like illnesses impacting the local population. By mid-April 2009, more than 850 cases of pneumonia and nearly 60 pneumonia-related deaths had occurred in Mexico City alone. Unfortunately, these cases were not limited to Mexico City and were quickly spreading throughout the country. They were quickly reported as influenza, but the particular strain was not identified until a few days later when the United States also reported similar cases. This H1N1 "swine flu" quickly spread through the United States. Initially there were two deaths in the United States—a Mexican toddler who was visiting relatives in Texas and a 33-year-old American woman in Texas. In both cases there were underlying health conditions that contributed to their deaths. By late April, the U.S. Food and Drug Administration issued emergency use authorization for the Strategic National Stockpile (SNS). Tamiflu (oseltamivir) and Relenza (zanamivir) were prepared from the SNS inventory for distribution and use in response to the growing number of cases. Days after this authorization, school districts in central and north Texas as well as other parts of the United States closed all schools and sporting events in response to H1N1 influenza cases appearing in their student populations. Over the next six weeks, the H1N1 outbreak continued to spread through countries in both the Northern and Southern Hemispheres and was ultimately declared a pandemic by the World Health Organization on June 11, 2009.[2] Because this event was multijurisdictional and required the response of multiple disciplines to ensure response was consistent and effective, many hospitals, health departments, and other peripheral health-support agencies turned to the utilization of social media to proliferate messages about preparedness and response related to H1N1. Most prevalent of these was the U.S. Centers for Disease Control and Prevention's (CDC) use of Twitter, YouTube, Widgets, RSS feeds, and internet-based maps to provide real-time response information, generating both situational awareness and specific protective action recommendations to the general public (Figure 2.1). For instance, between March 2009 and July 2009, the CDC's Twitter page jumped from approximately 1,000 followers to over 500,000 followers.[3] Clearly the utilization of a range of social media and Web 2.0 technologies during this global emergency helped meet the need and desire for information from the general public.

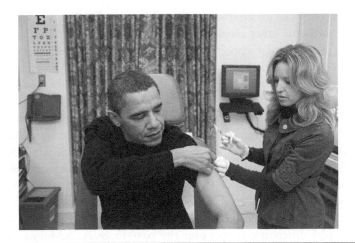

Figure 2.1 Obama receives H1N1 vaccination. (Official White House photo, Pete Souza.)

users of connected networks to communicate and share information. By the beginning of the next decade, websites were being established that began to consider the possibility of feedback and two-way communications with users throughout shared networks. These systems have since spawned all of the social media and Web 2.0 technologies that local emergency managers must consider for adaptation. This represents the functionalities that are further discussed throughout this book, including crowdsourcing, citizen control, applicable tools, and much more.

Every type of social media and Web 2.0 technology is based on the principles established in Chapter 1. These systems—especially when utilized by emergency managers—must encourage conversation, be transparent, and ultimately be cost effective. These three rules will be evident as social networks, blogs, microblogs, photo- and video-sharing sites, as well as numerous other types of social media are explained in greater detail throughout this chapter.

Social Networks

Social networking at its core is a sociological phenomenon that brings people with shared connections into mutually acceptable social constructs.[4] Over the past decade, technology has created numerous systems to help manifest this process further. Related to technology, social networks are online systems that allow for individual users to be grouped together based on common traits such as friendship, kinship, geography, school, or profession. There are numerous variations of this structure that are discussed; however, they all have similarities related to the establishment of a personal profile. This profile contains personal information, including shared or liked internet links, photos, videos, current status, email, and instant messaging. These social networks often also allow for collections of individuals into groups, categories, or other classifications based on shared or common interests (e.g., alumni of a particular school). Some social networking systems maintain open systems for external development of software, protocols, or engaged applications. These user-created applications are some of the most effective for consideration for emergency management professionals.

Most social media experts agree that the first significant social network was the establishment of SixDegrees in 1997, which allowed people to create personal profiles and connect them with friends, family, and acquaintances. SixDegrees was quickly followed up by Friendster in 2002 and MySpace and Facebook in 2004. Although SixDegrees closed its doors in 2001, it set the foundation for what social networks were to become. While Facebook currently is the most popular social networking site, that status has been controlled by Friendster and MySpace at different times and under different concepts over the past 15 years. Additional significant social networks include LinkedIn and Ning. With the gigantic rise in the popularity and usage of Facebook, each of the other systems has needed to focus on niche areas of networking, such as music and art (MySpace), professional networking (LinkedIn), topic-specific networks (Ning), or certain geographic areas (Friendster).

Online social networks often contain characteristics of all types of social media and Web 2.0 technologies. They are often capable of aggregating the tools and capabilities that exist in the other social media forms, including microblogging, blogging, video sharing, photo sharing, location-based data, instant messaging, internal messaging, and open-sourced information. However, this can also create a "Humpty-Dumpty effect" where the systematic size necessary to be capable to support this plethora of functionality can ultimately be too much to manage effectively, thus leading to a proverbial fall from the wall of their own success. As stated earlier, with the exception of Facebook, most social networks have had long-term success by establishing a targeted user base that maintains strongly shared common interests.

The application of social networks within the field of emergency management must strongly avoid the Humpty-Dumpty effect. While it is unavoidable to talk about Facebook as one of if not the most important tools currently available for the distribution of emergency management information during all phases of activity, it is critical for emergency managers to conceptually understand social networks well enough to utilize the specific concept and not necessarily the particular system.

This concept is most critically present in the balance between personal and professional use of social media systems. For instance, a local emergency manager may establish a personal profile on a social network such as Facebook to present information to his or her social network. The challenge to this setup is that the emergency manager who holds the profile can only create communication pathways with those individuals who "friend" him or her through the system. Moreover, this profile is both inherently and based on most social networking user systems for personal use and should not be utilized as an outlet for the release of professional information. Additional tools (called Pages and Groups on Facebook) are specifically designed to allow an organization, business, or collective interest to express opinions from a more communal approach. These pages and groups are often completely public with an available uniform resource locater (URL, or website address). These tools can be followed by social network users in a way that allows posted content such as public education, public information, pictures, and video to be immediately shared with those groups. Consequently, an open-access website that automatically distributes content is incredibly valuable for emergency management.

These types of tools must be implemented within the correct types of social networking systems. Emergency managers can utilize the size of Facebook (more than 800 million users) to nearly instantaneously generate a following related to their particular type of emergency preparedness, response, and/or recovery. However, this type of automatic following does not happen on every social networking site and cannot be generated by force or coercion. For instance, Microsoft unveiled a new location-based social networking site called Vine in April 2009 that was specifically targeted to support socially networked connections between friends and family to improve emergency preparedness and response activities during a disaster. The system allowed for text messaging and email technologies to be able to be used during an emergency to contact those within the user-established social network. However, by October 2010, Microsoft discontinued its support of Vine as a social network.[5] While no official word was given for their suspending support of the project, it can be presumed that social network users already active on sites such as Facebook, Friendster, or MySpace were reluctant to participate in a new social network, even one with a clear potential benefit. While the premise of Vine was excellent for emergency managers, it ultimately was a poor utilization of social networking for emergency communications and public information. It is this type of evaluation that emergency managers must be careful of as they begin to utilize social media and particularly social networking sites.

Moreover, social networking pages and groups are not effective when established at the time of an emergent incident. By delaying the establishment of these systems, the owner of the page or group has not allowed an organic trust to be developed by prospective followers and community stakeholders related to the information that will be distributed. Therefore, it is absolutely critical that the utilization of these systems occur prior to events to ensure the needed emergency or disaster information is not lost due to ineffectiveness or lack of use. This concept is further discussed in Chapter 4 and Chapter 11.

The final major consideration of social networks is the open source code established within most social networks. Open source code allows developers other than the system designers to manipulate the connectivity that already exists between individuals and their shared networks for free. Put more simply, software applications can be created that run on the social network. Although underutilized within the emergency management field, applications on Facebook already exist that allow emergency notifications (similar to Microsoft Vine), educational games about emergency preparedness, and incident awareness. The challenge of utilizing social network applications is the need for a software developer with a comprehensive knowledge of the source code related to the particular social network. Unfortunately, in most cases this is not available to the average emergency manager but could be overcome via strategic partnerships with internal or external organizations.

Blogs

Blogs are websites that are controlled and maintained by individual users who typically provide regular entries, commentaries, descriptions of activities, or other material such as pictures and videos. Much like the status entry within social networks, the postings are typically presented in reverse-chronological order with the most recent posting at the top of the blog. Most blogs allow for commentary and feedback from friends and followers, which can ultimately lead to a virtual conversation about a particular topic whether related or tangential to the original posting. According to blog aggregator BlogPulse, there are over 152 million blogs on the internet.[12] Interestingly, according to Technorati's State of the Blogosphere 2010 report, there is significant projected growth in the topics under discussion on blogs, a rise in the number of female bloggers, and an increase of the availability of blogs on mobile platforms. Moreover, nearly 50% of all bloggers believe that more people will get news and entertainment from blogs in the next five years than from traditional media outlets.[8]

Although not always immediately evident, the content of most blogs is usually centered on one central concept. This central concept can be related to a particular political, social, or cultural issue (e.g., tax relief) or simply revolve around the interests of the particular blogger. Traditionally, posting to a particular blog is handled by a single individual (or blogger), but the concept of groups of bloggers sharing one blog has grown over the past several years. This is particularly evident in the emergency management community where groups of like-minded emergency managers have posted content to blogs to facilitate local, if not regional or national, conversations about particular challenges in the field of emergency management.[6] Other prime examples of blogs that impact emergency management are those that are presented as journalistic outlets similar to an online newspaper. One of the best illustrations of this type of blog was the "In Case of Emergency, Read Blog" by the late John Solomon.[7] As a passionate citizen interested in improving emergency preparedness and response, he was able to provide a unique perspective from outside the industry to highlight best practices, question certain applications, and broaden the discussion about these issues. The concept and impact of citizen journalism is further discussed in Chapter 3.

The last major way emergency managers are utilizing blogs is through formal blogs for their organizations. While present at the local and state government levels as well as local and regional nongovernmental organizations (NGOs), some of the

MOST COMMON SOCIAL MEDIA SYSTEMS

Social Network—Facebook, MySpace, and LinkedIn
Blog—WordPress, Blogger, and TypePad
Microblog—Twitter, Tumblr, and Yammer
Photo Sharing—Flickr, Picasa, and Photobucket
Video Sharing—YouTube and Vimeo
Video Streaming—LiveStream, UStream, and Skype
Wiki-Sourcing—Wikipedia
Virtual Worlds—Second Life
Online Radio—BlogTalkRadio
Aggregators—TweetDeck and HootSuite

most well-organized, instructive, and mission-centric blogs are those run by federal emergency preparedness agencies and national NGO offices, including the Federal Emergency Management Agency,[10] the American Red Cross,[9] and the U.S. Centers for Disease Control and Prevention.[11] These blogs routinely share information about current events and often encourage conversation about current preparedness or response efforts, which ensures the transparency so necessary when utilizing social media.

Microblogs

Microblogging is a form of blogging that only allows the user 140 characters to post the content of the message. Because of this shortened structure, microblog posts are often abbreviated utilizing sentence fragments, abbreviations, and shorthand. Although they can have established privacy settings, they are often completely public and accessible to anyone with the URL (or web address). Moreover, because of the inherent brevity of microblogging messages, the topic of the content posted by

IN A NUTSHELL

Twitter posts in disaster struck areas and the areas that are indirectly affected were somewhat similar. Most of the tweets in disaster-hit areas were warnings, help requests, and reports about the environment. Official local authority Twitter accounts set up at the time of the earthquake were particularly useful, well followed and retweeted extensively, especially when warnings of an imminent tsunami were predicted.

—Adam Acar and Yuya Muraki[35]

individual users is often more erratic than blogs; however, they still typically stay within certain parameters of interest and knowledge.

The term *microblog* became prevalent among social media and internet users by end of 2007 as microblog services such as Tumblr and Twitter grew in usage and popularity.[13] In the relatively short time since microblogging became a legitimate social media practice, Twitter has quickly become the most influential and utilized system available. By October 2010, Twitter reported more than 175 million users with a growth rate of 15 million new users per month, which is significantly higher than the 300,000 new users per month that had been reported six months earlier.[15] On the other hand, Tumblr has also seen steady although less noteworthy growth. As of March 2010, Tumblr reported 2 million daily posts with a growth rate of 15,000 new users daily (or 450,000 per month)[16] with a user retention rate of 85%[17] compared to only 40% by Twitter.[18] Although retention rates are debatable due to statistical analysis and chosen definitions, it is important to strongly consider which sources are best for emergency management utilization.

For instance, although several studies have noted that the utilization of Twitter is relatively limited (10% of the most prolific users accounting for over 90% of all systematic postings),[14] the importance and effectiveness to the emergency management community cannot be understated. Specifically, Twitter has quickly become a primary source for breaking local, national, and global news. This phenomenon first became evident in 2008 during the Mumbai terrorist attacks on the Indian financial district. News about this event was first reported on Twitter by individuals who were observing the incident and reporting back real-time information (including pictures) about what was occurring around them.[19] Consequently, local and national media outlets routinely follow various Twitter users for breaking news, which often is posted well before traditional news wires such as the Associated Press release the information.[20]

Microblogs have become trustworthy to most media agencies because of one of the fundamental rules related to social media: Social media is inherently self-correcting. By establishing systems that encourage open and transparent conversation, there is a significant and often implied need for response or clarification if reported data is erroneous or misrepresented. Additionally, because social media information is exchanged nearly instantaneously throughout the globe (remember the Connecticut bicyclist from Chapter 1), news media outlets (and therefore emergency managers) can quickly feel confident that information being disseminated via this format is not intentionally inaccurate. It does not eliminate the possibility that these eyewitness reports via microblogs may be later clarified as the bigger picture of the event becomes clear. However, this phenomenon is inherent in eyewitness reporting and is not an intrinsic fault of the microblogging system. This becomes critical to emergency managers as well when incident information is being monitored for patterns and trends related to response. This secondary impact is further evaluated in Chapter 6.

Additional commercial microblogs like Yammer have also been utilized during emergency management and response activities. Yammer, unlike Twitter and

Figure 2.2 Snow coverage of 2010 "Snowpocalypse" from satellite. (From National Aeronautics and Space Administration [NASA]).

Tumblr, is limited to select users and thus creates a closed system for updates and information sharing. During the Deep Horizon oil spill in 2010, the U.S. Departments of the Interior and Fish and Wildlife Service utilized Yammer to communicate with various organizations and resource units involved in cleanup efforts in the Gulf of Mexico. By utilizing Yammer, the response efforts were able to utilize one robust source to discuss response ideas, questions, and collect field expertise about the challenges related to the spill. Additionally, Yammer was also utilized by the District of Columbia in 2010 to facilitate telework during a significant snow event that caused operational disruption for the working government and internal agencies.[21] (See Figure 2.2.) This integration of formalized response systems with social media is further discussed in Chapter 8.

The small size (typically up to 140 characters) of microblogs naturally allows for microblogs to be distributed via SMS text messaging. This is a possibility because SMS texting services often send small packets of data to increase the efficiency and efficacy of the system. Consequently, many of the microblogging services like Twitter have built-in functionality where the general public can follow certain users by SMS text message rather than through traditional or mobile internet browsing. (See Figure 2.3.) In some communities this has been utilized as a cost-effective alternative to commercial mass notification systems that have become commonplace in many communities, schools, and large businesses.[22]

Multimedia content is also frequently shared via microblogging services. This type of content includes photos, videos, and internet links that often support or connect to the posted message. This content is typically not uploaded to the microblogging service itself but rather to secondary sites or systems that have created an interface with these systems. Much like social networks, most microblogging services have open access to code development through advanced programming interfaces

Figure 2.3 **Social media systems are mobile and portable. (From Adam Crowe.)**

(APIs). The API for these systems allows various components to be maximized. An example of this utilization is for URL shorteners. Because website addresses are often long and complicated, it was critical to find a way to shorten their length to minimize the use of the limited number of characters available on microblogging sites. Consequently, URL shorteners like Bit.ly or TinyURL created new web addresses that are shortened in length. Another application of a microblog's API is the connectivity to secondary applications that allow for systematic management of comments, responses, and integrated messages. For example, there are numerous secondary applications such as TweetDeck, HootSuite, Twitterific, and Echofon that aggregate posted content, responded content, and direct messaging on various microblogging sites. These secondary applications are often also available for other social media systems such as geospatial systems and social networking. Nearly all of these applications are available for computer use and for mobile phone devices. The mobility and portability of social media systems is further discussed in Chapter 12.

The last major consideration for microblogging is the unique vernacular that is often associated with it—particularly Twitter. For instance, Twitter allows for the posting of original content (tweet), responding to original content (retweet), and private messaging (direct messages) between users. Much like the need for URL shorteners to preserve space, Twitter users needed to adopt a systematic approach to

COMMON EMERGENCY MANAGEMENT HASHTAGS

#SMEM—Social media and emergency management
#EM—Emergency management
#Gov20—Government 2.0 references
#HSEM—Homeland security and emergency management
#WX—Weather-specific tweets[37]

showing what kind of message was being posted. The answer to this issue was for retweets to be prefixed with "RT" before the message and direct messages to be prefixed with a "D." For both RT and D, the user to whom the message is in response or directed to is listed with an "@" sign in front of it. If an original message is being posted, there are no codes or terms included within the posting. This utilization of codes allows all users to understand the message and allow for filtering and organization of messages in secondary applications.

In addition, Twitter utilizes additional categorical tools called hashtags. These hashtags are combinations of letters, characters, and numbers that are prefaced by the pound sign ("#") and represent an issue, event, or condition of shared interest. For instance, citizens interested in posting messages about Halloween might use tags such as #halloween, #spooky, #costume, or #oct31. For emergency management, common hashtags include #EM, #HSEM, and #WX for emergency management, homeland security, and weather-related tweets, respectively. These hashtags can be generated by any user at any time. However, the portions of the Twitter community interested in those topics ultimately settle on a common hashtag or set of hashtags to cover certain areas.

Photo Sharing

There are numerous online repositories for photos within the social media realm. Much like the social networks, blogs, and microblogs discussed previously, these systems are established around users whose content is organized, described, and open to comment in open and/or controlled networks of friends and followers. The organization of photos and videos are generally based on a user-driven classification system called tags. These tags can be words or terms that describe the photo or video in any way the user desires. Tags can be limited to simple physical descriptions (trees, mountains, etc.) or to terminology that is arbitrary (good, bad, awesome, etc.). These terms are then gathered together to provide systemwide examples of that particular tag.

Common examples of photo-sharing sites include Flickr, Google Photos (previously Picasa), and Photobucket. These systems all support the same basic functionality. These particular systems all have basic, free accounts that allow for up to 300 MB,[23] 1 GB,[25] and 10 GB[24] storage, respectively. These photo-sharing sites are also owned by major corporations as part of their social media tool packages, which has impacted the usability and social media acceptance in a variety of ways. Flickr, for example, is owned by Yahoo and as of September 2010 had over 5 billion photos stored on its system.[26] Conversely, Google Photos is owned by Google with far fewer hosted pictures, but focus is centered on the capability to edit and manipulate pictures rather than storage. Lastly, Photobucket is owned by Fox Interactive Media and is focused on tools that create dynamic multimedia content such as slideshows, scrapbooks, and video integration.

The application of photo-sharing sites by emergency management professionals has primarily been utilized for preparedness activities. Organizations like the Federal Emergency Management Agency (FEMA) maintain photo-sharing sites that have pictures of all response and recovery activities that their personnel have been involved with. These pictures are available for public download and usable for educational activities. Interestingly, FEMA's photo-sharing site does not actually utilize free systems such as Flickr or Photobucket due to concerns about the photos usage even though they have adopted comprehensive utilization of many other social media systems.

Although a relatively new technology, some of these photo-sharing systems like Google Photos have facial recognition capabilities that attempt to help the user efficiently and effectively categorize pictures based on those individuals present. The system currently attempts to categorize faces with the tagging responsibility left to the user.[27] This type of technology may become widespread during homeland security and law enforcement investigations to begin to identify common contacts and known associates of suspects and criminal perpetrators. This will be particularly useful as users utilize the facial recognition capabilities to comprehensively add the names of friends and family to publicly viewable pictures. This concept of engaging these systems in support or replacement of commercial systems with Web 2.0 systems is expanded in Chapter 14.

Video Sharing

Like photo-sharing systems, video-sharing capabilities both as freestanding systems and integrated into other social media systems have become widespread on the internet. Sites such as Vimeo and YouTube have quickly grown from online storage for videos to public venues for statements from politicians, musicians, artists, citizens, and emergency managers. Vimeo typically processes approximately 4 billion video views per month and increased its user base by 1000% over one year.[28] Although impressive, YouTube far exceeds the current utilization of Vimeo by supporting nearly 2 billion daily video views with nearly 24 hours of video uploaded to the site each minute.[29] In most cases, a user's video-sharing page is referred to as a channel.

Like all social media systems, video-sharing sites are designed to encourage connections and networking between individual users. This is accomplished several ways. The most basic tool that establishes networks is the commentary feature available on most publicly posted videos. For instance, within YouTube, viewers are given the opportunity to provide text comments related to the video or the user channel as a whole. Similarly, viewers are allowed to provide more generic feedback that simply states whether they like or dislike the posted video. This feature is also available in many social networks like Facebook. Secondarily, YouTube users are also allowed to subscribe to other YouTube channels to receive updates about users who post content they want to follow. Much like status posts on social networks or microblogs, this strongly encourages the continued networking and potential conversation between two individuals.

In addition to direct feedback mechanisms like comment boxes, video-sharing systems also utilize tagging classification. Not only do these tags allow for greater search functionality within the video-sharing system, they also allow the system to generate lists of suggested videos that may be of similar or related content. This is a critical social media step to not only encourage conversation but also spread discussion and awareness about the topic of interest to individuals and groups outside the known network. For instance, if a video about hurricane evacuations was posted with tags such as "hurricane," "preparedness," "ready," and "evacuation," systems like YouTube might suggest that you watch another video on personal preparedness for emergencies that had similarly been tagged "preparedness" and "ready." For most videos, this happens on a relatively small scale; however, there are incidents where certain videos are viewed and shared so many times through these systematic connections that they are referred to as "viral." This viral video status is strongly sought by most social media users, including emergency managers using these systems.

There are numerous public and private emergency management professionals and related organizations who are utilizing these systems during preparedness, response, and recovery to spread educational and incident-related messages. Posted videos range from professional quality public service announcements (PSAs) to homemade videos about specific issues within the emergency management spectrum. Regardless, these videos are often connected through the tagging and classification system already discussed. Interestingly, YouTube also supports closed captioning capability for any video posted to their site.[30] As emergency managers continue to be challenged by providing equal preparedness and response activities for functional and accessible needs community members, this is a free tool that could aid in that process for certain functional characteristics. These challenges are further expanded on in Chapter 14.

Video Streaming

As a contrast to the static storage of photo and video sharing, there are some Web 2.0 technologies that allow live or streaming video to be presented from any computer or mobile device with a working web-ready camera and access to the internet.

Video-streaming systems like UStream.tv, Justin.tv, and Livestream allow users to establish live video streams that are broadcast through the internet via a pre-determined web address or channel. Like most of the other social media systems discussed, this streaming capability can also be embedded through APIs into websites and other secondary social media systems. Additionally, these systems create broadcast channels that integrate with live chat, social networks, and microblogging sites to encourage conversation and community around events that have live video streams.

Both Ustream.tv and Livestream were founded and released to the public in 2007. In the short period of time since their creation, both systems have been utilized by various politicians, musicians, artists, and other media figures to control and maintain a channel limited only to their perspectives and purpose. Within emergency management, the concept and utilization of live streaming is extremely limited. Professional conferences and workshops have capitalized on this technology as a business model to increase the number of individuals paying and capable of seeing and hearing the speakers; however, the operational implications of live streaming for emergency managers must also be considered. Specifically, all three major live-streaming systems provide mobile applications via their APIs that allow for the generation and watching of live streams from anywhere there is an internet-capable mobile phone. This type of utilization could be extremely beneficial for field work that requires command and control review but could also be challenging for emergency responders to completely control information available for citizens to video stream at an emergency or disaster scene. These issues are further discussed in Chapters 12 and 5, respectively.

Skype and Video Calling

Skype is a unique software application that is not easily categorized with other social media and Web 2.0 technologies. It is a variant of Voice over Internet Protocol (VoIP) technology that allows voice and video calling between computers via the internet. Additionally, the system allows voice calls to be made from computers to traditional landline phones or mobile phones anywhere in the world for a small fee. However, the more significant technology component is the capability to provide free video calling. Unlike traditional VoIP technology, Skype does not utilize hosted servers to process that information but instead utilizes the processing on the computers connected to make the call. This type of innovation was based on the peer-to-peer file-sharing systems that quickly arose during the early 21st century via systems like Napster and Kazaa.[31]

Although the original phone-based Skype system was developed in 2003, video conferencing between two users was introduced in 2006 and later expanded for up to five users in 2010. By late 2010, Skype had well over 500 million users with over 40 million daily users of one of the two forms of Skype.[31] Like other Web 2.0

systems, Skype maintains an API that allows third-party developers to construct additional functionality (e.g., sending faxes) not available as part of the standard Skype package. As of 2011, Skype also strategically partnered with Facebook to provide video chatting to all users.[36]

As an overall tool, the functionality of Skype is potentially valuable to emergency management professionals regardless of discipline. Specifically, many emergency management offices through budgeted or grant monies have purchased commercial video-conferencing equipment and routinely pay for subscriber and usage fees to utilize the video teleconferencing capability. While potentially more robust than Skype, these professional systems are extremely expensive and are often burdensome to setup, maintain, and utilize efficiently. Moreover, smaller and often rural emergency managers most likely lack the funds to support these costly professional systems. The challenge for most emergency managers in converting to Skype is not the cost versus benefit analysis but rather technological hurdles such as concerns over bandwidth and appropriate use policies.[31]

Although the overwhelming leader In this particular sector of Web 2.0 technology, Skype does have one growing competitor called ooVoo. This system is classified as an instant messaging client but supports much of the same functionality as Skype, including person-to-person video calls as well as group video conferencing.[32] The ooVoo system currently maintains 14 million users worldwide with a growth rate of around 700,000 per month. Based on other social media and Web 2.0 technologies, competition is not unusual or unexpected. Like all systems, the functionality that exists on both Skype and ooVoo presents fantastic possibilities for utilization within emergency management.

Other Systems

There are numerous other social media and Web 2.0 technologies available to emergency managers, including aggregators, online radio, wiki-sourcing, virtual worlds, and instant messaging; for the purposes of this book they are addressed as needed in other chapters to expand upon certain implementation or utilization challenges that exist for the field of emergency management.

However, there is one additional system that should be addressed to fully understand the landscape of how social media is being implemented in modern emergency management. In 2010 in response to findings from the 9/11 Commission,[34] the U.S. Department of Homeland Security (DHS) Science and Technology (S&T) Directorate's First Responder Technologies program released an online network called Communities of Practice. This network was intended to consist of active and retired first responders and emergency response professionals from all levels of government who could share information, ideas, and best practices to improve the readiness to respond to emergencies and disasters.[33] Because of the potential for sharing sensitive information as part of the discussions within the system, each user is vetted, approved, and assigned a user ID (userid) and password by DHS personnel.

The Communities of Practice system contains multiple working groups to focus discussion and cooperation among the first responders. Each of these working groups contains social media tools such as wikis, blogs, document storage, and discussion boards. Interestingly, these systems parallel the functionality of many of the social media systems already discussed but lack connectivity to them. While it was a peculiar decision to recreate a new social media system rather than optimizing structure and functionality that already existed and to require a highly secured access, these decisions were made to try and maximize participation from all types of emergency managers. This included those emergency managers and first responders who are used to controlled access systems (similar to other DHS products) and highly distrust the openness of common social media systems. While there are many other communities of practice attempting to embrace the adaption of social media to emergency management, it is important to consider that organized discussions and the sharing of resources is critical to the future successes.

Practitioner Profile: Hal Grieb, Previstar

Hal Grieb (Figure 2.4) currently serves as a training and implementation specialist for Previstar. Previous to this, Mr. Grieb served as the senior emergency planning

Figure 2.4 Hal Grieb.

specialist for Plano (Texas) Emergency Management and responded to several natural disasters while serving in the Florida Army National Guard, including Hurricane Katrina, Hurricane Rita, Hurricane Wilma, and Tropical Storm Ernesto. He handled the Prepared in Plano social media campaign and was recognized as one of the top 25 most influential social media personalities in Texas during 2011. While at Plano Emergency Management, Mr. Grieb began focusing on the rise and impact of social media and Web 2.0 technologies on emergency management. Specifically, Mr. Grieb said, "Social media has become a great tool in streamlining the communication to and from community members and allows for efficient online coordination in all phases of the emergency management cycle, which aids emergency managers in more efficient collaborative work flow." He continues by stating that a benefit is "cost effectiveness of not just the platforms, but also due to the lowering need for time and travel to meetings to engage stakeholders in multiple projects." In addition, Mr. Grieb believes that the understanding of social media is still in its "infancy" but that a "second, larger wave of adoption and implementation" has just begun. Regarding the future of social media in emergency management, Mr. Grieb stated that there will be "massive impacts in non-resource-rich jurisdictions and agencies in being able to communication and implement web-based tools to help their communities in times of need." Additionally, Mr. Grieb stated, "As more agencies use these systems, semantic aggregation of common terms and needs will begin to become more uniform and accepted into the programming thereby making these technologies even easier and faster to use when emergencies and disasters happen." In closing, Mr. Grieb looked to a future change in perspective by stating that "Sooner than later we will be asking the question 'could you imagine emergency management without social media or other web-based collaborative technologies?'"[34]

Chapter Terms

Social media: Internet tools that engage nearly instantaneous conversational information exchange through nearly free or free interfaces.

Blogs: Type of social media that allows for unlimited user-generated content posted in reverse chronological order with the capability to share text, photos, videos, and links, along with the capability to tag and categorize entries.

Microblogs: Type of social media that allows for limited user-generated (no more than 140 characters) content posted in reverse chronological order with the capability to share text, photos, videos, and links through secondary interface systems while maintaining internal shortcuts and codes to categorize information.

Social networks: Type of social media that allows for limited user-generated content posted in reverse chronological order with the capability to host and share text, photos, videos, and links through approved friends or contact lists.

Video sharing: Type of social media that allows for user-generated video content to be publicly shared with followers as well as to maintain the capability to tag and categorize entries to encourage the connectivity between videos and users.

Photo sharing: Type of social media that allows for user-generated photos to be publicly shared with followers as well as maintain the capability to tag and categorize entries to encourage the connectivity between photos and users.

Hashtag: Term for the process utilized by users of the microblog Twitter to categorize and sort posted content.

Humpty-Dumpty effect: Concept where technology systems become so large or influential that their growth begins to weaken the effectiveness of their products due to expansion, poor business decisions, or unmanaged innovation.

Chapter Questions

General Questions

1. Which of the following are microblogs?
   a. Facebook
   b. Twitter
   c. YouTube
   d. Flickr
2. True/False: Tags are terms attached to posted social media content that allow for the categorization and aggregation of similar information.
3. True/False: Social media and Web 2.0 technologies are the same thing.

Essay Questions

1. Why is social media important to the future of emergency management?
2. How should emergency managers utilize photo and video sharing as well as video streaming for preparedness, response, mitigation, and recovery?
3. Should the emergency management community utilize current social media systems for the development of these technologies or create new systems like the First Responder Communities of Practice?

Works Cited

1. Bradley, Anthony J. "A New Definition of Social Media." *Gartner Blog*, January 7, 2010. http://blogs.gartner.com/anthony_bradley/2010/01/07/a-new-definition-of-social-media/ (accessed October 27, 2011).

2. "Swine Flu Timeline." *About.com*. http://pediatrics.about.com/od/swineflu/a/509_timeline_2.htm (accessed January 11, 2011).

3. "Lessons Learned from H1N1." *Osmosis, Inc.*, July 16, 2009. http://www.slideshare.net/jmbhan/h1n1-influenza-how-social-media-improves-communication-collaboration-for-public-health (accessed January 11, 2011).

4. Hopkins, Mark. "Just What Is Social Media, Exactly?" *Mashable*, November 18, 2008. http://mashable.com/2008/11/18/social-media-defined/ (accessed January 11, 2011).

5. Arrington, Michael. "Microsoft to Shut Down Disaster Communication Service Vine." *TechCrunch*, September 10, 2010. http://techcrunch.com/2010/09/10/microsoft-to-shut-down-disaster-communication-service-vine/ (accessed January 11, 2011).

6. "iDisaster 2.0: Social Media & Emergency Management." *iDisaster 2.0*, November 18, 2008. http://idisaster.wordpress.com/ (accessed January 11, 2011).

7. Solomon, John D. *In Case of Emergency, Read Blog: A Citizen's Eye View of Public Preparedness*. http://incaseofemergencyblog.com/ (accessed January 11, 2011).

8. "State of the Blogosphere 2010." *Technorati.com*, November 3, 2010. http://technorati.com/blogging/article/state-of-the-blogosphere-2010-introduction/ (accessed January 11, 2011).

9. *American Red Cross Blog*. http://blog.redcross.org/ (accessed January 11, 2011).

10. *FEMA Blog*. http://blog.fema.gov/ (accessed January 11, 2011).

11. "Public Health Matters Blog." *Centers for Disease Control and Prevention*. http://blogs.cdc.gov/publichealthmatters/ (accessed January 11, 2011).

12. "Internet 2010 in Numbers." *Royal Pingdom*, January 12, 2011. http://royal.pingdom.com/2011/01/12/internet-2010-in-numbers/ (accessed October 27, 2011).

13. Naone, Erica. "A Brief History of Microblogging." *MIT Technology Review*, September–October 2008. http://www.technologyreview.com/computing/21227/ (accessed October 27, 2011).

14. "New Twitter Research: Men Follow Men and Nobody Tweets." *Harvard Business Review*, June 1, 2009. http://blogs.hbr.org/cs/2009/06/new_twitter_research_men_follo.html (accessed January 11, 2011).

15. Murphy, David. "Twitter: On-Track for 200 Million Users by Year End." *PC Magazine*, October 31, 2010. http://www.pcmag.com/article2/0,2817,2371826,00.asp (accessed January 11, 2011).

16. *Tumblr Staff Blog*, March 8, 2010. http://staff.tumblr.com/post/434982975/a-billion-hits (accessed January 11, 2011).

17. Dannon, Chris. "What the Hell Is Tumblr? and Other Worthwhile Questions." *Fast Company Blog*. May 13, 2009. http://www.fastcompany.com/blog/chris-dannen/techwatch/what-hell-tumblr-and-other-worthwhile-questions (accessed January 11, 2011).

18. "Many Twitters Are Quick Quitters: Study." *Reuters*, April 29, 2009. http://www.reuters.com/article/idUSTRE53S1A720090429 (accessed January 11, 2011).

19. Beaumont, Claudine. *The Telegraph*, November 27, 2008. http://www.telegraph.co.uk/news/worldnews/asia/india/3530640/Mumbai-attacks-Twitter-and-Flickr-used-to-break-news-Bombay-India.html (accessed January 11, 2011).

20. Ketz, Kris. Presentation, "How Social Media Impacts the Incident Command System," December 14, 2010, Kansas City, Mo.

21. *Yammer Blog*, September 7, 2010. http://blog.yammer.com/blog/2010/09/yammer-helps-in-times-of-crisis-.html (accessed January 11, 2011).

22. "JOCOAlert." Johnson County Emergency Management and Homeland Security. http://www.jocoem.org/CIT/jocoalert.shtml (accessed January 11, 2011).

23. "Flickr: Help—Free Account." *Flickr Blog,* 2011. http://www.flickr.com/help/limits/ (accessed October 27, 2011).
24. "Photobucket Now Has Unlimited Storage." *Photobucket Blog,* 2011. http://blog.photobucket.com/blog/2011/06/photobucket-now-has-unlimited-storage.html (accessed on October 27, 2011).
25. "Picasa Now Offering Virtually Unlimited Free Photo Storage, Brings Google+ Tapping." *Lifehacker Blog,* 2011. http://lifehacker.com/5817483/picasa-now-offering-virtually-unlimited-storage-brings-google%252B-tagging (accessed October 27, 2011).
26. "5,000,000,000." *Flickr Blog,* September 19, 2010. http://blog.flickr.net/en/2010/09/19/5000000000/ (accessed January 11, 2011).
27. Reisinger, Don. "Picasa Refresh Brings Facial Recognition." *Washington Post,* September 2, 2008. http://www.washingtonpost.com/wp-dyn/content/article/2008/09/02/AR2008090200873.html (accessed January 11, 2011).
28. O'Neill, Megan. "Vimeo Users, Plays, and Uploads Doubled in 2010." *Social Times,* December 27, 2010. http://www.socialtimes.com/2010/12/vimeo-2010/ (accessed January 11, 2011).
29. "YouTube Fact Sheet." *YouTube.* http://www.youtube.com/t/fact_sheet (accessed January 11, 2011).
30. "Captions and Subtitles." *YouTube Blog.* http://www.youtube.com/t/captions_about (accessed January 11, 2011).
31. "Skype." *Wikipedia.* http://en.wikipedia.org/wiki/Skype (accessed January 11, 2011).
32. "ooVoo." *Wikipedia.* http://en.wikipedia.org/wiki/OoVoo (accessed January 11, 2011).
33. "Connecting the First Responder Community." *Communities of Practice.* https://communities.firstresponder.gov/ (accessed January 11, 2011).
34. Interview with Hal Grieb on December 27, 2010.
35. "Twitter and Natural Disasters: Lessons from Japan." *Homeland Security Newswire,* 2011. http://www.homelandsecuritynewswire.com/twitter-and-natural-disasters-lessons-japan?page=0,1 (accessed May 11, 2011).
36. Guynn, Jessica. "Facebook Adds Video-Calling Skype at No Charge." *StarTribune Business,* 2011 http://www.startribune.com/business/125117979.html (accessed August 11, 2011).
37. *Social Media for Emergency Management,* www.sm4em.org (accessed November 15, 2011).

Chapter 3

Citizen Journalism: The Rise and Impact of New Media

The testimony of the independent, well-informed eyewitness is more vital than ever in our interconnected world...[but] how can this still be achieved when the technology and business of journalism is being transformed out of all recognition?

—**Timothy Garton Ash**, *Facts Are Subversive*[1]

Chapter Objectives

- To comprehend the impact of citizen journalism on emergency and disaster response scenes, emergency public information, and comprehensive emergency management
- To identify and consider characteristics of both traditional and public participatory journalism
- To identify the level of acceptance of citizen journalism characteristics by the general public and the traditional media
- To consider new paradigms of time and pacing of news cycles
- To identify the tools and systems utilized by citizen journalism
- To consider all systematic and structural challenges to citizen journalism

DISASTER FOCUS—MIRACLE ON THE HUDSON

At 3:24 p.m. EST on January 15, 2009, U.S. Airways Flight 1549 was cleared for takeoff from Runway 4 at New York's LaGuardia Airport for a routine flight from New York City to Charlotte, North Carolina. There were 155 souls aboard the Airbus 320 plane, including five crew members, with Captain Chesley "Sully" Sullenberger at the helm. Captain Sullenberger, 57, was a former fighter pilot who had been a commercial pilot for nearly 30 years since leaving the U.S. Air Force. Within six minutes of takeoff, the plane was struck by a flock of Canada geese (Figure 3.1). Subsequently, there was an immediate and complete loss of thrust from both engines. Captain Sullenberger and his flight crew quickly determined that they would not be able to safely return to any local airfield and instead decided to turn south to glide the plane into an emergency landing on the Hudson River near the USS *Intrepid* Museum. All occupants were safely evacuated by emergency services from the plane, which was amazingly still virtually intact although partially submerged and slowly sinking into the river. The entire crew of U.S. Airways Flight 1549 was later awarded the Master's Medal of the Guild of Air Pilots and Air Navigators and dubbed the "Miracle on the Hudson" by traditional media outlets.[2] Although an amazing story of heroics and courage in the face of adversity, it also marks one of the most amazing examples of citizen journalism recorded. Specifically, while on a trip to New York City from his Florida home, Janis Krums (@jkrums on Twitter) was, according to his website, "in the right place at the right time" to capture a cell phone picture of the airplane floating in the Hudson River.[3] Mr. Krums immediately posted the picture to Twitter from his iPhone and within 34 minutes was being interviewed by MSNBC as an eyewitness to the crash.[4] News coverage quickly followed on Google, FoxNews, and many other traditional news outlets throughout the world.[4] Since that time, Mr. Krums's picture has been downloaded over 635,000 times.[5] Additionally, numerous Facebook pages and groups have been created since the event celebrating both the heroism of Captain Sullenberger and the Miracle on the Hudson event. Clearly traditional news outlets now seek out and need the input of citizen journalists for real-time event-related pieces of news information.

Journalism—Traditional and Participatory

By any standard, journalism is the practice of reporting news. The challenge for both professional journalists and those individuals affected by news (everyone else) is that the understanding of what is news and what is professional news coverage is challenging, particularly as social media has become more prevalent. The foundation of news reporting started with Johannes Gutenberg's invention of the moveable type

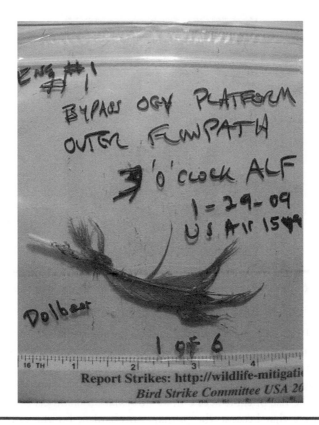

Figure 3.1 Bird feather found in left engine of U.S. Airways Flight 1549. (From National Transportation Safety Board [NTSB].)

printing press in 1456 (see Figure 3.2), which led to the widespread dissemination of information (and ultimately news). Most historians note that the first newspaper appeared in Europe in the 17th century. By 1702, the *Daily Courant* was the first daily newspaper with continued publication in the United States. Not long after, the British government adopted the Press Restriction Act, which required that the printer's name and place of printing be included on each publication.[10] This act ensured printers maintained professional acknowledgment and source transparency. This concept is of critical importance as it became a foundation of professional journalism and ultimately has been one of the biggest hurdles for the acceptance of the contribution of citizen journalism from (potentially) unknown and untrained individuals.

The next two major sources of professional journalism were created with the rise of radio and television. The capability for long-range radio transmission was first established by Guglielmo Marconi (Figure 3.3) in 1895 and first broadcast as a radio news program on August 31, 1920, by station 8MK in Detroit, Michigan.[11] Likewise, the technology of television was developed incrementally over the first 25 years of the 20th century with regular broadcasting debuting in New York

Figure 3.2 Copper engraving of Johannes Gutenberg, the inventor of the printing press.

City in April 1931. Regular network television broadcasts began on NBC in 1947 and on CBS and ABC in 1948 with numerous additional stations being established throughout the eastern part of the United States soon thereafter.[12] Quickly television news formats were established both at the national and local levels. Additionally, the rise of cable access news information channels by the 1980s created an industry that became the primary mechanism for the public to receive emergent information.[13]

By the end of the 20th century, the rise of the internet had created a new medium to distribute news-related information. This initially started as website extensions of traditional media formats in print or on television or radio. For example, CNN's traditional cable television news broadcast was mirrored (typically in text form) on the CNN website. By the beginning of the 21st century, original source and web content became more and more integrated with some significant coordination related to the distribution, dissemination, and timeliness of information on one or both of these formats. This process was further supplemented by news aggregators like Google News, the Huffington Post, and the Drudge Report that collected links to major news stories from various outlets and formats into one measureable interface. Direct internet reporting of news quickly became the fourth major source of information related to all events.

Even with these four major sources of news, one major question still remained: What is the role of citizens? With some minor exceptions related to internet news outlets (which are often tied to more traditional news organizations), the only role citizens have ever been granted in the news process is to collect and act on the information received. Interestingly, social media and Web 2.0 technologies created

Figure 3.3   Gugilelmo Marconi, the inventor of long-range radio.

an unprecedented empowerment of citizens to contribute, refine, and process news at a level similar to the print, radio, television, and internet media outlets. On the other hand, many professional journalists in all forms would disagree, stating various objections that include the need for an editorial review prior to distribution.[14] It is this juxtaposition between the empowerment and opportunity to act against appropriateness that throws citizen journalism into such stark contrast to traditional journalism.

FIVE TYPES OF CITIZEN ENGAGEMENT IN JOURNALISM

1. Audience participation at mainstream news outlets
2. Independent news and information websites
3. Full-fledged participatory news sites
4. Collaborative and contributory media sites
5. Personal broadcasting sites[14]

According to online blogger and journalist J. D. Lasica, citizen journalism can be classified into five broad categories.[14] These categories include audience participation at traditional news outlets, independent news and information websites, full-fledged participatory news sites, collaborative media sites, and personal broadcasting sites. The first of these participatory news categories includes public involvement at traditional news agencies in all four major formats discussed (newspaper, radio, television, and internet). Examples of this type of activity include staff editorial blogs that incorporate reader comments, approved blogs for public officials, discussion forums, and articles written by readers, as well as photo and video reports provided by readers or viewers.[14] The second type of citizen journalism includes independent news and information sites. These sites typically are topically oriented and include examples such as Gawker, Gizmodo, and the Drudge Report. These sites vary in their degrees of professional journalism, but all are heavily based on the contributions of amateur, independent, and contracted writers. The third type of citizen journalism is referred to as full-fledged participatory news sites, which are primarily international outlets that concentrate on first-person reporting of events and news. This type of citizen journalism often makes little to no attempt at staying objective when reporting. The fourth classification of participatory journalism includes collaborative media sites. These types of collaborative sites combine blogs, discussion boards, social media integration, and other user-created editorial content as well as links to other news sites—both traditional and participatory. Examples of this form of citizen journalism include Slashdot, Mashable, and many others. The success rate of this category of site is often boom or bust, with sites quickly failing or becoming high-volume drivers of media and content. The final type of citizen journalism includes personal or organizational broadcasting sites. This primarily includes audio and video sites that allow for news interviews and collection of event-driven content. The primary example of this type of citizen journalism is most often seen in online radio and video-streaming sites like BlogTalkRadio or UStream.tv, but can also be found in high-volume blogging sites. The function, message, and content of these sites are completely driven by the user and ultimately can report on news information without editorial review or agreed-upon professional standards. Although these definitions are a strong attempt to classify citizen journalism, they do not cover every website or social media form that allows for or encourages public involvement.[14] (See Figure 3.4.)

Citizen journalism has also had a profound impact on the profitability and sustainability of print media. Since 2007, 175 print news outlets in the United States have closed or moved strictly to web content.[15] The progression of closures over time is included in Table 3.1.[16] These closed outlets include publications of all sizes and reputations and some nationally recognized outlets such as the *Rocky Mountain News* and *Seattle Post-Intelligencer*. The reasons for these closures are multifaceted but are fundamentally related to readership and circulation that is in steep decline. According to the Pew Research Center's News Media Consumption Survey, newspaper readership was down to 25% when limited to print form.[17] Moreover,

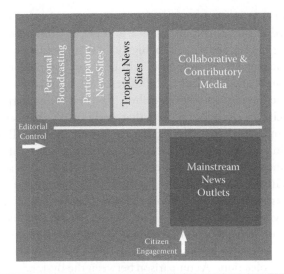

Figure 3.4 Complex spectrum of different types of citizen journalism. (From Adam Crowe.)

Table 3.1 Number of Print Media Closures 2007–2010

2007	2008	2009	2010	Total
1	40	109	25	175

Source: From "Closed Newspapers," *Paper Cuts.* http://newspaperlayoffs.com/maps/closed/ (accessed January 11, 2011).

additional research by the Pew Research Center's Internet and American Life Project determined that nearly 92% of Americans use multiple platforms to get their daily news[17] and that the internet is the second most-popular news platform behind local and national television news.[22] This ranking puts online news sources—including citizen journalism sources within the social media framework—ahead of national and local print newspapers as well as terrestrial radio.[18] Emergency managers and risk communicators must be aware of this change and consider it when utilizing news sources to send and receive information during emergencies and disasters.

Acceptance by the General Public

If citizens are involved in the generation and processing of news as citizen journalists, there must be some consideration of how and when they play this role. Specifically, citizen involvement is inherently at the incident source of event scene, which has long been defined in the context of response and public information. For instance, if a local building catches on fire, it is highly likely that the first person to notice the scene and provide any level of "response" will be a local bystander. This individual may or may not have any knowledge, ability, resource, or impetus to respond to the event, but until action is initiated (e.g., calling 9-1-1) no formal response is possible. Interestingly, social psychologists suggest that traditionally there are two responses from onlookers and bystanders. The negative response, called the "Bystander Effect," actually results in no response from event observers for a variety of reasons ranging from altruistic inertia or other social constraints.[6,7] Conversely, according to one study from the Greater Good, "[There is] positive influence we can exert as bystanders....[J]ust as passive bystanders reinforce a sense that nothing is wrong in a situation, the active bystander can, in fact, get people to focus on a problem and motivate them to take action."[7] Although not explicitly stated within the study, this type of altruistic momentum is the justification for so-called Good Samaritan laws, which protect these types of actions. A comparison between the Bystander Effect and active bystander activities is included in Figure 3.5.

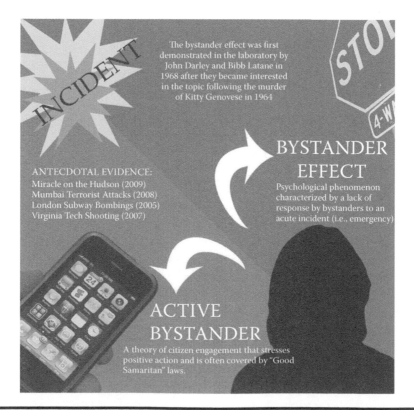

Figure 3.5 Bystander effect vs. active bystanders. (From Adam Crowe.)

IN A NUTSHELL

[There is] positive influence we can exert as bystanders....[J]ust as passive bystanders reinforce a sense that nothing is wrong in a situation, the active bystander can, in fact, get people to focus on a problem and motivate them to take action.

—Dacher Keltner and Jason March, "We Are All Bystanders"[7]

Additionally, there is significant anecdotal evidence to suggest that the Bystander Effect can be overcome more effectively with the availability of social media tools than perhaps any other method. Above and beyond the earlier mentioned utilization of Twitter and TwitPic by Janis Krums for the Miracle on the Hudson event, Twitter, Flickr, Facebook, and mobile video feeds have been documented as primary sources of information that were later utilized by traditional media in events including the terrorist attacks on the Mumbai financial district (2008), London subway bombings (2005), and the Southeast Asian tsunami (2005) to name a few.[8,9] In all cases, there were significant numbers of individuals willing to report, in light of significant personal risk, critical information about the disaster. These social and psychological conditions along with the influence of Twitter have redefined the disaster scene to empower the citizen observer to provide comment and context to the event through text, pictures, video, and location-based references.

Not only are citizen observers empowered by social media to become emergency reporters, they have also been heavily influenced by what New York University professor and communications expert Clay Shirky refers to as the "algorithmic authority."[19] He establishes that this authority is "the decision to regard as authoritative an unmanaged process of extracting value from diverse, untrustworthy sources, without any human standing besides the result saying 'Trust this because you trust me.'"[19] In other words, the impact and effectiveness of citizen journalism that lacks editorial control and "professional" oversight is based on predetermined networks of trustworthiness that are inherent throughout the social media formats. These participatory journalism sites often aggregate information from various nonvetted sources that collectively validate newsworthy or emergency information and become trusted sources for individuals and collections of individuals equally.

The best examples of this concept are Wikipedia and Amazon.com. Wikipedia is an online encyclopedia written, edited, and ultimately validated by individual users. This contrasts greatly to traditional encyclopedias that were written and edited by so-called experts on the given topics of the encyclopedia. The issue with the traditional model of encyclopedias was that if an error occurred or referenced information (e.g., geopolitical boundaries) changed, the content and therefore by extension the entire volume of encyclopedia was wrong and out-of-date. A Wikipedia entry, on the other hand, can be edited an indefinite number of times until the collective knowledge of all users creates an entry that is as accurate as possible at the given moment. Similarly, Amazon.com and most online retailers create user feedback mechanisms for products sold that are generally presented as a rating system of some kind. These ratings are left by individuals who, when reviewed by other individuals, may or may not have credibility. For instance, "Alice from Wichita, Kansas" is considering purchasing a new book that has been reviewed by "Joey from Pittsburgh, Pennsylvania." Due to geographical separation, it is highly unlikely that Alice would know Joey or have any reason to give him individual credibility. However, when "Joey from Pittsburgh," "Sandy from South Dakota," "Nick from New Jersey, "Matt from Montana," and "Dan from Delaware" have all provided feedback about the product, she has the capability to give collective credibility to the group.

This concept of collective credibility or algorithmic authority is critical for emergency managers and crisis communicators as disaster-related information is collected and processed through social media systems. One individual reporting an emergency or disaster may or may not have credibility, but if numerous individuals claim the same or similar circumstances related to the event, it is reasonable for emergency managers to take action in response to this information. This concept is one of the reasons why the National Weather Service (NWS) ultimately implemented a system to receive severe weather reports via Twitter.[19] Specifically, the NWS Twitter tool helps aggregate storm-related information that can then be processed in the same vein as traditionally credible sources such as phone reports, meteorological reviews, and radar measurements. The impact and benefit of crowdsourced information and additional aggregation tools is further discussed in Chapters 10 and 5, respectively.

Acceptance by News Media

Citizens report incident-related information on social media systems like Twitter and Facebook with or without any acknowledgment from traditional media sources like televised news. The acceptance of this information as news or newsworthy by traditional media outlets was slow to start but has exponentially increased in acceptance by all major outlets. Not only are many outlets directly engaging in social media systems for the dissemination and collection of information, there are also many media personalities actively engaging social media for news tips, leads, and breaks to stories that they may or may not have previously had. This implementation of social media as a primary source of information has had far-reaching implications, including impacts on traditional reporting mechanisms, reporting standards, speed of delivery, and the business model of news.

First and foremost, the speed of major news coverage, regardless of format or size, has sped up tremendously. Over the past several hundred years, the speed and

IN A NUTSHELL

Whomever can shout the loudest each second of each day, owns that second and the thousands of retweets, likes and traffic that go with it.

—Dominic Litten, "The 24-Hour News Cycle Is Dead"[21]

expected delivery time of news has exponentially increased with the establishment of each new major media form. Print, radio, and network television reduced the cycle of news from daily to several times a day. Cable television—particularly the establishment of CNN in 1980—established the 24/7 news cycle that was available at any time of day throughout the week.[20] This 24/7 news cycle continued as the expected speed for most of the rest of the 20th century; however, with the rise of social media systems such as social networks, microblogs, and blogs, that information cycle has been reduced to minutes or even seconds. Astute social media blogger and marketer Dominic Litten described this new paradigm as "Whomever can shout the loudest each second of each day, owns that second and the thousands of retweets, likes and traffic that go with it."[21] Consequently, the concept of a 24/7 news cycle should be replaced with a 60/60 news cycle requiring constant vigilance for 60 seconds of every minute for 60 minutes of every hour. News outlets have quickly set their goal not only to be the leading journalists but to have sustained business models as well. To accomplish this, many news outlets have begun to adjust to the speed of social media and find ways to adopt the information—no matter what form or accuracy.

In many ways due to the change in the length of the news cycle, the rise of social media and Web 2.0 technologies has also led to a change in acceptable standards of distributed media. This change in standards is comprised of the credibility of sources as well as the quality of material used in support of a story. Specifically, news agencies are not immune to the influence of the collective credibility created through social media channels. Consequently, an individual eyewitness who reports event details on a social network or microblog may not have enough credibility for traditional news agencies to use it to create a story. However, the collected information from multiple sources on social media sites is as effective as multiple eyewitnesses interviewed in a traditional manner. Not only is the information acceptable via social media sources, it is also a quicker way to move from event to reported story, which is critical for most traditional news outlets as they attempt to comply with the shrinking news cycle established earlier. In some newsrooms, social media outlets—particularly microblogs like Twitter and Tumblr—routinely deliver breaking news faster than traditional news wires (such as the Associated Press).[26]

In addition to the change in requirements for credibility, the influence of social media has also impacted the accepted quality of material utilized for stories. While most prevalent in television news, this change in quality also applies to print and sometimes radio news outlets. This change in standards includes grainy photographs, blurry videos, and fuzzy audio in various forms. These different formats come from citizens who utilize Web 2.0 technologies such as phone cameras, videocams, and webcams to post sharable content through social media systems such as video streaming as well as photo and video sharing. Interestingly, according to recent research, this acceptance of inferior quality media sources may actually be more palatable to the general public as social media and its standards become more and more pervasive.[23] Skype, in particular, has become very commonly used by television media outlets due to its ease of use and aid in shortening the period of time necessary to plan and prepare interviews on camera.[24] As before, this type of technology (and acceptance of its quality standards) helped reduce the news cycle tremendously.

Not only are traditional news outlets utilizing participatory journalism and the tools associated with it, it is clear that traditional media outlets are also seeking out formalized partnerships with new media outlets to further the distribution of news and information. For instance, Apple and NewsCorp launched *The Daily*, the first iPad-only news publication that will have no website or print edition and will cost a small fee to download.[25] Additionally, mergers between AOL and TechCrunch[27] as well as *Newsweek* and the Daily Beast[28] are strong indicators that the business model of traditional media outlets is quickly adjusting to profitability and journalistic benefits. With the rise of emergency technologies and the popularity of social media, it is difficult to imagine what traditional media will look like in the future, but clearly the traditional format is changing, if not dead.

Available Tools of a Citizen Journalist

Individuals throughout the world are beginning to utilize social media to report their surroundings, which includes emergency or disaster events that affect geographic locations "upstream" of the event. Citizen journalism is facilitated (and in some cases fueled) by various social media systems and Web 2.0 technologies that allow for the posting of status updates, pictures, videos, and streaming videos. It is through these systems that emergency event-related information can be shared and disseminated easily. Although the systems are important, the tools to engage these systems need to be addressed.

The most common and prevalent tool that facilitates the use of social media systems is the mobile or cellular phone. With nearly 300 million American cellular subscribers generating a 93% population penetration, the capabilities that exist on mobile phones are critical to understanding how many citizens will be reporting witnessed information.[29] In addition to the commonness of cell phones, 74% of surveyed Americans stated that they had used their cell phones during an

IN A NUTSHELL

The old saying is that a lie will travel halfway around the world before the truth gets its pants on. Should we change that to an on-the-scene tweet will make it halfway around the world before our vetted and approved half-truth gets its pants on?

—Jim Garrow, "Stop Pretending You Control Any Information"[37]

emergency, and an additional 41% stated that they used cell phones in their free time when unoccupied by other activities.[30] These findings are strong indicators that the general public associates cell phones with effective communication tools that are actively used and therefore particularly valuable to observe and document events related to emergencies and other high-pressure situations.

If cell phones are available and quickly utilized as tools, it is critical to consider what functionalities exist in those phones. For instance, according to Nielsen, by 2011 more than half of all mobile devices will be smartphones with the capability to run software applications and contain other embedded dynamic features such as photo and video cameras.[31] The combination of software applications and image-generating technology allows most smartphones to have the capability to utilize social media systems that have mobile interfaces to post text, photo, and video content. This citizen reporting could include textual updates about the event at hand or provide real-time visual reporting about how the event is progressing. In addition, most cell phones contain the capability to send and receive text messaging through the short messaging system (SMS) protocol. The SMS protocol delivers short packets of information that are no more than 140 characters, which has also quickly become a tool for the delivery of information to other cell phone users and as posts to social media systems like Twitter or Facebook. With nearly 72% of adults[34] and 88% of teenage cell phone owners[35] routinely texting, the utilization of this tool to facilitate citizen journalism is extraordinarily valuable and should be embraced as such by traditional media providers and emergency managers alike. The impact of mobile systems is further discussed in Chapter 12.

Challenges to Citizen Journalism

Although empowered by numerous tools and systems to upload and share information, citizen journalists face some challenges to this process. Perhaps most important is the question of who owns the shared content from a journalistic perspective. Unlike traditionally produced content distributed by mainstream media outlets

Figure 3.6 Rally in Bahrain during Arab Spring of 2011. (From WPM News/ Creative Commons CC0 1.0 Universal Public Domain.)

that is protected through copyright laws, social media content may be different. For instance, if a citizen posts a picture or video to his social media account that is then reproduced, reposted, or redistributed by traditional media outlets, is there a transfer of ownership or is source acknowledgment required? Although the journalistic ethics of this particular exchange are still under consideration, there was a 2010 international court case that confirmed social media content had to be credited and remunerated appropriately.[32]

Interestingly, there are some events where social media users resort to specific and dedicated citizen journalism because traditional media outlets will not cover the event to the size and scope expected by the community. For example, in 2010 significant flooding in Nashville, Tennessee, and 52 neighboring counties received minimal national mainstream media coverage but maintained significant levels of social media presence on Facebook, Twitter, YouTube, and other systems.[33] Likewise, during the so-called Arab Spring in 2011 (see Figure 3.6) where several countries in the Middle East such as Egypt dealt with public protests and citizen outrage about government suppression, local internet availability was stopped by local governments in an attempt to reduce the impact of social media on the spread of information related to the protests. However, much like the people in Tennessee, local citizens utilized older technologies such as dial-up modems, traditional landlines, and older satellite phones to circumvent the attempted government control of social media to continue to spread messages about the event.[36] This lack of traditional media coverage or attempted government control forced local citizens to create their own journalism, with reports about the event being

Figure 3.7   Tom Erickson.

posted to social media to advocate for issues related to the disaster. Social media systems provided not only a voice to impacted individuals but also a magnified voice to the entire community.

Practitioner Profile: Tom Erickson, Johnson County Sheriff's Office

Tom Erickson (Figure 3.7) is a well-respected law enforcement public information officer in the Greater Kansas City area who utilizes social media for situational awareness and media engagement. When asked why social media was important, Mr. Erickson stated, "[S]ocial media is the only tool available to emergency managers to communicate instantly and directly with their residents." He went on to say that "It would be impossible to have a full operating picture without its use in monitoring for situational awareness." When asked to address the implications of social media on contemporary journalism, he stated that "Not since the public implementation of the internet has anything had such a profound impact on journalism and communications [with]…the speed at which information is shared forcing journalists to create content on an increased schedule, push stories out to the masses on multiple platforms and utilize social media as a new primary source for information." Mr. Erickson identified that not all emergency managers have begun to embrace social media and its impact on citizen journalism. Instead he shared that "There are those [in the public] who will disagree with government in many instances and the only way to combat this is provide [them] with the correct information instead of being silent." Mr. Erickson is a strong advocate of active social media use and clearly understands its impact not only to emergency managers but to professional journalists as well.

Chapter Terms

Citizen journalism: Concept of reported media, in any form, that has had the participation and/or contribution of information from citizens, observers, or other nonprofessional or pseudo-professional individuals.

Participatory journalism: Secondary term used to describe citizen journalism.

Bystander Effect: Psychological phenomenon where event observers stay unengaged and do not initiate or facilitate appropriate and effective response.

Good Samaritan effect: Concept and legal protection that allows for and encourages event observers to be able to provide appropriate and necessary actions that are lifesaving or life preserving.

Algorithmic authority: Sociological phenomenon identified by Clay Shirky that stresses the capability of taking information from multiple sources with little to no individual credibility into a combined source that is vetted, trustworthy, and capable of being usefully transmitted or shared.

24/7 news cycle: Concept of a news cycle that must be aware of current conditions and prepared to report newsworthy information 24 hours a day, 7 days a week. This type of news cycle was initially created within the implementation of cable news networks in the 1980s.

60/60 news cycle: Concept of a news cycle that must be aware of current conditions and prepared to report newsworthy information 60 seconds a minute, 60 minutes an hour. This type of news cycle is strongly influenced by the rise and impact of emergency technologies such as social media.

Chapter Questions

General Questions

1. What is the name of the concept of news reporting that allows participatory functions by nonprofessional individuals in association with professional journalists?
    a. Algorithmic authority
    b. 60/60 news cycle
    c. Citizen journalism
    d. None of the above
2. True/False: The news cycle is becoming extended with more time in between reports about a given incident.

3. True/False: The Bystander Effect is the phenomenon where individuals respond quickly and effectively when they witness emergencies or disasters.

Essay Questions

1. Discuss the four major media forms, including the historical, social, and technological considerations for each.
2. Discuss the impact of editorial review on journalistic reporting.
3. Discuss the challenge of changing news cycles throughout the four major media forms.

Works Cited

1. Ash, Timothy Garton. *Facts Are Subversive: Political Writing from a Decade without a Name*. Oxford: Yale University Press, 2009.
2. "US Airways Flight 1549 Crew Receive Prestigious Guild of Air Pilots and Air Navigators Award." *GAPAN Press Release*. http://www.gapan.org/ruth-documents/Masters%20Medal%20%20Press%20Release.pdf (accessed October 27, 2011).
3. "Janis Krum." AboutMe. http://about.me/JanisKrums (accessed January 11, 2011).
4. Frommer, Dan. "U.S. Airways Crash Rescue Picture: Citizen Journalism, Twitter at Work." *Business Insider*, January 25, 2009. http://www.businessinsider.com/2009/1/us-airways-crash-rescue-picture-citizen-jouralism-twitter-at-work#ixzz19p4NQI8V (accessed January 11, 2011).
5. *TwitPic*, January 15, 2009. http://twitpic.com/135xa# (accessed January 11, 2011).
6. Darley, John M., and Bibb Latané. "Bystander Intervention in Emergencies: Diffusion of Responsibilities." *Library for Psychology in the New Millennium*, 1968. http://www.wadsworth.com/psychology_d/templates/student_resources/0155060678_rathus/ps/ps19.html (accessed October 27, 2011).
7. Keltner, Dacher, and Jason Marsh. "We Are All Bystanders." *Greater Good—The Science of Meaningful Life*, Fall–Winter 2006–2007. http://greatergood.berkeley.edu/article/item/we_are_all_bystanders/ (accessed January 11, 2011).
8. Glaser, Mark. "Did London Bombings Turn Citizen Journalists into Citizen Paparazzi? *OJR: The Online Journalism Review*, July 12, 2005. http://www.ojr.org/ojr/stories/050712glaser/ (accessed January 11, 2011).
9. "Mumbai: Twitter's Moment." *Forbes.com*, November 28, 2008. http://www.forbes.com/2008/11/28/mumbai-twitter-sms-tech-internet-cx_bc_kn_1128mumbai.html (accessed January 11, 2011).
10. "History of Journalism." Wikipedia. http://en.wikipedia.org/wiki/History_of_journalism (accessed January 11, 2011).
11. "History of Michigan AM Broadcasting." *Michigan's Radio and TV Guide*, 2011. http://www.michiguide.com/history/am.html (accessed October 27, 2011).
12. "National Broadcasting Company." *Museum of Broadcast Communications*, 2011. http://www.museum.tv/eotvsection.php?entrycode=nationalbroa (accessed October 27, 2011).

13. "Press Accuracy Rating Hits Two Decade Low, Public Evaluations of the News Media: 1985–2009." *Pew Research Center for the People and the Press*, September 13, 2009. http://people-press.org/report/543/ (accessed January 11, 2011).

14. Lasica, J. D. "What Is Participatory Journalism." *Online Journalism Review*, August 7, 2003. http://www.ojr.org/ojr/workplace/1060217106.php (accessed January 11, 2011).

15. Winer, Dave. "DaveNet: What Is a News Aggregator?" *DaveNet Blog*, October 8, 2002. http://scripting.com/davenet/2002/10/08/whatIsANewsAggregator.html (accessed October 27, 2011).

16. "Closed Newspapers." *Paper Cuts*. http://newspaperlayoffs.com/maps/closed/ (accessed January 11, 2011).

17. "Newspapers Face a Challenging Calculus." *Pew Internet Center for the People and the Press*, February 6, 2009. http://pewresearch.org/pubs/1133/decline-print-newspapers-increased-online-news (accessed January 11, 2011).

18. "Understanding the Participatory News Consumer." *Pew Internet and American Life Project*, March 1, 2010. http://www.pewinternet.org/Reports/2010/Online-News.aspx (accessed January 11, 2011).

19. "Storm Reports via Twitter." *National Weather Service*, April 15, 2010. http://www.weather.gov/stormreports/ (accessed January 11, 2011).

20. "CNN Changed News—For Better or Worse." *Taipei Times*, May 31, 2005. http://www.taipeitimes.com/News/editorials/archives/2005/05/31/2003257358 (accessed January 11, 2011).

21. Litten, Dominic. "The 24-Hour News Cycle Is Dead." *Point to Point Blog*. July 8, 2010. http://www.pointtopoint.com/2010/07/sources-the-24-hour-news-cycle-is-dead/ (accessed January 11, 2011).

22. "Internet Gains on Television as Public's Main News Source." *Pew Research Center*, January 4, 2011. http://people-press.org/report/689/ (accessed January 11, 2011).

23. "Video Quality Less Important When You're Enjoying What You're Watching." *Rice University Press Release*, August 12, 2010. http://www.media.rice.edu/media/NewsBot.asp?MODE=VIEW&ID=14616 (accessed January 14, 2011).

24. "Skype Surges as TV Interview Tool." *CBC News*, September 2, 2010. http://www.cbc.ca/arts/media/story/2010/09/02/skype-tv-news.html (accessed January 14, 2011).

25. "Is Rupert Murdoch's iPad-Only Newspaper the Future of Journalism?" *Mashable*, November 21, 2010. http://mashable.com/2010/11/21/the-daily-ipad-journalism/ (accessed January 14, 2011).

26. Presentation by Kris Ketz, KMBC News Anchor, Kansas City, Missouri, December 14, 2010.

27. Ostrow, Adam. "AOL Acquires Technology Blog Network TechCrunch." *Mashable*, September 28, 2010. http://mashable.com/2010/09/28/aol-acquires-techcrunch (accessed January 14, 2011).

28. Brown, Tina. "Daily Beast, Newsweek to Wed!" *Daily Beast*, November 11, 2010. http://www.thedailybeast.com/blogs-and-stories/2010–11–11/the-daily-beast-and-newsweek-to-wed/ (accessed January 14, 2011).

29. "U.S. Wireless Quick Facts." *CTIA Advocacy*. http://www.ctia.org/advocacy/research/index.cfm/aid/10323 (accessed January 14, 2011).

30. "Americans and Their Cell Phones." *Pew Internet and American Life Project*, April 3, 2006. http://www.pewinternet.org/Reports/2006/Americans-and-their-cell-phones.aspx (accessed January 14, 2011).

31. Entner, Roger. "Smartphones to Overtake Feature Phones in U.S. by 2011." *Nielsen Wire*, March 26, 2010. http://blog.nielsen.com/nielsenwire/consumer/smartphones-to-overtake-feature-phones-in-u-s-by-2011/ (accessed January 14, 2011).

32. Mullin, Joe. "Court to AFP: Pics Aren't Free Just because They're on Twitter." *PaidContent.org*, December 29, 2010. http://paidcontent.org/article/419-court-to-afp-pics-arent-free-just-because-theyre-on-twitter/ (accessed January 14, 2011).

33. Sellers, Bob. "What the Media Missed in the 'Nashville' Flood." *Huffington Post*, May 10, 2010. http://www.huffingtonpost.com/bob-sellers/what-the-media-missed-in_b_570686.html (accessed January 14, 2011).

34. "10 vs. 50—Texting: Adults vs. Teens." *Pew Research Center*. http://pewresearch.org/databank/dailynumber/?NumberID=1089 (accessed January 14, 2011).

35. Lenhart, Amanda. "Teens, Cell Phones and Texting." *Pew Internet and American Life Project*, April 20, 2010. http://pewresearch.org/pubs/1572/teens-cell-phones-text-messages (accessed January 14, 2011).

36. Macedo, Diane. "Egyptians Use Low-Technology Gadgets to Get around Communications Block." *FoxNews*, January 28, 2011. http://www.foxnews.com/sci-tech/2011/01/28/old-technology-helps-egyptians-communications-black/ (accessed February 16, 2011).

37. Garrow, Jim. "Stop Pretending You Control Any Information." *Face of the Matter Blog*, 2011. http://jgarrow.posterous.com/stop-pretending-you-control-any-information (accessed January 17, 2011).

Chapter 4

Mountains or Molehills: Engagement Challenges in the Application of Social Media

Asking who should be doing social media is like asking who should have a phone on their desk. Assume everyone is on social media.

—Warren Whitlock, co-author of *Twitter Revolution*[1a]

Chapter Objectives

- To analyze the benefits and challenges of social media application and implementation for emergency management
- To identify return-on-investment (ROI) strategies for proper implementation of social media
- To identify privacy and security issues for the implementation of social media
- To understand the impact of the Freedom of Information Act (FOIA) and "sunshine laws" on social media use by emergency managers
- To identify functional considerations and components of social media policy

DISASTER FOCUS—DEEPWATER HORIZON OIL SPILL

On April 20, 2010, methane gas from a high-pressure Gulf of Mexico oil drilling well on a rig called the Deepwater Horizon expanded out of the drilling column, causing a significant explosion. Fire quickly engulfed the drilling platform. Many of the workers escaped the Deepwater Horizon rig by lifeboat; however, 11 workers were never found despite prolonged searches by the U.S. Coast Guard and were later presumed dead. After burning for nearly a day and a half, the Deepwater Horizon sank on the morning of April 22, 2010. On the afternoon that the rig ultimately sank, an oil slick began to spread around the former rig site (Figure 4.1). The source of the oil spill was ultimately identified as a sea-floor oil gusher from the damaged drilling pipe previously utilized by the Deepwater Horizon. This oil leak flowed for three months during the summer of 2010 and was eventually stopped by a procedure called a "static kill" that sealed the leak using a mixture of cement and heavy drilling mud. According to some estimates, by the time the leak was stopped it had released about 4.9 million barrels or 205.8 million gallons of crude oil. The Deepwater Horizon oil drilling rig was owned by Transocean, operated by Halliburton, contracted by British Petroleum (BP), and inspected for safety by the U.S. Minerals Management Service. This division of responsibilities quickly became the focus of response and recovery activities. Traditional media as well as the general public through social media channels began to question who was accountable for the loss of life and environmental impact of the explosion on the Deepwater Horizon. Although the U.S. federal government ultimately focused responsibility for the event on BP, the public relations consequences were profoundly magnified through the application (or lack thereof) of social media by the major players. Specifically, BP did not engage social media in earnest to present its version of response to the oil spill until several weeks into the spill response. Moreover, their actual Twitter and Facebook accounts were significantly overshadowed by parody and boycott pages established on Twitter and Facebook, respectively. In retrospect, BP's oversight related to the proper and effective implementation of social media for disaster communications cost them millions of dollars in revenue through significant impacts to brand imaging and loss of clients.[1,2,3,4]

Hurdles and Hindrances

One of the most significant hurdles for the average emergency management office to implement effective and appropriate social media programs is the fear of doing it wrong. Ironically, this fear is paradoxical considering the example set during the Deepwater Horizon oil spill where doing nothing was as dangerous to sensitive public messages as doing it "wrong." This chapter focuses on the proper application

Figure 4.1 Vessels conduct skimming operations in the Gulf of Mexico near the site of the Deepwater Horizon incident May 16, 2010. (From U.S. Navy, Stephanie Brown.)

of social media systems, including models of execution, policy implementation, and challenges—both legal and structural—that exist for emergency managers.

To begin this process, emergency managers regardless of discipline must look at a "2.0" model of practice. Since most emergency managers exist within the governmental or quasi-governmental model, Andrea Di Maio's five essentials for government 2.0 should be strongly considered as an excellent model for beginning the 2.0 conversion (Figure 4.2). The first of these essentials was the concept that this new model of government creates a paradox between politicians and governmental operators. Specifically, Di Maio states that government 2.0 models will only "succeed when [politicians] stop trying to meet political requirements, such as increasing people's trust in government, and start addressing service delivery and resource management challenges."[4] Additionally, government 2.0 must also concentrate on being a part of the social media conversation rather than the host. Government—emergency managers included—are accustomed to hierarchal structures where information is managed through command and control situations. Unfortunately, this is not the form established within the social media community. This operational difference is based on the necessity of two-way conversations through social media channels versus traditional one-way communication facilitated by governmental entities still functioning under traditional "1.0" models. The third and perhaps most important essential concept highlighted by Di Maio, and one that ties into the fourth and fifth concepts, is the need for an alignment between government 2.0 initiatives and organizational strategic goals. In other words, emergency management organizations attempting to implement the government 2.0 model cannot apply social media simply for the sake of having

GOVERNMENT 2.0 CONSIDERATIONS

1. Government 2.0 and politics don't mix.
2. Government 2.0 is not about being the host but being a guest in the conversation.
3. Government 2.0 is not a platform, it's a toolkit.
4. Government 2.0 is about more than conversation.
5. Government 2.0 initiatives must align with business goals.[17]

such systems. Rather the application should support organizational needs such as public education, crisis communications, situational awareness, and the development of operational tools.

Programmatic Implementation

The consideration of implementing the government 2.0 model and thus social media systems is divided into three categories: active, passive, and stationary. Each of these three models of social media application has challenges and complex considerations that must be evaluated by emergency managers prior to implementation (Figure 4.2). The difference between these models is primarily related to the degree of social media monitoring, analysis, and validation as well as information dissemination applied by the end user or organization. For instance, the active model of social media application involves the routine utilization of social media systems for the dissemination of information and vigorous monitoring of the social media conversation related to the given community. For instance, if a given community is concerned about a hurricane that is forecasted to impact their community, an emergency manager who has actively implemented social media would monitor conversations on social networks, blogs, and microblogs to determine community response to incident-related actions such as evacuation, household mitigation, and personal preparedness. On the other hand, passive application of social media systems by professional emergency managers does not support the robustness of the active model. Passive models are defined by the support of only information dissemination or information analysis, but not both. Given the emergency scenario of the forecasted hurricane described above, emergency managers utilizing passive application of social media would either be disseminating information about evacuation routes and other preparedness strategies via social media systems or monitoring the social media conversation about the event. Lastly, the stationary social media model is the complete opposite of the active model because it utilizes social media to neither disseminate information nor monitor event-related communications. This stationary model is the "do nothing" form of social media application that some emergency management

Figure 4.2 **There are different levels of social media engagement for emergency events such as hurricanes. (From National Aeronautics and Space Administration [NASA], Jeff Schmaultz.)**

professionals continue to embrace rather than considering either the active or passive models.

The major issue with the stationary model of social media application is that the emergency management organization risks the same issues that British Petroleum (BP) did during the Deepwater Horizon oil spill in the summer of 2010. Not being active in social media systems can be extremely impactful when a significant event threatens a given organization or jurisdiction because (based on the BP model) organizations cannot implement effective social media utilization *after* an event or disaster has occurred. To put this into perspective, a fake Twitter account (@ BPGlobalPR) was created soon after the initial explosion on the Deepwater Horizon drilling rig that quickly became a primary source of public information. By the middle of July 2010, this fake parody account had 116,000 followers, which was more than 10 times the number of followers on the official BP Twitter account.[5]

Consequently, it is careless and negligent not to implement at least a passive social media strategy considering the public safety responsibility that is fundamentally granted to emergency managers across all disciplines and functions.

Although active and passive implementation strategies are significantly more effective than the stationary model of social media implementation, there are also considerable challenges to their application. These challenges include privacy, security, policy implementation, and acceptance by leadership, as well as return-on-investment (ROI) justifications. Each of these challenges contains unique issues for any emergency management application of social media and Web 2.0 systems. These challenges, however, can be overcome through systematic review and implementation by the modern emergency manager.

The Challenge of Privacy

The first of these challenges is to ensure privacy is paramount regardless of the social media system or technology applied. This includes situations that require both the dissemination and the monitoring of information by emergency managers using social media systems (see Figure 4.3). For example, emergency managers working in the health and medical field are required to abide by the Health Insurance Portability and Accountability Act (HIPAA). The HIPAA privacy regulations were created to protect the privacy of an individual's health information. Consequently, it is extremely important within this sector of emergency management to evaluate the impact of social media on HIPAA standards before any information can be distributed or collected. This becomes a challenge when social media provides opportunities to streamline the sharing of information during emergency medical situations. For example, it would be conceivable for emergency medical technicians working in an ambulance in route to a hospital from an emergency scene to utilize cell phones and social media systems like Twitter to photograph the patient's condition (e.g., wounds) and forward them to the emergency room medical staff for review and preparedness prior to arrival. While potentially extremely useful to the improvement of emergency response, considering the uncontrolled and potentially public nature of utilizing social media sites and Wi-Fi signals, this type of scenario would clearly put this type of activity in violation of HIPAA guidelines.

Privacy considerations related to the implementation of social media relate not only to the potential professional utilization of social media in emergency management but also to the personal use of these systems by emergency managers. This type of personal utilization can often be a blurred line with professional employment, which can cause significant confusion on where privacy rules and general appropriateness are correctly applied. While not directly related to emergency management, there was a prime example of this issue among nursing students at Johnson County Community College in Overland Park, Kansas, in late 2010. Specifically, Doyle Byrnes, a senior nursing student at Johnson County Community College

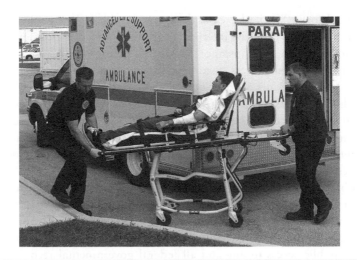

Figure 4.3 Paramedics must balance the benefit of utilizing social media with preexisting privacy rules and regulations. (From U.S. Navy/Mass Communication Specialist Seaman Patrick J. Cook.)

(JCCC) posed with a picture of a human placenta that was being studied in the nursing lab. She was immediately dismissed once the picture was discovered posted to Ms. Byrnes's personal Facebook page. Although the event was called a "momentary lapse in judgment" and a "lesson hard learned" by Ms. Byrnes and the JCCC administration, respectively, it is a profound example of where personal and professional boundaries can blur within social media systems.[6]

Additionally, the challenge of privacy for social media implementation by emergency managers also involves the security of operational data and the impact of information disseminated by external sources. For instance, there are significant types of data controlled by emergency managers—especially those responsible for law enforcement and homeland security—that are sensitive in nature and often limited, if not completely guarded, from public view. The attempt to secure this information is often to ensure investigative and response efficacy. However, there have been situations such as the 2010 release of nearly 250,000 secret U.S. embassy cables through an online site called Wikileaks that put such efforts at risk. These documents revealed internal U.S. diplomatic and operational considerations within the framework of known foreign policy that resulted in both embarrassing and politically sensitive declarations about internal relationships and foreign partnerships.[7]

This type of security challenge is inherent when government begins to adopt, engage, and respond to social media systems like Wikileaks. As the name implies, Wikileaks is a wiki-sourcing website like Wikipedia that is designed to allow the collection of information about a particular topic (in this case governmental communications) that can be edited, vetted, and organized by users who collectively have access and knowledge about certain issues that transcends the knowledge of the individual (or in Wikileaks' case, the general public). This wiki concept is of growing importance within the internet community and is critical for emergency managers to understand. For instance, Wikileaks claims to be a wiki outlet for the collection of "untraceable mass document leaking and analysis...[of] oppressive regimes in Asia, the former Soviet bloc, Sub-Saharan Africa and the Middle East, but [can] also...be of assistance to people of all regions who wish to reveal unethical behavior in their governments and corporations."[8] This type of purpose may seem altruistic and benign on the surface but can clearly become extremely impactful to governmental or private entities that have confidentiality and privacy concerns and/ or mandates such as might exist in homeland security.

In addition, many governmental and quasi-governmental emergency management programs have been impacted by freedom of information requests for information on various components of information. The Freedom of Information Act (FOIA) originally passed by the federal government in 1966 was designed to allow the general public access to any and all federal governmental records. The only FOIA exceptions were classified into nine categories that included disclosure protection for issues related to national defense, personnel rules, trade secrets, medical records, certain financial records, and some related to law enforcement investigations.[9] Most states quickly followed this model by creating freedom of information legislation commonly referred to as "sunshine laws." Much like the FOIA exceptions, most states with sunshine laws also have limitations to what types of information are exempted. Unfortunately, most legal experts consider social media as equivalent to other governmental materials and thus must comply with freedom of information requests if categorically allowed. Consequently, it is critical that emergency managers evaluate the legal requirements in their jurisdictions about the retention and preservation of messages and then evaluate what impact this may have on social media usage. In most cases, social media sites used by governments are public and therefore collected by the particular social media system, allowing them to be reviewed at any time by anyone in the public. There are, however, some systems that can more quickly search stored public social media messages and aggregate these for both freedom of information requests and for operational purposes. These systems are further discussed in Chapter 7.

Policy Implementation

Establishing localized policies and procedures for freedom of information requests is just skimming the surface of issues related to social media policy implementation. There are additional issues that must be addressed in policy to ensure effective, efficient, and accountable application of social media by emergency managers. The benefits to implementing robust and vetted policies include the protection of an organization's reputation, the clarification of murky legal issues, and an increase in organizational brand awareness.[10] The process of writing and later implementing a social media usage policy should be vetted across an organization's core functions and/or representatives and should have vertical support from users to elected leadership and executive management. These core functions include human resources, information technology, risk management, legal, and of course emergency management and their respective partners. This will ensure the social media policy complies with all current internal policies and local ordinances, as well as state and federal laws. An effective social media policy must create a framework of rules and guidelines to address eight key characteristics: employee access, account management, acceptable use, employee conduct, content, security, legal issues, and citizen conduct. Each of these characteristics is unique and must be completely developed to ensure a thorough social media policy.

The first policy consideration is related to the level of access allowed to an organization's employees. One study from Webroot of 1,000 companies in the United States and the United Kingdom determined that 40% of the companies had policies that prohibited employees from visiting Facebook, 30% blocked access to Twitter, and 27% prohibited employees from visiting video-sharing sites like YouTube or Vimeo.[13] This indicates that more than half of the companies surveyed did not strictly prohibit access to social media systems. It is this balance that must be struck by each organization, but with particular consideration of the potential emergency management implications. In some cases, organizations have maintained that employees should only have limited (if any) access to social media

FUNCTIONAL CONSIDERATIONS FOR SOCIAL MEDIA POLICY IMPLEMENTATION

LEGAL

- Privacy laws
- Freedom of information laws
- Record retention

TECHNICAL AND RISK MANAGEMENT

- Internet bandwidth capacity
- Antivirus and malware protection
- Network and information security
- Protection of patient/client data

HUMAN RESOURCES

- Employee behavior
- Jurisdictional representation
- Productivity

for fear that their productivity will suffer due to distraction. Interestingly, some studies have shown that employee productivity actually increases with open access to social media systems.[12] This increase is hypothesized to occur for several reasons, including an improved capability and desire to multitask by younger generations.[11] Other organizations have maintained this limitation based on concerns that the organization's internal network and all related functional systems are at greater risk due to exposure from social media systems to system limitations as well as viruses, malware, and other malicious forms of technological attack.

The second major policy consideration is related to account management. Account management refers to those social media sources officially approved, managed, and instituted by the organization. Although this seems relatively straightforward, it is critical that a structure be established to set the framework for account management that includes the secured collection of user identification (userids) and passwords as well as identified employees who have the responsibility for content on the sites. These types of protocols help ensure that the information ultimately disseminated via official social media systems is of the type and quality required by the organization and does not ultimately reflect poorly on the organization. The role of account management is also closely related to the overall strategy of social media implementation. Specifically, if not handled correctly, organizations can quickly become overcommitted to social media systems and be unable to either properly manage or to monitor officially established systems.

The third characteristic that must be considered when evaluating social media policy implementation is related to acceptable use of these systems by employees and representatives (see Figure 4.4). The acceptable use consideration is closely related to employee access and conduct. Since social media is fundamentally based on transparent, two-way conversation, governmental and quasi-governmental agencies must define what types of conversation will be conducted on officially approved systems. For instance, some organizations will not allow or will significantly moderate

Figure 4.4 Maintaining a strong and effective policy is critical to successful social media usage. (From Federal Emergency Management Agency [FEMA], Leif Skoogfors [image] and Jennie Crowe [graphic].)

any public postings or comments related to officially posted social media content. Although this is a fundamentally flawed approach to try and manage social media accounts, it is one end of the spectrum when considering approved usage of these systems. The other end of that spectrum is an open and accessible system that posts conversational content that encourages and facilitates conversation that could be perceived as either positively or negatively reflecting on the organization. Predictably, most emergency management organizations fall between these two extremes, with many emergency managers preferring to lean toward the more controlled and moderated end of the spectrum. Regardless, leadership, management, and the employees ultimately responsible for the social media systems must be on the same page to ensure this process is managed efficiently and effectively.

As stated earlier, the approved use of social media is closely related to policy considerations about employee conduct. This interconnectivity occurs for two reasons. First, employees who create social media content on behalf of their organizations must be careful to create a social media "voice" that is consistent with organizational policies and philosophies but does not ignore the social media foundations of transparent conversation. This is often extremely difficult to do as the general public will often respond in extremely casual, sometimes argumentative or confrontational tones—especially when the topic relates to the spectrum of emergency management issues that may be discussed. The second reason that employee conduct is important is that employees—whether on official or personal social media systems—may be perceived as representing their employer on issues related to their employment. For example, if an employee posts on one of her personal social media sites (such as Facebook) that she thought a recent emergency management training session was a waste of time and taxpayer money, there is a reasonable interpretation that these comments could be referring to her employer regardless of the intention of the employee. Consequently, it is critical to create a framework for employees to understand how they are supposed to engage the general public on official sites as well as their expected behavior on personal sites. For personal social media sites, this component of a social media policy is typically handled by simply instructing employees when posting to their personal sites to add a phrase similar to "This is not the official opinion of [insert employer]" when discussing issues that are professionally related or might have ethical implications. Including a procedural mandate to include this type of simple disclaimer by the employee will alleviate or minimize any issues that may arise due to confusion about the official nature of messages.

Official content is an additional consideration for social media policy implementation, specifically regarding what type of content can be posted and in what forms. For instance, many organizations mandate that all social media systems link back to primary sources such as the organization's website or to trusted sources. For emergency management, this might include state emergency management offices, FEMA.gov, and Ready.gov. Maintaining consistent linkage helps ensure officially posted content is trustworthy and supports the organization's mission and image within the given community or industry sector. Additional content considerations may surround the type of content allowed for official distribution. This particular issue arises with content posted and/or shared on systems such as internet radio, video sharing, photo sharing, and video streaming. These formats allow for content that is either somewhat improvised (online radio) or potentially requires a certain technical skill or capability to achieve materials that are of a professional quality that is acceptable and cohesive with current organizational standards.

There are also numerous legal issues that must also be considered when implementing a social media policy for emergency management offices. These legal issues include consideration of harassment, use of copyrighted or trademarked materials, employee privacy, and censorship.[13] Considering the relative newness of social media and the limited legal opinions available, these issues are not always as clear-cut as some governmental concepts that need legal consideration. For instance, privacy on social media is a unique concept. In most cases, public postings on public social media sites cannot be considered private; however, this issue is further complicated by social networking systems that have varying levels of privacy settings that can be easily misunderstood by the system user. Consequently, organizations have the capability to monitor employee behavior or comments on those public systems but cannot make discriminatory decisions based on information discovered about race, gender, political opinion, or sexual orientation. This interpretation is further compounded by the source of access to these systems. The concept of privacy for an employee or citizen is not as concrete if social media systems are accessed and/or the data is stored on servers and/or internet portals that are controlled, operated, or owned by the organization.

In addition to privacy considerations, there is a strong need to specifically address use of copyrighted or trademarked materials in governmental social media systems. This becomes a challenge because many citizens—including government employees—have the misperception that if a picture, logo, or other created content is available to be downloaded (for free or for charge), they are eligible to be utilized in any reproduced materials. Unfortunately, this understanding of the use of intellectual properties is inaccurate. In most cases, these materials must be approved for use by the creator or innovator prior to their inclusion in official social media outlets. In some cases, owners of the copyrighted material are hiring external firms to track down unauthorized usages and push for maximum penalties for use, which have included a $150,000 fine and a seizure of the domain that posted the content.[14] Most governmental agencies, including emergency managers, seeking to utilize protected intellectual property to improve public education campaigns need to be careful to be specific within social media policies when determining what type of content is and is not allowable for official use.

Citizen content is the final consideration for policy implementation. The definition of social media citizen content can sometimes be confusing, especially for those individuals who are not actively engaged in these systems. Specifically, content is only those materials (text, photo, audio, video, etc.) posted on the page or site controlled by the organization. However, because most social media systems require individuals to create specific userids with corresponding social media sites, there is inherently a link when an individual posts a response, comment, or selects to follow another social media site. For instance, if the Central City Emergency Management Agency posts on its Facebook page about a new public education campaign, they are inherently opening their official page for public comments and content. This content must be reviewed and controlled under the Central City social media policy. However, if citizen John Smith posts a response to the Central City Facebook page and another citizen "Jane Doe" clicks on "John Smith," the Central City Emergency Management Agency cannot be held responsible for any content that is viewed after that point. This content falls under the control of the citizen, or in this case "John Smith." These content streams, while similar in nature, are not accountable in the same ways. This is a critical point within social media streams because an overly restrictive policy will potentially negatively impact the actual content of the site.

Challenges to Implementation

Although social media programmatic and policy implementation is critical to the successful utilization of social media by emergency managers, there are significant challenges and hurdles that must be considered during this process. These hurdles include evaluations of systematic effectiveness such as return on investment (ROI), benchmarking, management and facilitation challenges, and proper public engagement. The management and facilitation of social media systems starts with proper commitment from executive leadership and elected officials. Without buy-in from these levels of the organization, proper systematic implementation will be difficult if not impossible. If leadership commitment is present, specific organizational issues must be considered, such as size of the jurisdiction and organization as well as the demographics of the local community. These considerations are critical to ensure that social media duties are assigned strategically and given appropriate weight in comparison to other duties. It should be noted, however, that the size of a jurisdiction or the organization managing that jurisdiction should not be an excuse to not programmatically implement social media. This book, as well as the numerous anecdotal stories of the importance of social media on the future of emergency preparedness and response, should support the fact that an inactive implementation strategy is not sufficient in modern times.

Once the level of engagement is determined by organizational leadership, there will be an expectation to establish the return on investment (ROI) for social media implementation. Unfortunately, establishing ROI analysis on social media implementation and utilization is difficult because of the nontraditional structure of these systems. Some systems have been developed, such as Klout, that help measure influence of common social media systems like Twitter, but these are sometimes incompatible with governmental analysis of ROI. Additionally, benchmarking for social media application is challenging and often is based simply on emulating systems and approaches utilized by organizations that appear to be successful. Consequently, most organizations adopt rudimentary output models of analysis rather than evaluating social media results based on the more complex outcome analysis. In other words, nearly every social media system allows for complex analytics tools that will quickly process number of followers, fans, subscribers, posts, response comments, and many other pieces of information over a period of time. These measurements allow for basic analysis about whether social media systems are continuing to increase in the number of followers and provide quality social media discourse. Various aspects of social media analysis are further discussed in Chapter 6.

Another challenge to implementation and effectiveness is the difficulty of communicating through social media systems in a way that is professional and analogous to organizational standards of communication while maintaining a quality social media "voice" that is genuine, transparent, and conversational in tone (see Figure 4.5). Organizations that do not utilize this type of voice or that strictly implement automated messaging are often ignored by the general public, and the benefit of communicating via social media systems is lost. Unfortunately, governmental and quasi-governmental organizations can overreach in their attempts to have a unique social media voice. For instance, in 2010, after the U.S. Transportation Security Administration (TSA) as a division of the U.S. Department of Homeland Security instituted body scanners at airports, there was significant public outcry about the process, including calls that it invaded the privacy of passengers and was unnecessary to secure the protection of the traveling public. Among other strategies, TSA implemented a social media strategy that included Twitter as an opportunity to provide feedback from the general public about their concerns. Unfortunately, the voice TSA utilized was cynical and often times rude and clearly was incongruous with the other primary communication pathways utilized by TSA. For example, during the Thanksgiving flight season of 2010, the TSA Twitter account posted flippant responses related to seasonal themes and casual responses to legitimate concerns from the general public.[16] It is clear that governmental social media outlets cannot speak in the same tone and frankness of the general public; however, with some considerations and analysis of real-life examples, an effective voice can be developed that is consistent and dependable.

The last challenge that impacts effective implementation of social media for government is the growing need to provide support and communication for citizens with functional or special needs. Although various definitions exist, one emergency management survey created five categories for functional or special needs populations: language proficiency, age vulnerable, physical limitations (or disabilities), economically disadvantaged, and culturally/geographically isolated.[15] Although these categories are extremely broad and contain much subcontext, the use of social media may or may not be effective in reaching these community sectors. For instance, communities that are culturally or geographically isolated (e.g., Amish

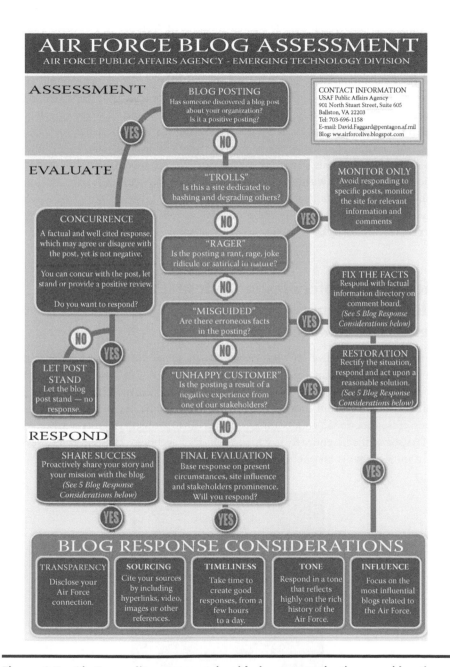

Figure 4.5 Air Force discovery matrix aids in communication considerations. (From U.S. Air Force.)

communities) and not exposed to technology or have the infrastructure to support social media could not effectively be communicated with via social media or Web 2.0 technologies. On the other hand, utilizing some of the Web 2.0 technologies that exist to convert written messages to audio text (e.g., podcasting) or to convert them into secondary languages within communities (e.g., Spanish) would be an effective strategy to provide communication to the language proficiency subgroup. Regardless, the use of social media to reach these communities is not significantly different than communities as a whole considering the need to utilize social media as part of a comprehensive strategy for communication and technology integration. Understanding this perspective is critical for all governmental agencies but particularly important within emergency management as professionals continue to evaluate how to communicate with the public during crisis situations to ensure as many citizens as possible receive the protective actions statements necessary during emergencies or disasters.

Practitioner Profile: Jason Lindesmith, Federal Emergency Management Agency Headquarters

Jason Lindesmith (Figure 4.6) has served as the social media lead for the Federal Emergency Management Agency (FEMA) since 2010. He has significant experience in strategic and crisis communication, emergency management, organizational collaboration, and most importantly, social media. At FEMA, his job is to deliver cross-functional collaboration and critical problem solving within all of FEMA's social media endeavors, which includes Facebook, Twitter, YouTube, and Ready.gov, and he is an energetic administrator who supports and utilizes social

Figure 4.6 Jason Lindesmith.

media freely and with significant candor. When asked why social media is so important to the future of emergency management, Mr. Lindesmith responded, "It connects people directly with avenues for critical information and eliminates the need for disaster survivors to have to wait for news and official information during a rapidly changing situation." In addition, Mr. Lindesmith indicated that the watershed moment for emergency management and social media was the 2010 earthquake in Haiti where emergent technologies (e.g., Facebook and Twitter) "coupled with thousands of disaster survivors led to cries for help that transcended ways previously seen by emergency responders." As an expert in strategic implementation of social media, Mr. Lindesmith stressed that procedural and policy application are critical for social media to be successful in emergency management because it reflects how an organization acts toward disaster survivors. This engagement helps ensure organizations are perceived as trustworthy and responsive during emergencies. Interestingly, when asked if social media was a long-term component of emergency management, Mr. Lindesmith responded by saying that social media might not be around but the objective of "connecting people and organizations directly with other people will continue to be extremely valuable for disaster response." Mr. Lindesmith unmistakably has a keen understanding and comprehension of not only how social media is being utilized but also how to strategically implement it within modern emergency management.

Chapter Terms

Government 2.0: Processes, protocols, and procedures utilized by government and quasi-government agencies to facilitate a modern form of community engagement that focuses on the integration of new technologies and the prioritization of two-way conversation with the general public.

Active implementation: Official governmental implementation of social media that utilizes social media monitoring, analytics, and information dissemination.

Passive implementation: Official governmental implementation of social media that utilizes one or two but not all of the following: social media monitoring, analytics, and information dissemination.

Stationary implementation: Official governmental implementation of social media that does not conduct social media monitoring, analytics, or information dissemination.

Wiki-sourcing: Type of social media system that collects information about a particular topic that is open to the collective editing of a group of people with shared interests about the topic.

Freedom of Information Act (FOIA): Legislation passed by the U.S. government to mandate the public availability of government-generated materials with the exception of materials related to national defense, personnel matters, trade secrets, medical records, certain financial records, and some related to law enforcement investigations.

Sunshine laws: Common term for state laws that address the public accessibility to government-generated information and meetings. These laws were often based on the foundation established by FOIA, including the exemptions from this type of law.

Return on investment (ROI): Concept that analyzes what benefit is returned from an initial or ongoing investment into a particular project. ROI is critical for social media implementation to ensure the continued support and commitment from executive management and policy decision makers.

Benchmarking: Concept that attempts to create a comparison between organizations, processes, and applications that are realistic and fair due to shared or similar demographics or foundational considerations (e.g., population size).

Functional needs populations: Certain components of the general population who have functional or accessible needs. These populations are often categorized by language proficiency, age vulnerability, physical limitations (or disabilities), economic vulnerability, or geographic isolation.

Chapter Questions

General Questions

1. True/False: The use of social media analytics and information dissemination only is referred to as the stationary model of social media implementation.
2. True/False: Governments utilizing a "2.0 model" should consider participation in social media as a guest rather than the host.
3. What of the following is not a functional consideration for social media implementation?
   a. Privacy laws
   b. Internet bandwidth capacity
   c. Employee behavior
   d. Record retention
   e. None of the above

Essay Questions

1. Discuss three of the biggest challenges to emergency managers in their attempt to implement social media.
2. Discuss the effectiveness of active, passive, and stationary models of social media implementation.
3. Discuss why it is important for emergency managers to write policies and procedures related to the use of social media.

Works Cited

1a. Whitlock, Warren and Micek, Deborah. (2008). *Twitter Revolution: How Social Media and Mobile Marketing is Changing the Way We Do Business & Market Online*. Xeno Press.

1. Alford, Ben. "Five Months, Eight Days: A Timeline of the BP Oil Spill." Takewaway. org, September 21, 2010. http://www.thetakeaway.org/blogs/takeaway/2010/sep/21/ five-months-eight-days-timeline-bp-oil-spill/ (accessed January 20, 2011).

2. "The National Commission on the Deepwater Horizon Oil Spill and Offshore Drilling Ceased Operations on March 11, 2011." *National Commission on the Deepwater Horizon Oil Spill*, 2011. http://www.oilspillcommission.gov/ (accessed on October 29, 2011).

3. Hoch, Maureen. "New Estimate Puts Gulf Leak at 205 Million Gallons." *PBS Newshour*, August 2, 2010. http://www.pbs.org/newshour/rundown/2010/08/new-estimate-puts-oil-leak-at-49-million-barrels.html (accessed on October 29, 2011).

4. Van Buskirk, Elliot. "BP's Social Media Campaign Going About as Well as Capping That Well." *Wired*, June 9, 2010. http://www.wired.com/epicenter/2010/06/bps-social-media-campaign-going-about-as-well-as-capping-that-well/ (accessed January 20, 2011).

5. "BP's Global PR vs. BPGlobalPR." *Newsweek*, June 3, 2010. http://www.newsweek. com/2010/06/04/bp-s-global-pr-vs-bpglobalpr.html (accessed January 20, 2011).

6. "Placenta Photo Gets Kansas Student Expelled." FoxNews. http://www.foxnews.com/ us/2011/01/02/placenta-photo-gets-kan-nursing-students-expelled/ (accessed January 8, 2012).

7. "WikiLeaks U.S. Embassy Cables: New Documents Released." *Huffington Post*, November 28, 2010. http://www.huffingtonpost.com/2010/11/28/wikileaks-us-embassy-cables-documents_n_788893.html (accessed January 20, 2011).

8. "Wikileaks: About." *Wikileaks*. www.wikileaks.org/wiki/Wikileaks:About (accessed January 20, 2011).

9. "Your Right to Federal Records Questions and Answers on the Freedom of Information Act and the Privacy Act, 1992." *Electronic Privacy Information Center*. http://epic.org/ open_gov/rights.html (accessed January 20, 2011).

10. Henricks, Mark. "Why You Need a Social Media Policy." *Entrepreneur*, January 6, 2011. http://www.entrepreneur.com/article/217813 (accessed January 20, 2011).

11. Vara, Suzanne. "How Social Media Actually Improves Your Productivity at Work." *Social Media Today*, 2010. http://socialmediatoday.com/suzannevara/237190/how-social-media-actually-improves-your-productivity-work (accessed January 20, 2011).

12. Ward, Toby. (2009). "Insights from Insidedge: Intranet 2.0 Increases Employee Engagement." In the Know Newsletter, Vol. 1, Issue 4. http://www.insidedge.net/ intheknow/emails/archive/US/7.09_newsletter.html (accessed January 10, 2012).

13. Saper, Daliah. "An Introduction to Legal Issues Surrounding Social Media." *Saper Law*. http://www.slideshare.net/DaliahSaper/legal-implications-of-social-media (accessed January 20, 2011).

14. Pullen, John Patrick. "Las Vegas's Copyright Crapshoot Could Maim Social Media." *CNN Money*, January 6, 2011. http://tech.fortune.cnn.com/2011/01/06/las-vegas-copyright-crapshoot-could-maim-social-media/ (accessed January 20, 2011).

15. "Special Needs Report for the Greater Kansas City Area." Special Report to the Metropolitan Emergency Managers Committee (MEMC). 2005 (accessed January 20, 2011). Available on request from the Mid-America Regional Council (MARC).

16. "The TSA Needs to Opt-Out of Tweeting." *Gizmodo.* http://gizmodo.com/5698460/the-tsa-needs-to-opt-out-of-tweeting (accessed January 20, 2011).
17. Di Maio, Andrea. "5 Necessary Truths about Gov 2.0." *Federal Computer Week,* December 8, 2010.

Chapter 5

The Yellow Tape Conundrum: Citizen and Responder Responsibility

I hope we don't ever see a situation where a bystander, eager to cover an event like [the Virginia Tech Shooting], puts himself in harm's way and comes to regret it.

—Brian Montopoli, political blogger on CBSNews.com[12]

Chapter Objectives

- To understand the impact of social media and Web 2.0 technologies on incident scene preservation, emergency responder safety, and citizen welfare
- To understand the ethical challenges that exist in the usage of social media in emergencies and disasters
- To evaluate public expectations for the usage of social media during emergencies and disasters
- To comprehend the impact of citizen and responder social media actions on emergency response activities
- To establish social media usage rules during emergencies and disasters

DISASTER FOCUS—VIRGINIA TECH SHOOTING

On Monday, April 16, 2007, a school shooting took place on the campus of Virginia Polytechnic Institute and State University (Virginia Tech) in Blacksburg, Virginia, that ultimately killed 32 people and wounded many others. The perpetrator, a senior English major at Virginia Tech named Seung-Hui Cho, used two firearms during two separate attacks on campus. He started at West Ambler Johnston Hall where he killed 2 students and then moved across campus to Norris Hall where another 30 people died before Cho committed suicide. The shooting is the deadliest peacetime shooting incident by a single gunman in the history of the United States. While much of the post-event media attention circulated about Cho's previous history of mental instability and the lack of gun control laws related to these conditions, the impact of social media is profoundly important to this disaster.[1] For perspective, the first 2 people were killed at Virginia Tech at approximately 7:00 a.m. EDT while the next 30 were killed during the second shooting between 9:30 and 9:50 a.m. EDT. While Virginia Tech students, staff, and faculty were initially informed via email to remain indoors, official communications from the university were slow to come. By the time Virginia Tech officials held an official press conference at 12:00 p.m., they only confirmed 21 deaths and 28 injuries. (See Figure 5.1.) The Virginia Tech community as well as friends and family of students and faculty quickly began to utilize social media sites to facilitate the collection of additional information about the remaining victims. While Virginia Tech officials confirmed the final death toll (but not their names) by 2:13 p.m., the collection of social media sources like Facebook served to identify the names of victims prior to that point. Although none of the multiple lists on various social media outlets contained all names, the total compiled list correctly identified all 32 victims. Moreover, there was some evidence that these names were in different orders on different systems, which indicated to disaster sociologists that this organic process was happening simultaneously through multiple avenues.[2] Although sociologically amazing that the collection of people with loosely held social connections could come to this level of information accuracy in a mere few hours, it is a prime example of the need to consider ethics within the use of social media during emergencies and disasters. Should the general public collect and/or engage in disasters through social media? Should emergency managers and first responders utilize this information? These are critical concepts to the future application of social media in modern emergency management.

Figure 5.1 President George W. Bush comforts a Virginia Tech student during the Convocation on the Virginia Tech campus honoring students, faculty, and staff who died or were injured. (From White House, Eric Draper.)

A Change in Public Expectations

Much like the Virginia Tech shooting, numerous emergencies and disasters over the past decade have been greatly impacted by social media. Moreover, there is growing evidence that the expectations of the general public are exponentially increasing with regard to how emergency managers of all disciplines should respond to social media reports related to emergencies and disasters. For instance, a 2010 American Red Cross survey found that 20% of citizens who could not reach 9-1-1 would try to contact responders through social media or Web 2.0 technologies. Additionally, 35% stated that they would post a request for assistance directly on an emergency management or first responder's Facebook or Twitter page.[3] Perhaps the most profound result of this survey was that 69% of those surveyed stated an expectation that first responders should be monitoring social media sites to initiate emergency response as deemed necessary. Since social media—especially active monitoring—is not universally applied within the emergency management field (see Chapter 4), this level of public expectation creates a significant challenge for both emergency managers and citizens at large. This range of expectations and capabilities can lead to ethical dilemmas that impact the safety of citizens and responders and can potentially impact the effectiveness and efficiency of response and recovery activities related to an emergency or disaster.

The rise in the prevalence of social media users converging through these shared systems is not sociologically unexpected. Sociologists who study the collective behavior of people have long noted a convergence of behavior when there is a shared basis for physical, spatial, temporal, and emotional response. Several researchers have categorized these convergent groups into seven categories: returnees, anxious, helpers, curious, exploiters, supporters, and memorializers.[17] These seven characteristics help draw people to emergent situations that can quickly develop into emergencies or disasters. If this convergence is natural and organic, the use of new technologies and connective systems available through social media is a natural extension and may merely expedite this connectivity or move it into a virtual environment. Consequently, it is critical for emergency managers across all disciplines to thoroughly begin to evaluate how to handle how this convergence affects the efficiency and effectiveness of response activities as well as any impacts to the safety of responders and victims.

Specifically, emergency responders and citizens need to establish and accept rules for proper use of social media during emergencies and disasters to ensure responder and citizen safety as well as incident preservation. For instance, emergency incident scenes have long been controlled (or at least defined) by protective barriers such as the proverbial "yellow tape." (See Figure 5.2.) However, as the use of mobile-phone-integrated photos and videos continues to rise, this traditional scene control nearly evaporates. Real-time, potentially accurate information can be posted via text, video, or photo by any citizen with a clear view of the scene. This level of access can be dangerous to both the general public and first responders.

Figure 5.2 Changes in scene control are critical with the rise in use of social media technologies. (From U.S. Army.)

Rise of New Systems

When social media systems are created, they are often built on the foundation that members desire to communicate and share information in nearly instantaneous ways. In turn, these systems often end up focusing on certain niche community groups or geographic locations. An example of this concept was the rise of MySpace as a successful social networking site that ultimately encouraged the concentration of connections based on music, bands, and other art forms. This type of natural growth has similar application related to emergency and disaster management. Over time, many social media and Web 2.0 technology systems have become real-time repositories of emergency and disaster-related information. This information exchange related to emergencies and disasters is not just parallel to traditional media outlets but has also many times served as a primary source of information. For instance, the 2008 Mumbai attacks were first reported on Twitter with some experts estimating that Twitter was receiving 70 updates (or tweets) every five seconds when the news of the event first broke, which far outpaced traditional media output.[6] This pace of disaster-related information was being exchanged significantly faster than information was being received and processed by traditional media outlets throughout the world. As was mentioned in Chapter 1, the number and pace of Twitter messages during emergencies, disasters, and incidents of national and international significance continue to rise with every subsequent event as more and more people become active within the system. Consequently, those same traditional outlets quickly embraced the availability of information from Twitter as a primary source of information.

In addition to the rise of Twitter as a powerful new tool for citizen reporting, wiki-sourcing has quickly become a powerful tool for the collection and validation of information related to emergencies and disasters. The wiki concept supports public sites that can be edited by registered users numerous times to provide as much (or little) information as needed about respective topics. These topics are often cross-referenced against external sources (such as online news outlets) and with one another to create an intricate network of topics and concepts on these issues. Wikipedia, the most common wiki-sourcing website, contains over 3.5 million pages with more than 850,000 posted files of pictures, audio files, and related content. These pages have been edited over 440 million times, which averages approximately 19 edits per page.[7] For example, the Wikipedia entry on the 2007 Virginia Tech shooting has 129 separate reference entries that support and create the composite entry.[8] While not every Wikipedia page has been edited a significant number of times, it is evident that the vast majority of these entries have considerable validation. In fact, much like Twitter, this level of validation has created a primary source of information regarding any number of issues related to emergencies and disasters.

In addition to Wikipedia, the U.S. Department of Homeland Security has adopted the First Responder Communities of Practice as a conduit for information for the implementation of social media and new technologies for first responders and emergency managers. Within this system there are numerous topical communities that maintain wiki sites that allow for the collection and editing of content related to that particular system. For instance, system users can post policies or best-practice protocols at any given time that can be appended if newer concepts are added or can be removed if they have become outdated or determined to be incorrect. Much like Wikipedia, as this system (or ones like it) grows in usage and users, the validity of the shared data will create fantastic tools for the emergency management community to utilize freely and effectively.

Photo- and video-sharing sites like Flickr and YouTube have also quickly become tools for citizens to share multimedia content about emergencies, disasters, and emergent situations as well as for emergency managers and first responders to use as incident information and intelligence. These systems primarily utilize groups, tags, and counter-references to facilitate organic public engagement about common issues or events. For instance, from 2004 to 2007 there were at least 29 different Flickr photo groups established to collect and categorize pictures from seven different major disasters (e.g., Hurricane Katrina, Virginia Tech shooting, and Southeast Asia tsunami).[17] Each of these groups had varying levels of photos and members, but all were effective in drawing together individuals who shared a physical or emotional connection to the event.

The standard Facebook interface has already significantly changed the exchange and distribution of information during emergencies and disasters. However, Facebook has implemented several modifications to its primary systems that have further increased the capability and suggestion for citizens at large to contribute to broader social conversations—whether they are routine or related to an emergent event. The first of these was the establishment of a Facebook advanced programming interfaces (APIs) that allowed third-party websites to create interfaces on their websites where Facebook users could log in and engage in the conversation being created via the virtual environment. An example of this interface was the CNN Forum that was developed during the 2008 presidential election to allow the Facebook interface to be utilized to allow friends and sometimes strangers to publicly discuss and argue about the various political issues of the day.[9] This type of interface has not yet been adopted by governmental organizations—much less emergency managers—but does define the beginning expectations of the general public to have real-time response and conversation to public events and activities. Media coverage of disasters and emergencies are certainly not immune from this potential treatment. Similarly, Facebook has also created the OpenGraph API interface that allows users on various websites to log in to the third-party website through the user's Facebook account information. This feature has allowed a Facebook user's preferences and opinions about a variety of issues to be shared through a broader spectrum than just Facebook itself.

Regardless of the system, the primary question still exists as to whether these systems can be fairly and ethically used during crisis situations. On the one hand, traditional media outlets have utilized these new social media interfaces to secure breaking news as quickly as possible; however, the validity of public reports and the ethics of confirmatory journalism are sometimes sacrificed to meet this need. For example, CNN utilizes a Web 2.0 technology interface called iReporter to allow the general public to provide content—both text and multimedia—through an easily accessible interface. As of January 2010, there were over 50,000 posted iReports with nearly 36,000 having been vetted and confirmed within their system.[10] Although CNN initially started this concept in 2006, its utilization by the public and emphasis by both CNN and traditional media was after the 2007 Virginia Tech shootings where graduate student Jamal Albarghouti captured the sounds of local gunfire while he used his mobile phone to capture video of the scene.[11] Interestingly, some sources noted that Albarghouti's video was so compelling that CNN paid him an undisclosed amount of money for exclusive use of it, which is counter to the principles of social media and Web 2.0 technologies as well as morally ambiguous for a traditional and legitimate news agency. This model of creating easy access formats for citizen journalists is commonplace across all media platforms, including FoxNew's uReport and many variations at local news agencies using terms such as "uLocal."

On than other hand, the increasing utilization of citizen journalism and external integration of social media systems can have ambiguous moral and ethical consequences. For instance, in late 2010, a 56-year-old single mother checked into a hospital in Eau Claire, Wisconsin, complaining of chest discomfort. Within a few hours, the woman lapsed into a coma; local doctors determined that she had sustained a significant stroke, causing paralysis. Due to various compounding conditions that were unusual for her age, her conditions rapidly deteriorated and doctors feared the worst. Because the woman lived far away from any close family members and her son could only provide limited health information about the woman, doctors were challenged to determine a proper treatment until one doctor identified that the woman had a Facebook profile page. Through her Facebook profile page, the doctors quickly utilized her Facebook status postings over the previous few weeks to establish an accurate timeline for how her current condition had developed. The establishment of her medical history allowed the team of doctors to determine that the woman had a hole in her heart and had thrown blood clots, which allowed a successful treatment plan to be implemented and ultimately saved the woman's life.[13] While certainly a wonderful example of the lifesaving potential of social media for personal medical emergencies, it is also a prime example of how ethically challenging social media has become for both citizens and responders. Should doctors have had access to her Facebook page, which in many ways violated this woman's privacy even though it resulted in her medical survival? Although most people would support this type of violation if the results were this positive, the success of that result cannot be guaranteed and is ultimately the crux of the issue.

Incident-Based Risk

As an example of incident-based risk, what if a local law enforcement response agency responded to a local neighborhood based on a report of a hostage situation related to domestic violence? Law enforcement, emergency medical service, specialized response teams, and other response personnel (sometimes from multiple jurisdictions) would be simultaneously responding to one central physical location. An incident commander or unified command would quickly be established to determine leadership and scene control. Because of the complexity of this response scene, numerous citizens in the impacted neighborhood and some simply in the vicinity would be drawn to the scene and would be witnesses of all activities therein. (See Figure 5.3.)

Because of the numerous social media and Web 2.0 tools already discussed, this level of public presence could quickly lead to dozens (if not more) comments, texts, photos, and/or videos posted to Facebook, Twitter, and YouTube (just to name a few) by the general public because they are shocked, concerned, or otherwise interested in the scene and fascinated by the novelty of what they are seeing. These social media posts could be simple updates or multimedia reports that incorporate details of the scene, including where responders are located, current levels of support, and other similar details. Because the scene observations are shared via social media, the person of interest holding the hostage is now potentially aware of many of the response actions the law enforcement agency has taken, including description of team uniforms, response tactics, positions of personnel, and type of equipment in use. This level of awareness means that the traditional tactical advantage and protective strategies in place are potentially vulnerable because of this use of social media. If the tactical advantage and protection is minimized and/or eliminated, first responders are at significantly greater risk than previously thought or planned for by emergency managers.

This very scenario happened in 2011 when Utah police cornered a man named Jose Valdez in a Salt Lake City hotel room where they were trying to serve a bench warrant on him. Local Special Weapons and Tactics (SWAT) teams maintained a perimeter around the hotel room for 16 hours because Valdez had a woman with him who was believed to be his hostage. During the time of the standoff, Valdez made six posts to his Facebook page, with his friends posting approximately 100 comments in return. These comments ranged from positive support to urgent requests for him to "do the right thing." Perhaps the most striking of these was a comment stating that a SWAT member was hiding in the bushes outside the room. In response, Valdez simply stated, "Thank you homie...good looking out." Valdez later shot himself as SWAT members stormed his room. Local law enforcement authorities openly admitted afterward that they were not sure how to handle Valdez's Facebook friends who so openly provided him response intelligence. Some local community leaders even suggested that Valdez's friends should be charged with a crime for their use of social media.[20]

This type of situation can also put local citizens in significant danger from the disaster conditions. In some ways, this phenomenon occurred during the terrorist

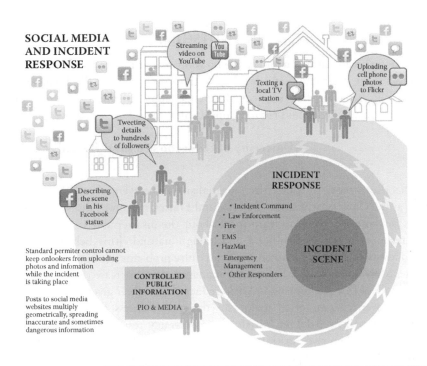

SOCIAL MEDIA AND INCIDENT RESPONSE

Streaming video on YouTube

Texting a local TV station

Uploading cell phone photos to Flickr

Tweeting details to hundreds of followers

Describing the scene in his Facebook status

INCIDENT RESPONSE

• Incident Command
• Law Enforcement
• Fire
• EMS
• HazMat
• Emergency Management
• Other Responders

INCIDENT SCENE

CONTROLLED PUBLIC INFORMATION

PIO & MEDIA

Standard permiter control cannot keep onlookers from uploading photos and infomation while the incident is taking place

Posts to social media websites multiply geometrically, spreading inaccurate and sometimes dangerous information

Figure 5.3   Scene control and preservation is potentially significantly impacted by the presence of individuals utilizing social media tools. (From Mid-America Regional Council [MARC], Barbara Hensley.)

attacks of the Mumbai financial district in November 2008. In this particular event, numerous local citizens took photos of the terrorists moving through the impacted areas. In some cases, these pictures clearly showed the weapons and incendiary devices being carried by the terrorists and were later used by traditional media outlets like CNN to report real-time updates about the event.[4,5] Clearly, if these individuals were close enough to capture images and multimedia content of the terrorists via cell phones, these citizens were at increased risk to be harmed by those same terrorists. Consequently, there is a significant question whether these citizens put themselves at greater risk by utilizing social media during this event. Is the benefit of having that level of incident-related information and intelligence worth the risk to citizen journalists?

Likewise, if a natural disaster such as a tornado or earthquake were happening in a local community, many local citizens would seek ways to capture information about the disaster—including pictures, videos, and firsthand accounts, which can quickly be shared via social media systems through mobile devices regardless of the current status of traditional infrastructure (e.g., local internet access). This public response is caused by many factors, including the novelty of such an event impacting their lives as well as the encouragement of local and national media outlets like

> **IN A NUTSHELL**
>
> Disaster breeds curiosity for those who want to learn more about the disaster and see the destruction and response activities first-hand….[T]hough natural, [this behavior] has been called "disaster tourism" and can significantly impact rescue, relief, and recovery operations.
>
> **—University of Colorado's Natural Hazards Center**[14]

CNN's iReporter to provide citizen journalism of the event. According to research done at the University of Colorado's Natural Hazards Center, "disaster breeds curiosity for those who want to learn more about the disaster and see the destruction and response activities first-hand….[T]hough natural, [this behavior] has been called 'disaster tourism' by some…and can cause problems if it hinders rescue, relief, and recovery operations."[14] Emergency managers must increase their awareness and acceptance of this phenomenon to help reduce risk in their given communities.

Moreover, citizens often make this desire to witness the event the priority rather than calling 9-1-1 to initiate the emergency response process. For example, in 2009, when two Australian girls (aged 10 and 12) got lost in a stormwater drain in Adelaide, they posted to their Facebook pages from their mobile phones rather than calling the Australian equivalent of 9-1-1. Although these young girls might not have felt imminent danger, the mere thought that they would post to a social media site is a new phenomenon for most emergency management and first responder disciplines.[15] Interestingly, this phenomenon also cannot be only attributed to youthful ignorance. In 2009, an Atlanta City councilman spotted a woman having a seizure on a nearby street corner. Much like the Australian preteens, the councilman posted to Twitter that there was a woman in need of medical assistance rather than dial 9-1-1 to report the condition. Within seconds, the councilman's Twitter followers retweeted the message and some called 9-1-1 directly. After the fact, the councilman reported that his decision to use Twitter rather than the emergency number was due to low battery life on his phone.[16] Even if this was the case, this example validates the growing perception for users of social media that the robustness and connectedness of social media sites are more effective than traditional mechanisms to report emergencies. This possibility of modern emergency notification and messaging is further discussed in Chapter 8.

First Responder Responsibility

Maintaining a high level of fairness and application has long been a benchmark of emergency managers and first responders alike. This concept is echoed in the oft-stated axiom "Do the most good for the most amount of people." Emergency managers and their partners must not make preparedness and response decisions based on favoritism or bias but merely on the most efficient and effective processes that ensure the preservation of life and property of impacted citizens and those responding to their needs. A prime example of this process is the need for law enforcement to maintain and train on a use of force spectrum that provides guidance on what is and what is not appropriate when dealing with a particular event. For example, should a law enforcement officer use his service weapon to shoot a local citizen who jaywalks or runs a stop sign? Of course not! These first responders are most often trained to maintain a response that is as least impactful as possible. Unfortunately, social media is a moral and ethical challenge for emergency managers of all disciplines that does not yet have the same level of appropriate use as the mentioned force spectrum.

If ethical and reasonable response is already an accepted model for emergency managers and first responders within the various disciplines and response specialties, this should be no different for the use and impact of social media. With some inspiration from the U.S. Air Force's social media utilization policy,[18] emergency managers of all disciplines should adopt six basic rules of use related to social media and emergencies or disasters. These rules consist of statements to ensure that all uses of social media maintain confidentiality, privacy, accuracy, and trustworthiness. The adoption of these rules is critical to ensuring the public is comfortable and confident that all materials utilized by emergency managers are of the same level of accuracy and reliability as any other piece of information distributed or utilized by emergency managers of any discipline.

The first of these components is to ensure accuracy of all information used and disseminated by emergency managers. First and foremost, emergency managers must establish some rules about how to verify information received from the general public through social media systems about emergencies or disasters. These rules suggest that a social media source be confirmed and/or verified by no fewer than three sources with at least one as a traditional media outlet (that already has established rules about verifiability). Although this number is completely arbitrary,

RULES FOR FAIR AND SAFE USE OF SOCIAL MEDIA BY EMERGENCY MANAGERS

1. Utilize only materials posted by three or more trusted sources (preferably one of these a traditional media source).
2. Publicly post the dates and times when official social media systems will be monitored for incident-related issues.
3. Do not divulge incident-critical (aka classified) information.
4. Do not violate privacy of victims or their families.
5. Do not use trademarked or copyrighted materials.
6. Admit mistakes and do not lie.[18]

it supports the need to identify some level of implementation that emergency managers at their organizations, if not industry-wide, can learn to accept and apply during emergency preparedness and response. In addition, these rules also suggest that emergency managers must uniformly admit mistakes and avoid duplicity when presenting disaster-related information to the general public.

In addition to accuracy, emergency managers must also seek out ways to ensure the reliability of the information they are receiving and disseminating via social media systems. The foundation of reliability starts with establishing a timeframe for when social media systems will be utilized. Clearly, the primary way emergency managers have justified their use of social media is the knowledge that it would be utilized during an emergency or disaster as a secondary system for the distribution of emergency public information, warnings, alerts, and other critical pieces of information. However, the question that many emergency managers must evaluate is what to do with their social media systems when preparedness and mitigation activities are underway and there is no known response activity. (See Figure 5.4.) Establishing these proverbial "hours of operation" is critical to ensure that the growing expectations of the public (as established by the American Red Cross survey) about the monitoring capability of social media sites is maintained at reasonable levels.

Additionally, the general public and emergency response partners must ensure that they respect the privacy, intelligence, and intellectual property connected to disaster-related events. This includes components of information related to victim's

Figure 5.4 Emergency managers must determine how to use social media during preparedness and mitigation activities that are common between disasters. (From FEMA, Marilee Caliendo.)

health information and emergency response intelligence, as well as copyrighted and trademarked materials. For instance, people have borrowed or utilized images found on the internet that they do not have permission to use. This type of careless use of social media is dangerous and disrespectful in the process of maintaining positive usage of social media within a community. Maintaining this level of transparency (as is expected within the social media community) ensures emergency managers will be perceived as trustworthy and reliable, which is critical during response operations.

Citizen Responsibility

Much like the operational considerations related to the use of social media during emergencies and disasters, emergency managers also have a responsibility to inform the general public what responsibilities citizens have related to the use of social media during emergencies. Much like 9-1-1 emergency systems that are now pervasive throughout the United States, citizens may or may not completely understand the impacts of their choices when it comes to the use of social media during emergencies. (See Figure 5.5.) For instance, 9-1-1 emergency systems have long been plagued by misuse and errant calls that include hang-ups, prank calls, and non-emergency calls.

Figure 5.5　Think Safe, Tweet Safe. (From Adam Crowe.)

CITIZEN RESPONSIBILITIES FOR THE SAFE AND EFFECTIVE USE OF SOCIAL MEDIA DURING EMERGENCIES AND DISASTERS

1. I will not put emergency responders and other public safety officials in harm's way by using social media.
2. I will not put myself or those around me at risk by using social media.
3. I will not redistribute disaster-related content unless it has been confirmed by two different trusted sources.
4. I will not expect a social media response from an emergency response agency unless they have stated that this will be supported.

To address these issues, 9-1-1 dispatch centers have implemented over time a variety of response tactics, including technology upgrades, law enforcement intervention, implementing 3-1-1 systems, and perhaps most importantly, increasing the education of citizens about proper use of their local 9-1-1 system.[19] This requisite and necessary education provided clarification for citizens as to appropriateness of calls, procedures when calls are made, and consequences for misuse.

As the public expectations about the use of social media continues to grow, so too does the level of official implementation by emergency managers. The same type of education that was necessary for 9-1-1 systems is absolutely necessary for social media. If this education and public awareness is not implemented, the potential impact and usefulness of social media during emergencies and disasters may be significantly hindered due to fears and misunderstandings. Moreover, as already established, there is also a significant potential risk to the personal safety of citizens and first responders if there is not a shared, common platform and protocol to use social media during events. Local citizens, traditional media, emergency managers, and local community leaders need to identify certain rules to follow when using social media during emergencies or disasters to ensure the safety of citizens and responders alike. Most of these suggested rules are focused on increasing the situational awareness of the individual utilizing social media. While many of these rules are routine to emergency public information and response activities, they are paramount to the successful implementation of social media into traditional emergency management and response systems. Although these rules may require the pace of social media distribution to slow slightly to ensure the proper actions are taken, it will be worth it in the end to ensure that the safety of both citizens and first responders is maintained as paramount. Although these rules are again subjective and arbitrary, they help set the foundation for future successes when utilizing social media during emergencies and disasters.

Social Media "How" versus Social Media "Why"

The ethical dilemmas of social media application in all phases of emergency management have been largely ignored. Most emergency managers are merely focused on the "when" and "how" social media systems can be used before, during, and after emergencies or disasters. The challenge with this mind-set is that it often neglects the "why," which may be critical to ensure the full incorporation of these concepts into traditional management and response structures and assumptions.

Emergency managers of all disciplines are good at what they do, and they maintain plans, procedures, and operational protocols based on years of best practices and community observations. Unfortunately, this operational and planning model does not often lend itself to the incorporation and development of new strategies and technologies such as social media and Web 2.0 technologies. The concept of how social media is impacting traditional response scenes, situational awareness, and public information as discussed within this chapter is merely the beginning of this conversation. Emergency managers across all disciplines and levels must be engaged to get practitioner feedback and buy-in to ensure these concepts can be fully embraced. Unfortunately, this type of implementation cannot occur using traditional methods of time and repetition. Rather, a concerted effort must be made to apply standards that are flexible and dynamic to ensure that they can quickly be modified or altered to address current needs or capabilities.

If this style of implementation can be adopted that allows for quicker decisions, the effectiveness of social media as well as the safety of citizens and first responders can be better preserved. As such, the rules included within this chapter to address the responsibilities of first responders, emergency managers, and the general public are merely starting points. These rules and expectations are subject to change and should be modified by the emergency management community continually to ensure their continued effectiveness. At no point in time should this suggested structure become rigid and closed from improvement and review. Rather, every emergency or disaster event—no matter how big or small—should be reviewed immediately to analyze and apply any findings regarding the impact of social media on that particular event.

Practitioner Profile: Alisha Griswold, Medical Reserve Corps, Kansas City

Ms. Griswold (Figure 5.6) is a disaster response specialist who specializes in biological and radiological disaster planning and response and is the executive vice chair to the Medical Reserve Corps of Kansas City (MRCKC). Additionally, she actively utilizes social media systems like Twitter to leverage professional development,

Figure 5.6   Alisha Griswold.

improve volunteerism, and engage this community. Because of her unique combination of professional involvement and passion for social media and volunteerism, Ms. Griswold was tasked by the International Association of Emergency Managers (IAEM) to develop a new committee to focus on emergency technologies such as social media and Web 2.0 systems. When asked about why social media was important to the future of emergency management, Ms. Griswold stated, "By leveraging social media tools, such as Twitter, I am able to share my daily activities within my community…[which] as a taxpayer and citizen I appreciate having the opportunity to get a better understanding of how other government agencies operate." She continued, "I don't believe that most emergency managers have a good understanding of social media or any other emerging technologies….[However] this is a pseudo-generational issue, where the previous 'generation' of emergency management professionals acquired their duties by demonstrating specific skills in another discipline and the new 'generation' is completing course work specifically for emergency management." When Ms. Griswold was asked to address why emergency managers across all disciplines continue to be reluctant to embrace emerging technologies, she said, "Many individuals hesitate out of concern for unforeseen repercussions such as legal or command and control issues." In conclusion she said, "We are witnessing the beginning of a new world order…where virtual emergency response begins as soon as a disaster strikes [such that] volunteers can lend a hand from anywhere in the globe…[and] where access to cellular devices can help fledgling democracies overthrow oppressive tyrants and vacationers can unintentionally provide live commentary on the takedown of the FBI's most wanted criminal." Ms. Griswold's passion and leadership will be critical to the future of emergency management as practitioners across the globe attempt to tackle how to successfully implement social media.

Chapter Terms

Citizen journalism: Firsthand reporting and documenting of emergency or disaster events by citizens via social media formats that can be used and/or translated by traditional and mainstream media outlets.

Wiki-sourcing: Collection and validation of information to a website or virtual concept through a process that uses the collective editing and validation of a large group of individuals.

Social media ethics: Attempt to create an ethical framework for the use and application of social media during emergencies and disasters that ensures the safety of first responders and citizens as well as scene preservation.

Incident-based risk: Risk of social media impacting the emergency response activities of a given scene due to preexisting relationships (and therefore social media connections) of those involved or impacted by the scene.

Chapter Questions

General Questions

1. True/False: Surveys indicate that citizens have a low expectation for the use of social media during disasters.
2. What allows Facebook to be utilized as a tool to facilitate citizen journalism?
   a. Facebook API
   b. Social status
   c. Millions of users
   d. All of the above
3. True/False: Responders and citizens should abide by predetermined rules when utilizing social media during disasters.

Essay Questions

1. Discuss how changing public expectations are changing how social media impacts disaster response scenes.
2. Discuss the importance of ethics in the utilization of social media during emergencies and disasters.

3. Discuss the suggested rules for citizens and responders when using social media during a disaster. Are they sufficient? Do they need to be expanded or contracted?

Works Cited

1. Hauser, Christine, and Anahad O'Connor. "Virginia Tech Shooting Leaves 33 Dead." *New York Times*, April 16, 2007. http://www.nytimes.com/2007/04/16/us/16cnd-shooting.html?pagewanted=all (accessed October 29, 2011).
2. Vieweg, S., et al. "Collective Intelligence in Disaster: An Examination of the Phenomenon in the Aftermath of the 2007 Virginia Tech Shooting." Proceedings of the fifth international ISCRAM conference, Washington, D.C., May 2008.
3. "Web Users Increasingly Rely on Social Media to Seek Help in a Disaster." *American Red Cross Press Release*, August 9, 2010. http://www.redcross.org/portal/site/en/menui tem.94aae335470e233f6cf911df43181aa0/?vgnextoid=6bb5a96d0a94a210VgnVCM 10000089f0870aRCRD (accessed January 26, 2011).
4. Busari, Stephanie. "Tweeting the Terror: How Social Media Responded to Mumbai." *CNN.com*, November 27, 2008. http://articles.cnn.com/2008-11-27/world/mumbai. twitter_1_twitter-tweet-terror-attacks?_s=PM:WORLD (accessed January 26, 2011).
5. Heussner, Ki Mae. "Social Media a Lifeline, Also a Threat?" *ABCNews.com,* November 28, 2008. http://abcnews.go.com/Technology/International/story?id=6350014&page=1 (accessed January 26, 2011).
6. Beaumont, Claudine. "Mumbai Attacks: Twitter and Flickr Used to Break News." *UK Telegraph*, November 27, 2008. http://www.telegraph.co.uk/news/worldnews/asia/ india/3530640/Mumbai-attacks-Twitter-and-Flickr-used-to-break-news-Bombay-India.html (accessed January 26, 2011).
7. "Statistics." *Wikipedia.com*. http://en.wikipedia.org/wiki/Special:Statistics.
8. "Virginia Tech Shooting; Sequence of Events." *Washington Post*. http://www.washingtonpost.com/wp-srv/metro/interactives/vatechshootings/shootings_timeline.html (accessed October 29, 2011).
9. Parr, Ben. "10 Great Implementations of Facebook Connect." *Mashable.com*, January 12, 2009. http://mashable.com/2009/01/12/facebook-connect-implementations/ (accessed January 26, 2011).
10. "CNN iReport." *CNN.com*. http://ireport.cnn.com/ (accessed January 26, 2011).
11. "Student Shot Video of Campus Shooting." *CNN.com*, April 16, 2007. http://www. cnn.com/2007/US/04/16/vtech.witness/index.html (accessed January 26, 2011).
12. Montopoli, Brian. "Citizen Journalists, Dangerous Settings." *CBSNews. com*, April 17, 2007. http://www.cbsnews.com/8300-500486_162-500486. html?keyword=Jamal+Albarghouti (accessed January 26, 2011).
13. Gingrich, Newt, and Kamar Thapar. "Facebook Is—Literally—a Life Saver." *AOL News*, December 5, 2010. http://www.aolnews.com/2010/12/06/facebook-is-literally-a-lifesaver/ (accessed January 26, 2011).
14. Hughes, Amanda L., et al. "'Site-Seeing' in Disaster: An Examination of On-Line Social Convergence." Proceedings of the fifth international ISCRAM conference, Washington, D.C., May 2008. http://www.jeannettesutton.com/uploads/ OnlineConvergenceISCRAM08.pdf (accessed January 26, 2011).

15. Cashmore, Pete. "Trapped Girls Updated Facebook Status Instead of Calling for Help." *Mashable.com*, September 7, 2009. http://mashable.com/2009/09/07/trapped-girls-facebook/ (accessed January 26, 2011).
16. "Atlanta Councilman Chooses Twitter over 911 to Report Emergency." *EMSWorld.com*, May 18, 2009. http://www.emsworld.com/web/online/Top-EMS-News/Atlanta-Councilman-Chooses-Twitter-Over-911-to-Report-Emergency/1$9546 (accessed January 26, 2011).
17. Liu, Sophia B., et al. "In Search of the Bigger Picture: The Emergent Role of On-Line Photo Sharing in Times of Disaster." Proceedings of the fifth international ISCRAM conference, Washington, D.C., May 2008. http://www.jeannettesutton.com/uploads/OnlinePhotoSharingISCRAM08.pdf (accessed January 26, 2011).
18. "New Media and the Air Force." *Air Force.* http://www.af.mil/shared/media/document/AFD-090406–036.pdf (accessed January 26, 2011).
19. Sampson, Rana. "Misuse and Abuse of 911." Problem-Oriented Guides for Police Series, Guide No. 19, *U.S. Department of Justice*, August 22, 2002. http://www.popcenter.org/problems/pdfs/Misuse_and_Abuse_of_911.pdf (accessed January 26, 2011).
20. Dobner, Jennifer. "Utah Man Updated Facebook Status during Standoff." *Yahoo News*, June 22, 2011. http://news.yahoo.com/utah-man-updated-facebook-status-during-standoff-212608080.html (accessed June 26, 2011).

SOCIAL MEDIA POLICY, PROCEDURE, INTEGRATION, AND ANALYSIS

If your reputation sucks, none of it matters. People with lousy products, crummy business practices, and shady backgrounds get found out. And word spreads with frightening speed.

—Sonia Simone, marketer and blogger at Remarkable Communication[12]

Chapter 6

Who's the Sheriff in These Parts? Monitoring and Analysis of Social Media Information

Social awareness has three levels: when everybody knows something, when everybody knows that everybody knows, and when everybody knows that everybody knows that everybody knows.

—Clay Shirky, *Here Comes Everybody: The Power of Organizing Without Organizations*[1]

Chapter Objectives

- To comprehend the utilization and benefits of using monitoring and analytics systems to measure impact and success of social media systems before, during, and after an emergency
- To understand systematic monitoring of social media systems during emergencies and disasters
- To evaluate the importance of comprehensive monitoring of social media systems during emergencies and disasters

DISASTER FOCUS—*SEVEN SIGNS OF TERRORISM* VIDEO

In 2008, the Michigan State Police's Division of Emergency Management and Homeland Security developed an educational video campaign called "The Seven Signs of Terrorism." This campaign called for citizens to watch for and report any of seven common signs of terrorism: surveillance, information gathering, testing security, planning, suspicious behavior, rehearsal, and positioning.[2] To date, the State of Michigan released this video through their website and via DVD upon request. Because of the relatively positive response to this video, the Citizen Readiness Subcommittee of the Regional Homeland Security Coordinating Committee in the Greater Kansas City area decided to produce a professional-quality video that was similar to the video produced by the State of Michigan. The Kansas City version of *The Seven Signs of Terrorism* was produced using local residents against a backdrop of regional landmarks unique to the city. After the video was produced, the committee decided to post the video on a Friday afternoon to a recently created YouTube channel that was managed and controlled by the Mid-America Regional Council (of governments). By the power of social media and the inherent capability of information to be shared and spread through the internet, the video generated more than 33,000 views by the next Monday morning, with well over 250 comments posted to the video. Most of the comments were negative with a perception that the video was inciting panic in the community with many specific accusations of fear-mongering. The regional emergency managers responsible for citizen readiness quickly had to adopt a process to review comments and feedback in the context created in social media. Because this monitoring and response did not occur while the event was progressing, it was difficult to manage the situation properly and is a strong indicator of why social media must be monitored to watch for public feedback and provide engaged feedback when possible. (See Figure 6.1.)

- To evaluate social media monitoring tools for efficiency and effectiveness
- To consider the measurement and importance of return-on-investment evaluations of social media systems

Traditional Media Monitoring

Social media monitoring and analysis is a complex issue due to the many systems available, varying levels of reliability, and the necessary resources to address these issues. However, much like the Clay Shirky quote that opens this chapter, initiating protocols and systems to monitor social media conversations—particularly

Figure 6.1 Command personnel assigned to planning or intelligence branches will need to monitor social media for real-time situational awareness. (From FEMA, Patsy Lynch.)

during disasters—is critical for both emergency public information and situational awareness. As was addressed in the first section of this book, the exchange of information and opinions is occurring within social media systems with or without the presence and participation of emergency managers and other governmental officials. Consequently, one of the easiest ways to become a part of (rather than control) this conversation is to use available tools to monitor what is being said and for what purpose.

Traditionally, emergencies and disasters have been monitored through the observation and inspection of popular media sources. When newspaper was the dominant media form for mass communication, monitoring was as simple as reading the paper and identifying any stories related to the event in question. Likewise, radio and television sources were monitored during emergencies at regular intervals that correlated to the daily broadcast. The first major shift in the event monitoring timeline was the rise of cable news outlets like CNN. This shifted the traditional news production cycle to 24 hours a day, 7 days a week (24/7). Although 24/7, event monitoring was still dependent on highly produced media formats that required stages, sets, resources, and other technical equipment in concert to report any information gleaned about the event. To support this process, traditional wire news services provided by the Associated Press (AP), Agence France-Presse (AFP), United Press International (UPI), and Reuters were utilized to collect national and international breaking news and distribute it to news agencies within their shared network.

However, as the use and implementation of the internet increased by both citizens and traditional media outlets, the formalized structure of news monitoring undertook a major overhaul. Various forms of the internet began to report disaster-related news more quickly and without the procedural and resource over-head necessary for traditional media outlets. This process was further impacted by the rise of social media. Social media moved beyond the idea of traditional media-controlled disaster-related information, allowing citizens to contribute to all forms of journalism as previously described in Chapters 3 and 5. This shift to shared journalistic responsibility moved news reporting to nearly simultaneous to the actual events occurring.

Social Media Monitoring

Consequently, as media reporting shifted, so did the need for media monitoring. While traditional media outlets in print, radio, and television continue to exist and have an impact on event monitoring, systems needed to be created to track the distribution and exchange of information on the internet and through social media systems at the same speed the information was distributed. This social media searching and monitoring capability is possible due to the open advanced program-ming interfaces (APIs) available in most social media systems. These APIs allow third-party systems to access the data and information included on public social networks, microblogs, blogs, photo-sharing sites, video-sharing sites, and other social media systems.

Emergency managers can utilize social media monitoring for both situational awareness and emergency public information activities. In both cases, the collection and review of social media information must be real-time and reflective of all pri-mary and secondary issues related to the particular event. For example, if a tornado impacted a given community, it would be critical to know all information being discussed on social media for damage assessment and power outages as well as sec-ondary issues such as mass care sheltering and debris management. For situational awareness, this kind of information is utilized operationally to ascertain necessary adjustments needed to ensure an efficient and effective response to the incident under consideration. Within the National Incident Management System (NIMS) framework, this kind of information could be assigned to an intelligence branch in the operations or planning section depending on the event conditions and the incident commander in charge. Likewise, the public information officer function is monitored by a public information officer often located in the Joint Information Center (JIC). This operational utilization of social media monitoring is further discussed in Chapter 10.

The other primary application of social media monitoring by emergency man-agers is within the emergency public information process. This process would typi-cally be assigned to the public information officer in the Joint Information Center in conjunction with an Emergency Operations Center (EOC) activation for a par-ticular organization. The JIC is fundamentally responsible for information analy-sis, information dissemination, and media monitoring. It is this final component that must be adjusted to incorporate social media monitoring and application. Specifically, the JIC must be able to pull from all social media systems real-time incident-related information that can gauge misinformation and the need for additional information. This real-time information should be searchable by time, users, phrases, location, connectivity, attitude, analytics, and influence.

Social media monitoring is heavily dependent on certain systematic classification characteristics such as hashtags, keywords, internal coding, and tags. As was discussed in Chapter 2, these systematic classification characteristics are foundational to the connectivity that exists in social media and Web 2.0 technologies. In all cases, these characteristics allow for the collection and gathering of similar information. Interestingly, these characteristics are user generated and have no formal structure or rules for their creation or establishment. Twitter monitoring, for instance, is heavily dependent on the creation and use of hashtags (or a random assortment of letters and numbers that is associated with a certain topic). Similarly, photo- and video-sharing sites like Flickr and YouTube are driven by tagging. Social networks, like Facebook, are the exception to this classification rule. Some monitoring systems use keyword searches for these types of systems, which sometimes creates less accurate results than some of the other social media systems. This difference is partially what requires the need for aggregation and validation of social media as well as monitoring. The aggregation and validation of social media data are further discussed in Chapter 7.

Real-Time Instantaneous Monitoring

The first major type of monitoring relates to those systems that provide real-time individualistic and instantaneous capabilities. Specifically, these systems are capable of gathering information related to a topic, category, event, name, or other incident-related information at any given moment. (See Figure 6.2.) However, real-time instantaneous monitoring systems have no capability to collect these same categorizations over time. There are numerous social media monitoring systems that currently exist, with many of them focusing on specific social media sites such as Facebook and Twitter; however, some of these sites can monitor multiple sites simultaneously.

The Twitter-specific sites that perform real-time instantaneous monitoring include Monitter, Topsy, Trendsmap, BackTweets, Twubs, and Twitter's Advanced Search. Although these systems all allow for the opportunity to monitor incident-related data, the specific filter available in each system is different. For instance, Monitter (spelled with two "t"s like Twitter) is a web-based Twitter monitoring tool that allows users to insert keywords or phrases and a geographic search parameter (based on mileage from a certain ZIP code). An additional benefit of this type of system is that it does not require any login, password, or connectivity to social media system. Moreover, this type of monitoring is very effective for emergency managers due to its capability for localized searching for real-time information. For

Figure 6.2 Effective monitoring of social media may help address public issues that can more quickly be resolved than traditional monitoring. (From FEMA, Michael Medina-Latorre.)

emergencies and/or disasters with local or regional impact, Monitter would be an extremely efficient tool to gather tweets in real-time. For instance, areas that heavily utilize outdoor warning sirens for emergency public notification are often burdened by occasional malfunctions, which can lead to confusion of the general public. Monitoring social media for these types of issues can identify the issue and shorten the time necessary to distribute public information to address the malfunction.

Another excellent real-time Twitter-specific monitoring tool is Trendsmap. While Monitter utilizes geographic vicinity to provide a list of matched tweets, Trendsmap looks for popular hashtags and presents them on a map. This type of approach can quickly indicate trends in the interests and opinions of the general public at any particular moment. For instance, if local emergency managers are interested in monitoring the public response to emergency snow removal activities during a blizzard, Trendsmap could quickly provide this monitoring capability through the organic terminology utilized in generated Twitter hashtags. For instance, in this case, if a hashtag such as #plowfaster or #plowmore were being monitored by Trendsmap, it would be a strong indicator to local emergency managers that local citizens were not satisfied with the pace and productivity of local emergency snow removal.

The last and perhaps most powerful Twitter-only monitoring tool is the Advanced Search tool available through Twitter itself. This Advanced Search tool allows for searching by words, people, places, dates, attitude, and others. Each of these search parameters has multiple entry capabilities. For instance, the people filter has the capability to look for tweets from, to, or about a particular Twitter account. Interestingly, it also allows unique search constraints related to emotions and for connectivity to other sites or web links. This is advantageous to emergency managers for a variety of reasons as they monitor an emergent situation during emergency or disaster response. For instance, much like the Trendsmap already mentioned, the collection and accounting for emotional statements (e.g., how many use happy or sad emoticons) related to a particular event would be very valuable in ascertaining the effectiveness and efficiency of response and/or acceptance of information by the impacted general public. This functionality would be exceptionally beneficial in the determination of how well protective action recommendations (e.g., issuances of a tornado warning) are being accepted and acted upon by local citizens. Additionally, the capability to measure how many times posted web links have been redistributed would also be valuable to determine the diffusion of the related message within the community.

Although powerful monitoring tools, these Twitter-centric capabilities do contain challenges to their effective use. First, regardless of what monitoring system is utilized, the effectiveness is dependent on the number of social media users engaged in the measured system at any given time. For instance, if 1,000 people have posted in response to a particular event but only 100 have used the same hashtag, official monitoring by local emergency management would only be based on 10% of those actually reporting about the incident. Additionally, the power of these monitoring systems is only as effective as the familiarity of the emergency managers using these systems. If emergency managers of all disciplines do not routinely use these systems during non-emergency events (community festivals, exercises, etc.), they will not be effectively used during an event. The final major challenge to Twitter-centric monitoring systems is the dependency on systematic naming within Twitter. Twitter is

REAL-TIME INSTANTANEOUS MONITORING FOR TWITTER

Twitter Advanced Search
Trendsmap
Monitter
Topsy
Twubs
BackTweets

heavily dependent on unique user identifications (userids) that may or may not be clearly associated with the actual name and geographic location of the user. This challenges monitored data to actually ascertain whether it is relevant to the event being monitored, which is why aggregation and validation is critical.

In addition to the Twitter-specific real-time monitoring systems, there are similar systems that collect instantaneous information about content being publicly posted to Facebook. Unlike Twitter monitoring tools, Facebook tools are strictly limited to keywords or phrases rather than classification terms (e.g., hashtags), geographic locations, and expressed feelings. As monitoring tools for Facebook continue to develop, these filtering tools may become available but currently are not supported. The two primary real-time monitoring tools dedicated to Facebook are Open Facebook Search and Openbook. Both of these systems have a simple search box that quickly collects all real-time references that match the request. From a monitoring perspective, the only significant difference between these systems is that Openbook allows for search filtering by gender. Regardless of the Facebook system utilized, the challenge to effective real-time monitoring of Facebook for instance-related information is the growing attention given toward the need for Facebook users to tighten down personal user settings, which in turn would minimize or eliminate their availability through current monitoring systems.[3]

Although monitoring systems are powerful tools, emergency managers (like most social media users) should be seeking out the most efficient and effective way to monitor all social media information related to a particular incident. This means that monitoring systems that allow for the simultaneous collection of information from multiple social media outlets would be valuable. If these were effective, they would be valuable tools to monitor emergencies or disasters with the limited tools available to most emergency managers. Fortunately, tools with this capability do exist. These multifunction monitoring tools include Kurrently, Social Mention, and Topsy. With the exception of Kurrently, these systems utilize powerful search and monitoring tools that have dynamic filters and selective sourcing that contribute to the search algorithm and ultimately the monitored results. Conversely, Kurrently simply lists in reverse chronological order any Facebook or Twitter post that meets the search criteria without any particular filter capability. Because of its simplicity, it is similar in structure and effectiveness to Openbook with the only real improvement being the addition of Twitter posts. Social Mention and Topsy both use parameters that can be filtered across a multitude of systems and web-based access. For instance, Social Mention allows for search filtering by blogs, microblogs, networks, bookmarks, images, videos, and audio as well as advanced monitoring of selected social media systems including Facebook, YouTube, Twitter, MySpace, Flickr, Friendster, and many other systems. This functionality is a tremendous asset in all monitoring capabilities for emergency managers due to the proverbial "one stop shop" potential. While similar, Topsy does not provide the depth of searching available through Social Mention. These aggregation sites search major social media sites and can filter by photos, videos, and web content. While

---

REAL-TIME INSTANTANEOUS MONITORING FOR FACEBOOK

Kurrently
Social Mention
Open Facebook Search
Openbook
Topsy

---

not as comprehensive as Social Mention, Topsy does provide the collection capability that would benefit emergency managers.

Real-Time Collective Monitoring

There are additional real-time monitoring systems that gather social media information in a collective fashion. For instance, in addition to the instantaneous information collected by the systems previously discussed, these systems will gather information that meets the search parameters and collect the data over time for analysis and comparison. For instance, if a local emergency manager wanted to monitor comments, responses, and feedback about his or her particular organization over time, one of the most straightforward ways to achieve this purpose would be to utilize one of these collective monitoring systems to watch over time the changing perspectives. This observation timeframe would be anything from minutes to hours to days or more depending on the events and activity of a particular organization. (See Figure 6.3.) Examples of real-time collective monitoring tools include Google Alerts, Yahoo Alerts, Social Mention Alerts, TweetDeck. Seesmic, and HootSuite.

Google Alerts, Yahoo Alerts, and Social Mention Alerts all provide similar email or text alerts about the posting of certain web content that meets preestablished alert criteria. For instance, if a local emergency manager wanted to monitor the appearance of his organization's name in social media and/or on a web posting, an alert such as these listed would work effectively. This is particularly effective to monitor internet postings from traditional media outlets to controlled web extensions of their traditional output. For instance, if that same local emergency manager is interviewed by a local television station who posts a video and text article on its website, an alert mechanism would be generated and sent to anyone who had established the appropriate search parameters. The Google and Yahoo alerts are similar in that they provide the opportunity for keyword filtering against web content, news, and breaking information related to the search parameter. Google has a slightly more robust filter that includes blogs, discussions, and videos. Unfortunately, these filters may or may not be on independent social media sites like Facebook and Twitter but could simply be incorporated into secondary

Figure 6.3 Without proper social media monitoring, critical incident-related information can be lost in the overwhelming quantity of information.

media sites. The Social Mention Alert is the most robust real-time collective alert for social media content. As already discussed, the Social Mention system allows keyword filtering and also allows for content and alerts checked against one or multiple social media systems.

The final three real-time collective monitoring tools are TweetDeck, Seesmic, and HootSuite. In all three cases, these social media monitoring and collection systems are multiplatform, multifunction systems capable of capturing tremendous amounts of social media data over short or long periods of time. Each of these systems is available through web browsing, desktop applications, and mobile applications. The concept for these tools is to provide an interface to the social media user that allows for the monitoring of social media comments, responses, private messages, pictures, video, and other shared content from one central location rather than from a variety of original sources. Specifically, TweetDeck, Seesmic, and HootSuite all support connectivity to Twitter, Facebook, LinkedIn, and FourSquare with some additional social media outlets supported on the individual monitoring systems.[4,5,6] The practicality of this type of interface is primarily related to time management.

REAL-TIME COLLECTIVE MONITORING TOOLS

Google Alerts
Yahoo Alerts
Social Mention Alerts
TweetDeck
Seesmic
HootSuite

Although these systems are utilized as much for social media output as monitoring, they are very effective at collecting a vast amount of information.

Unlike the individual real-time instantaneous and collective system already discussed, TweetDeck, Seesmic, and HootSuite allow for the preservation of all functionality available on the original systems. For instance, the Twitter interface on these systems is divided into followed content, responses, direct messages, and systematic searches in the Twitter system based on keywords, users, or hashtags. Each search category and/or collected information is typically listed in columns with the most recent content match appearing at the top of the column (in reverse chronological order). This content—especially in systems like Twitter—is generated instantaneously but maintains this list of information until the number of postings exceeds the maximum allowed in the list (e.g., TweetDeck's default is 200 comments or posts). For emergency managers, this is perhaps the most beneficial type of single monitoring tool. Multiple systems can be utilized for the distribution of information and the monitoring of information during preparedness, response, recovery, and mitigation related to an event, disaster, or community issue. TweetDeck, Seesmic, and HootSuite are very similar in style and presentation with only minor functional differences. Most end users would only utilize one of these systems based on personal preferences related to display, access, and technological inclinations.

Much like the real-time instantaneous monitoring, the collective monitoring systems have some limitations and challenges as well. For the systems that generate alerts, they can provide limited and/or inconsistent results if the search parameters are not specific enough. For instance, jurisdictions with common names (e.g., Athens or Johnson) can create incorrect results if they not are specific to the area in question. Additionally, for emergency managers, these false positive results can also be generated if the incident in question is generic. For instance, creating an alert for "snow," "tornado," or even "hurricane" most likely would not be sufficient due to the fact that these types of events are often occurring or have occurred in multiple areas at nearly the same time. Instead, the search parameters should be set as specific as possible including geographic or common terminology related to the event (e.g., "Hurricane Katrina" rather than just "hurricane"). (See Figure 6.4.) Likewise, systems like TweetDeck and HootSuite can actually be so effective at gathering information that significant monitoring and/or assessment of the information being generated can be difficult to manage because there is too much information. Ironically, this proverbial avalanche of information is so overwhelming that almost no positive value can be achieved during this process. For instance, 4,064 tweets were sent in one second during the 2011 Super Bowl, which would be nearly impossible to monitor and track for similar or related information.[7] While the Super Bowl is a global event with millions of viewers (both through traditional and social media), it is not unbelievable that a major disaster like the Deepwater Horizon oil spill or Japan earthquake and tsunami would generate significant social media traffic that would be difficult to monitor without well-organized personnel

Figure 6.4 Social media monitoring can only successfully be implemented when deferential and specific categorical terms are utilized to determine one disaster from another. (From FEMA, Tim Burkitt.)

systems utilizing very specific search parameters to help better manage the situational awareness related to the event.

Basic Monitoring Analytics

In addition to external monitoring tools, nearly all major social media systems provide some internal measurement system that analyzes basic information about the effectiveness of the social media account. These measurement tools are often called analytics when referring to social media sites and are typically accessible by a particular user about that particular user's accounts, pages, and applications. For instance, Facebook provides analytics (called Facebook Insights) related to how Facebook pages are followed and interacted with by those followers. Specifically, aggregate demographical data such as gender, age, and location are available as well as a breakdown of what percentage of those users are routinely interacting with the page. These measurements are available over a selected period of time since the establishment of the page under review. In addition to the formal Facebook Insights that look at user measurements over time, Facebook also provides immediate feedback on each page post. Specifically, the system will generate the number of views and the level of engagement (based on responses or comments) within a short period of time. These two measurement tools provide immediate monitoring capabilities particularly to determine how well a distributed messaging is disseminating during an event or related to a certain issue.

Similar to Facebook, YouTube also maintains a strong analytics tool called YouTube Insights. Specifically, YouTube Insights provides analytics measurements for the number of video views, method of video discovery, viewer demographics, feedback style and frequency, and viewer engagement. All of these features are available over any selected time since the creation of the page and/ or individual video. The method of discovery is potentially a valuable monitoring tool because this feature will subdivide if the video was viewed directly from YouTube, through related videos, on mobile devices, or as posted on external sites. Knowing the source of the public intake is important considering it may reflect a positive or negative outlook. For instance, if the *Seven Signs of Terrorism* video mentioned in the disaster profile was posted to several antigovernment and extremist group sites (which it was), this would have been a strong indicator that the video was not being well received. The feedback style and frequency analytics features help categorize the feedback from viewers into common words or phrases (good, bad, terrible, etc.), designation as a favorite feature, and number of rated stars. This tool can also be a strong indicator of how well a video is being perceived or understood by the general public. (See Figure 6.5.) The last demographics tool is related to the level of engagement, which YouTube refers to as Hot Spots. According to YouTube, Hot Spots show "the ups-and-downs of viewership at each moment in [the] video, compared to videos of similar length [with] the higher the graph the hotter your view…[which] is an overall measure of [the] video's ability to retain its audience."[8] This type of feedback mechanism is an effective monitoring tool particularly for preparedness and educational components in emergency management to determine how interesting and engaging these are to the general public.

In addition to the embedded analytics tools that help monitor social media sites for an aggregate sense of engagement and understanding, Google Analytics is a third-party tool that is capable of providing embedded analytics measurements on some additional social media systems like blogs or websites. Specifically,

Figure 6.5 Negative public views like this protest are difficult to measure on social media systems without proper monitoring. (From FEMA, Marvin Nauman.)

when activated through a Google user account, Google Analytics generates specific HTML code that can be dropped into customizable blog sites such as Blogger, WordPress, and TypePad. Google Analytics helps measure site usage, visitor overview, geographic location of engagement, sources of connectivity, and content measurements over a selected period of time. Site usage includes breakdowns based on page views, bounce rates, average time on site, and new users visiting the measured site. Additionally, the sources of connectivity show what websites, search engines, or other media interfaces are connecting to the measured site. Much like the similar functionality available through YouTube Insights, this type of connectivity when monitored is a strong indicator of a positive or negative public acceptance of the posted content.

Much like the other monitoring tools already discussed, there are also challenges to the effective use of standard analytics tools available through some social media systems or specifically supported by Google Analytics. Because emergency management is almost universally defined through the phases of preparedness, response, recovery, and mitigation, social media content that is not related to specific disasters is often shared or redistributed in areas and disciplines not originally connected to the project. For instance, educational campaigns like Preparedness Piggy, Freddy the Ready Frog, and PrepE Penguin that are originally created in individual parts of the country (or world) are shared in other parts due to the universality of its purpose and message. This redistribution of social media data can often skew the basic analytics tools away from accurate reflections of local citizens. Similar to the challenge of alerts, generic disaster-related information may also skew basic analytics because of confusion about where a particular event is occurring—particularly when the event is commonplace (severe thunderstorms) or widespread (massive snowstorm).

Measuring Influence and Success

Although many systems exist to monitor the exchange of information on various social media outlets, it is also important for emergency managers to find ways to monitor the success of efforts to distribute information via social media before, during, and after disasters. These assessments are generally divided into two categories: influence and return on investment (ROI). This subdivision allows for the determination of how certain social media users are perceived by other users as well as mechanisms to utilize traditional measurements of success or failure to be applied to social media usage and effectiveness. These determinations are particularly critical to emergency managers who are often assessing the efficiency of efforts dedicated to the use of social media before, during, and after a disaster, including the continued justification of its use.

The first measurement to evaluate is social media influence. Measuring influence of social media is extremely challenging due to the ever-changing application and interconnectedness of individuals, users, and pages within the various social media systems. This is exponentially more challenging to create an aggregated measurement across multiple social media platforms like Facebook, Twitter, YouTube, blogs, and the many other common systems. Fortunately, the measurement of influence can be measured on major systems like Facebook and Twitter in ways that create effective and efficient classification, comparison, and evaluation.

Twitalyzer is a Twitter-based tool that provides an impact score for an individual user account as well as an influence category. This impact score is based on the number of users, unique references, frequency of retweeted material, and the relative frequency of posts.[9] The classification categories are everyday users, reporters, social butterflies, trendsetters, and thought leaders. These classifications help categorize and create comparisons and benchmarked standards for Twitter accounts to be compared to others. In addition, Twitalyzer also identifies shared networks and common terminologies associated with the account in particular. There are also lists of benchmarking capabilities that show influence results in comparison to other Twitter users through filters based on number of followers, appearances on lists, engagement, and influence. Unfortunately, this type of benchmarking is ineffective for emergency managers who most effectively would be compared against other emergency managers with similar populations, response capabilities, or systems utilized rather than the general social media user.

In addition to Twitalyzer, Klout is an extremely effective tool for monitoring the influence of Twitter and Facebook user accounts. Klout divides its analysis between a categorical score and a score analysis. The actual score is comprised of 35 variables divided into three components: true reach, amplification, and network.[10] This overall score measures the influence on a scale of 1 to 100, with higher scores representing a wider sphere of influence. Of the subcategorizes, true reach is based on the system followers who actively listen and react to posted messages; amplification is the likelihood that generated messages will generate systematic actions (e.g., retweets, responses, and direct messages). The score analysis assesses these categorizes over time for the particular user. Additionally, Klout creates an influence matrix that categorizes the user account into one of 16 categories (e.g., explorer, observer, conversationalist) and establishes the influencers of the account as well as those influenced by content distributed by the user.

Beyond influence, it is also important for emergency managers to be able to establish a return on investment (ROI) for the time and resources dedicated to the support of social media systems. Initially, social media ROI was measured by "soft" metrics such as systematic followers or fan likes. However, a more comprehensive ROI analysis has been established by both traditional marketers and ultimately emergency managers who all seek to justify continued programmatic utilization and development of social media. For emergency managers, the ROI analysis is fundamentally a measurement of how well distributed information is being received by the general public. The capability to ascertain ROI before, during, and after emergencies or disasters would be particularly valuable but is exponentially more difficult.

A recent eMarketer survey of marketing officers suggested that new ROI evaluations include more comprehensive measurements than previously had been identified. For instance, the measurements most often noted were site traffic, number of positive comments, number of mentions, and number of contributors, to name a few, with over 90% of all surveyed indicating that measuring ROI was critical to future success.[11] Additionally, this same survey indicated that Facebook and Twitter engagement as well as an open rating system resulted in some of the highest social media ROI. Conversely, organizational blogs and YouTube provided some of the lowest ROI of all measured systems.[11] Unfortunately, surveys and assessments like this are often marketing-centric and costly to conduct, which makes the applicability of ROI data for emergency or government application limited at best. With only one source of evaluation related to social media ROI, it will be challenging for emergency managers to find effective ROI tools to support social media efforts. However, regardless of the challenge, it is critical that modern emergency managers continue to find ways to consider and evaluate this issue.

Practitioner Profile: Ethan M. Riley, Arizona Division of Emergency Management

As a public information officer with the Arizona Division of Emergency Management (ADEM), Ethan M. Riley has a variety of communications responsibilities,

Figure 6.6 Ethan Riley.

including having co-developed the Arizona Emergency Information Network (AzEIN), which serves as the State of Arizona's online source for emergency bulletins, preparedness and hazard information, and multimedia sources that use a variety of different social media and Web 2.0 applications. Mr. Riley has additionally given numerous national presentations on the strategic integration of the AzEIN into crisis and emergency public information. When asked why social media was important to the management of emergencies and disasters, Mr. Riley stated that "Social media does as much to fell the fourth wall (theatrical term to describe the separation between the audience and performers) between the public and emergency management as any tool yet commercialized by bridging the rift between governments and their publics." He went on to say that some emergency managers consider social media an "affront to the status quo…[with] devotees to the 'old ways' of information sharing, awareness and coordination dismissing social media as a novelty or a security threat." When asked about why it is important for emergency managers to monitor social media before, during, and after a disaster, Mr. Riley stated, "Conversations about [individual agencies] are being had in an emergency…and despite the self-correcting nature of social networks, people will disseminate misinformation and disinformation," which means that emergency managers must engage in monitoring through "empathy, actionable advice and clarification when able." Finally, when asked to consider the role of social media in strategic planning and implementation, he stated that "Communication is transactional, meaning that people responded better to conversation than being told what to do…and [mobile phones] are ubiquitous, consequently, pictures and videos of emergencies are equally pervasive…[which] can alert you as to what things might look like on-scene and foreshadow challenges that haven't been considered." Mr. Riley's knowledge and understanding provides clear insight into the need for organizational adaptations to social media that are purposeful and effective.

Chapter Terms

Advanced programming interface (API): Interface built by social media systems to allow third-party developers to build external interfaces that utilize the original system.

Hashtags: User-generated systematic categorical classification device used in Twitter to allow users to search for certain issues or topics.

Monitoring: Activities and systems necessary to actively or passively observe information on social media systems related to emergencies or disasters.

Influence: Consideration of how an organization's social media usage influences the opinion, feelings, and actions of other users.

Return on investment (ROI): Consideration of how much value is achieved in utilizing social media systems when compared to the time and resources invested in social media activities.

Chapter Questions

General Questions

1. True/False: Instantaneous monitoring will aggregate over time all noted items that are being monitored.
2. The systematic categorical classification system used in Twitter is called a
   a. Tweet
   b. Hashtag
   c. Post
   d. Retweet
3. Which of the following is not a social media monitoring tool?
   a. Facebook
   b. Kurrently
   c. Monitter
   d. Topsy

Essay Questions

1. Discuss why ROI is important for emergency managers when considering the use of social media.
2. Why is monitoring important for emergency management and response activities?
3. Discuss the difference between real-time instantaneous and real-time collective monitoring.

Works Cited

1. Shirky, Clay. *Here Comes Everybody: The Power of Organizing Without Organizations.* New York: Penguin Press, 2008, p. 163.
2. "DVD Released—The Seven Signs of Terrorism." *National Terror Alert Response Center*, August 7, 2008. http://www.nationalterroralert.com/2008/08/07/dvd-released-the-seven-signs-of-terrorism/ (accessed March 30, 2011).
3. Kirkpatrick, Marshall. "Why Facebook Is Wrong: Privacy Is Still Important." *ReadWriteWeb*, January 11, 2008. http://www.readwriteweb.com/archives/why_facebook_is_wrong_about_privacy.php.
4. "TweetDeck." Wikipedia. http://en.wikipedia.org/wiki/Tweetdeck.
5. "HootSuite." Wikipedia. http://en.wikipedia.org/wiki/HootSuite.
6. "Seesmic." Seesmic. http://www.seesmic.com/.
7. Indvik, Lauren. "Twitter Sets New Tweets per Second Record during Super Bowl." *Mashable*, February 9, 2011. http://mashable.com/2011/02/09/twitter-super-bowl-tweets/.
8. "YouTube Insight Overview." *YouTube*, February 4, 2008. http://www.youtube.com/watch?v=Xo6HBKTyIzQ.

9. "Twitalyzer Profile." *Twitalyzer*. http://twitalyzer.com/profile.asp?u=jocosheriff&elapse d=6&tc=4&em=&rl=97.

10. "Klout Score." *Klout.com*.

11. Swallow, Erica. "Marketers Optimistic about Finding Social Media ROI." *Mashable*, February 8, 2011. http://mashable.com/2011/02/08/social-media-roi-2/?utm_ source=feedburner&utm_medium=email&utm_campaign=Feed:+Mashable+(Masha ble).

12. "25 Insightful Social Media Quotes." *Ghostwriter Dad*, March 22, 2011. http://ghostwriterdad.com/25-insightful-social-media-quotes/.

Chapter 7

White Hot or White Noise? Aggregation and Validation of Social Media Information

It's not information overload. It's filter failure.

—Clay Shirky[21]

Chapter Objectives

- To understand the processes required to aggregate and validate social media information for use during situational analysis
- To consider the impact of demographics on aggregation and validation of social media information
- Identify specific aggregation and validation tools available for use by emergency managers and disaster responders
- Explore the theory of social validation and its impact on social media monitoring and aggregation
- Evaluate the opportunity and prevalence of bias in social media reporting

DISASTER FOCUS—FORT HOOD SHOOTING

At 1:34 p.m. local time on November 5, 2009, Nidal Malik Hasan, a U.S. Army major serving as a psychiatrist, entered the Soldier Readiness Center at Fort Hood, a U.S. military installation just outside of Killian, Texas. (See Figure 7.1.) The Soldier Readiness Center was a facility for military personnel to receive routine medical treatment prior to and returning from official deployment. He was armed with a semi-automatic pistol that he had purchased from a local gun store. According to eyewitnesses, Hasan sat at a nearby empty table for a few seconds and then stood up and opened fire on those soldiers within the facility. Army Reserve captain John Gaffaney and civilian physician Michael Cahill both tried to challenge Hasan but were both wounded in the process. As Hasan moved through the facility, he passed several opportunities to shoot civilians, instead focusing on soldiers in uniform. Ultimately, Hasan was shot and taken into custody by Army police officers and is now paralyzed from the chest down. By the end of the event, Hasan had killed 13 people and wounded 29 others. During the investigation of the event, there were 146 spent shell casings recovered inside the building and 68 casings collected outside, for a total of 214 rounds fired by Hasan and responding police officers. Moreover, medics who treated Hasan later reported that he was still carrying 177 unfired rounds of ammunition in his pockets. In the first few hours after the event, two other soldiers were believed to have been involved but were later released. By the end of the event, multiple agencies responded to the Fort Hood shooting, including the U.S. Army Criminal Investigation Command, Texas Rangers, Texas Department of Public Safety, Bell County Sheriff's office, and Federal Bureau of Investigation officers. As a military officer, Hasan was later charged with 13 counts of murder and 32 counts of attempted murder under the Uniform Code of Military Justice.[6] With the size and scope of the response and impact of this act of terrorism, the public desire and need for information was immense. Traditional media sources and citizen journalists alike quickly moved to report on any pieces of information that were available about the event. Unfortunately, without reliable sourcing and tools to aggregate and validate the plethora of rumors, anecdotes, and buzz-worthy information, it was challenging for impacted individuals to get a clear, concise, and accurate picture of what had happened.[7]

Figure 7.1   Darnall Hospital at Ft. Hood, Texas, where the Soldier Readiness Center is located. (From U.S. Army, Michael Heckman, III Corps PAO.)

Impact of Demographics

Social media information can be monitored and analyzed with a variety of tools. However, due to the sheer number of sources and the complexity of the interconnectedness between various social media systems, monitoring the information distributed and exchanged via social media is useless unless there are mechanisms that allow for the aggregation and validation of this information. If these mechanisms are not utilized properly, social media information and activity simply becomes undistinguishable white noise that neither alerts nor corrects, which can be disastrous when quick and effective response is critical, such as in emergencies and disasters where timely information is the currency of efficiency and success.

For instance, if a community were in the middle of responding to an earthquake, local emergency managers would be keenly interested in assessing where localized power outages were occurring. While some areas have utility providers that publicly provide this information, these types of systems may sometimes be unavailable or only viewable to a limited viewing audience. Consequently, without using aggregation tools to validate information, the emergency manager may hear via Twitter, Facebook, and a blog that power was out in a certain area, but perhaps in reality all three sources are from the same person. Clearly, if that were the case, it would be an inefficient response to push resources and response personnel in reaction to this information rather than to other areas of the community that may actually have a more extensive power outage. This lack of control over resource management is not acceptable in modern emergency management, which has been highly impacted in recent years by shrinking budgets and limited personnel.

Table 7.1 Age Demographics by Category

Category	Age
Pre-Millennials	Under age 18
Millennials	18–33
Gen X	34–45
Younger Boomers	46–55
Older Boomers	56–64
Silent	65–73
G.I.	Over age 73

Source: From "Generations 2010: What Different Generations Do Online," *Pew Internet,* December 16, 2010. http://www.pewinternet.org/Infographics/2010/Generations-2010-Summary.aspx

One of the first and most practical tools for aggregation and validation of social media information is to understand the demographics of social media users. According to Pew Internet, basic demographics can be divided into seven categories: Pre-Millennials (under age 18), Millennials (ages 18–33), Gen X (ages 34–45), Younger Boomers (ages 46–55), Older Boomers (ages 56–64), Silent (ages 65–73), and G.I. (ages 74+). While all seven generational categories spent 90% of their internet time utilizing email and internet searching, only the Pre-Millennials, Millennials, Gen X, and Young Boomer generations used more than 50% of their internet time on social network sites like Facebook.[1] Likewise, nearly all seven demographics categories uniformly spent the least amount of internet time on blogs and virtual worlds. These demographic considerations can provide strong validation for event-related information depending on source, content, and utilized system (see Table 7.1).

The demographics of culture, ethnicity, and gender also play a significant role in the validation of monitored and collected information. For instance, some research indicates that Latinos and African Americans who use the internet are more than twice as likely as Caucasians to utilize Twitter, with about 18% of active Twitter users being Hispanic, 13% being African American, and only 5% being Caucasian within each cohort.[2] Likewise, Facebook usage via mobile phone was 36% for Latinos, 33% for African Americans, and 19% for Caucasians.[3] Social media usage by gender is often slightly higher in women, especially for Facebook and Twitter. Income, however, is somewhat of an exception to the stereotypical breakdown of social media users. Specifically, users with incomes $25,000 to $75,000 were the highest users, followed by those who make between $75,000 and $100,000, with significant reductions in usage both above and below these ranges on nearly all major social media systems.[4] Interestingly, education level also had plateaus of usage. For instance, nearly all systems maintained highest usage for those individuals with some college or a bachelor's degree but had significant reduction for both limited education (e.g., high school only) and advanced education (e.g., graduate degree).[4] Much as it does with age breakdowns, understanding the cultural, ethnic, and sociodemographic considerations potentially helps strongly validate disaster-related information. Unfortunately, there is currently very limited data on how accessible and functional needs populations (children, elderly, those with physical handicaps, economic challenges, etc.) use social media sites (especially during disasters). When this data is available, it will be particularly valuable to emergency managers for validating effective communications because these populations are of growing importance, particularly as there is national emphasis to plan for the "whole community."[5]

It is also critical to understand the limitations that exist when utilizing demographics as an aggregation and validation tool. Sociological tradition would hold certain inherent characteristics about each generation. For example, Gen X citizens are often tagged with stereotypical labels such as "lazy" and "unmotivated" while older generations (especially when compared to Gen X) are "hard workers." Unfortunately, according to New York University professor Clay Shirky, this change has less to do with inherent differences but rather is more directly related to the opportunities available to these generations.[21] This misidentification of cause is referred to as the fundamental attribution error or correspondence bias.[22] Put in straightforward terms by Mr. Shirky, "[T]he fundamental attribution error is at work when we explain our own behavior in terms of the constraints on us but attribute the same behavior in others to their character."[21] Having this measured parameter is important when considering using demographics as an aggregation and validation tool.

In addition to the need to consider demographics, basic analytics about a given site are strong mechanisms for validation in the broadest sense. Typically, basic analytics include crude cumulative observations about a particular social media system including followers, responses, comments, and so forth. Consequently, if a social media site is established by a local emergency manager and followers are quick to follow, like, or subscribe to the site, there is significant validation that the information and relationship established on that site are approved by the general public and therefore are going to be effective. Moreover, it ensures the information disseminated via that social media system will be available to those followers, which is the ultimate purpose of each of these sites.

Power of Aggregation

Aggregation is critical to the validation of time-sensitive social media information. This type of information is most common in disasters and emergencies due to the

IN A NUTSHELL

Get very good at filtering and aggregating content. Deliver it to people at the right time, the right size, the right amount.

—John Jantsch at the Influencer Project Conference

ever-changing flow of information during an event and immediately afterward as the picture comes into focus. It is critical to understand whether information is event related or simply undistinguishable white noise. Ensuring information has maximum validation is not easily done within social media systems. In most cases, emergency managers assign public information officers within the joint information systems (or centers in physical environments) to aggregate and validate information from all media sources. Likewise, for operational considerations, this process is facilitated through intelligence components that are assigned to operations, logistics, and/or planning functions.

From a global perspective, one of the most powerful aggregators is Google's Crisis Response tool. Google's Crisis Response tool was an initiative of Google.org (Google's philanthropic branch) that utilized Google's various online tools to organize emergency alerts, news updates, donation opportunities, and other disaster-related information for globally significant emergencies or disasters. Specifically, Google Crisis Response created disaster-related interfaces for Cyclone Nargis (2008), Sichuan earthquake (2008), Hurricane Gustav (2008), Hurricane Ike (2008), Red River floods (2009), L'Aquila earthquake (2009), Santa Cruz wildfires (2009), Typhoon Morakot (2009), Haiti earthquake (2010), Chili earthquake (2010), Pakistan floods (2010), Deepwater Horizon oil spill (2010) (Figure 7.2), Queensland floods (2011), and the Brazil floods and landslides (2011). Because of the resources available to Google and the dedication to the improvement and validation of disaster-related information, Google's Crisis Response has also facilitated the development of collaboration tools such as Person Finder and Resource Finder, which have helped verify information quickly and effectively.[8] Google's Person Finder is further discussed in Chapter 14.

An additional aggregation tool that a growing number of emergency managers and social media experts have begun to use is called Paper.li. This is a Twitter and Facebook aggregation system that allows individual users to create online "papers" that collect and summarize key information posted and shared by identified users. For Twitter papers, the aggregation is based on certain topics mentioned or addressed in association with certain account names, hashtags, or Twitter lists, while Facebook pages aggregate based on keywords posted on public Facebook sites. These "papers" can be aggregated on a routine basis (e.g., hourly or daily) and then used to re-engage the providers of that content within the measured system. This type of tool, much like the alerts discussed in Chapter 6, are excellent tools

Figure 7.2 Deepwater Horizon oil rig on fire in Gulf of Mexico. (From U.S. Coast Guard.)

to automate aggregation opportunities related to disasters or broader emergency management concepts or issues.

The third example of a common aggregation tool used by emergency managers utilizing social media is Twitter lists. Twitter lists are groupings of Twitter users based on arbitrary characteristics of the list generator. Any Twitter user can generate a list based on any number of characteristics; the user simply has to tag another user to that particular group.[9] For instance, emergency managers might create Twitter lists based on other emergency managers, local media, elected officials, or other similar groups. Interestingly, mere days after Twitter established the list functionality, the Fort Hood shooting happened and the tool was quickly utilized by some emergency managers and more widely by traditional media outlets trying to cover the event. News organizations such as the *Huffington Post, Los Angeles Times,* the *New York Times,* CNN, *Dallas Morning News,* and the *Washington Post* were the first to set up lists of trusted Twitter sources, including Texas emergency managers, military members, and citizens as well as a Twitter account called @Fthoodshootings that had been spontaneously generated minutes after the event by journalists at the *Austin American-Statesman.*[10]

By analyzing the web traffic and social media interest, the potential impact of Twitter lists was emphasized during the Fort Hood shootings. Specifically, according to Pew Research Center's New Media Index, 20% of internet links to news-related stories from blogs were about the Fort Hood shooting as well as 38% of the Twitter activity. But these numbers only partially reflect the size and scope of internet interest in this disaster. Specifically, these indicators were measured on the final day of the measurement cycle. Consequently, by including the next day (and the first of a new evaluation cycle), 67% of the blog links and 88% of the Twitter activities were related to the Fort Hood shootings.[11] Utilizing Twitter lists during events of this magnitude and public interest would be extremely valuable to help aggregate and validate disaster-related information in a real-time fashion. Without strong tools like these, it would be nearly impossible for emergency managers to effectively determine if social media information is incident critical or extraneous.

Theory of Social Validation

One of the primary reasons social media works as a mechanism that can be aggregated and validated is the theory of social validation. According to Dr. Susan Weinschenk, this psychological theory can be summarized as "When [humans] are uncertain about what to do we will look to other people to guide us...and we do this automatically and unconsciously."[12] This type of confirmation is critical to humans to effectively perform a function or engage in a particular action with the confidence that it will be conducted correctly and within social norms. Social validation can facilitate both directed and facilitated action. For example, when online purchases are conducted through merchant sites like amazon.com, the purchaser often looks to the aggregated opinions and ratings of others who have purchased the items or similar items to gain some collective confirmation of its quality or value. On the other end of the spectrum, social validation can also facilitate people's drive to exceed their current level of work or output, especially when one's work quality or quantity is highlighted or hidden when presented to the public.[12]

Social media is a powerful and modern tool for the application of social validation. Specifically, the self-correcting aspect of social media is primarily driven by this social construct. When information is posted erroneously, all social media systems will eventually correct the information because both the original poster as well as those within the shared system want validation that their information is correct and is thus solidified by the presence of those persons within the shared community. In turn, the knowledge and desire for both the social validation and self-correcting mechanism in social media reduces the intentional posting of

IN A NUTSHELL

When [humans] are uncertain about what to do we will look to other people to guide us...and we do this automatically and unconsciously.

—Dr. Susan Weinschenk[12]

> ## IN A NUTSHELL
>
> Misinformation and rumor have the potential to spread very quickly through online social networks due to the Internet's informal structure and capabilities for unverified publication…the collective 'wisdom of the crowd' has been shown…to have the capacity for self-correction as those invested in a particular topic or subject matter monitor online behaviors and content posting corrections as necessary.
>
> **—Dr. Jeanette Sutton, "Twittering Tennessee: Distributed Networks and Collaboration Following a Technological Disaster"[13]**

misinformation, particularly during time-sensitive and community-centric events such as emergencies and disasters. According to disaster sociologist Dr. Jeannette Sutton, although "Misinformation and rumor have the potential to spread very quickly through online social networks due to the Internet's informal structure and capabilities for unverified publication…the collective 'wisdom of the crowd' has been shown…to have the capacity for self-correction as those invested in a particular topic or subject matter monitor online behaviors and content posting corrections as necessary."[13]

This social media phenomenon of self-correction through social validation is not limited to large-scale events that have significant traditional media coverage as well as widespread public outcry. For example, on December 22, 2008, a waste containment pond at the Tennessee Valley Authority's Kingston Fossil Plant in Roane County, Tennessee, spilled more than 5.4 million cubic yards of coal fly ash into a nearby valley and tributaries of the Tennessee River. (See Figure 7.3.) Individuals in the impacted area reported a variety of health issues presumably linked to poor air quality and increased levels of heavy metals such as arsenic, cadmium, lead, and thallium in the soil and water. Within the first few days of the incident, media coverage was minimal and limited to local reporting from regional sources such as the *Tennesseean* and the *Knoxville News*. Because of this lack of media advocacy, Twitter served as the primary means for the impacted individuals to distribute and share information about the local disaster, which was otherwise unrecognized and uncontrolled by traditional mechanisms. Consequently, one researcher stated that "The small network of self-professed [local] activists and green advocates… [self-organized] helped to sound the alarm about a devastating technological failure…[by] policing the accuracy of posted content, correcting misinformation, and dispelling rumors."[13]

This ability of social media systems to self-correct is juxtaposed against the use of anonymous sources in traditional media. Often mainstream media will utilize a source under anonymity to provide protection to the sources so they will potentially be more willing to share information about the covered topic. The ethics of

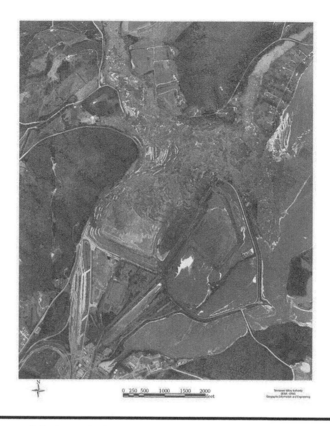

Figure 7.3 Aerial view of Kingston Fossil Plant the day after incident. (From Tennessee Valley Authority.)

journalism often require these sources—whether anonymous or not—to be confirmed by at least one additional source to ensure the validation of the pending media report. In many ways this type of validation is no more accurate or biased than the social validation and self-correction mechanism available in social media. This is an important reflection considering the fact that one of the concerns often presented in regard to social media—particularly by emergency managers—is about the perception that social media is rampant with inaccuracies and biased views. However, due to the psychological and sociological foundations already established, social media in its aggregate form is no more or less subject to these concerns than traditional media utilization.

The Power of the Virtual Voice

The discussion of social media can sometimes become fixated on the individual systems and minute considerations rather than on the collective power, influence, and voice of the millions of people throughout the world who utilize these systems for personal and news-reporting systems. In the most basic terms, it is the proverbial problem of looking at the trees instead of the forest of information about a particular issue or situation. The individual systems and users are important but only gain the impactful influence when considered as a whole. Much like statistical analysis that often eliminates outliers to level the statistical review, governmental officials and emergency managers are often guilty of the same response to individual citizens. If one person objects, he or she can be pushed aside as an outlier or fringe component; however, when 10 or 100 or 1000 state the same issue, quick response (or resolution) often follows.

As discussed earlier, this type of collective voice can be monitored in common systems like Twitter and Facebook but is also present through another category of new technology often referred to as social news sites. Examples of social news sites include Reddit, StumbleUpon, Digg, Newsvine, ShareThis, and AddThis. Reddit, StumbleUpon, Digg, and Newsvine are all based on the premise of posted web content whether from professional or amateur sources and allow users to rate the link positively or negatively. This functionality may exist as a thumbs up/thumbs down interface (StumbleUpon) or as digging/burying feature (Digg) but ultimately allows for the creation of user-driven popularity lists related to recently posted content. AddThis and ShareThis are embeddable website widgets that allow people to immediately link web content from blogs (e.g., www.mashable.com) and news sites (e.g., www.kansascity.com) to these various social news sites with corresponding positive or negative comments. To put the use of these sites into perspective, StumbleUpon has over 10 million users[14] and Digg has over 5 million users per month.[15] Interestingly, with the advent of the Facebook platform interface, many of these same websites have added or replaced some of these social news sites with the capability to "like" the site (just like in Facebook) and in essence provide the collective rating without having to visit the social media system itself.

The capability and importance of these social news sites to emergency managers is twofold. First, the capability to see public perception related to news content is invaluable, particularly during emergencies or disasters where corrective or protective actions are required for the public safety. Utilizing social news sites and the collective virtual voice of affected citizens is a valuable addition to the capability to validate incident-critical information. In addition to the aggregation capabilities, social news sites also allow for the facilitation of collective community action. For example, after the 2010 Haiti earthquake, Reddit challenged its users to generate slightly more than $30,000 in direct support of earthquake relief activities. This initial challenge was met within five hours of being posted as a web link on Reddit. A second challenge was issued to raise an additional $30,000. This additional challenge was achieved within seven more hours. This process continued with 3,787 individuals donating a total of more than $185,000 for emergency relief.[15] This type of modern donations management is impressive and is discussed further in Chapter 9.

RSS and Other Aggregation Tools

The last major type of social media aggregation tool is RSS. RSS, which is most often expanded as Real Simple Syndication, is a tool that captures and summarizes web content from multiple sites through readers or aggregators. For example, if a local citizen or emergency manager wants to monitor online content from various media sources like CNN, MSNBC, FoxNews, local media outlets, and various community blogs, it would be extremely time consuming to visit each of these sites at regular intervals to truly have an accurate picture of current conditions. This difficulty is exponentially greater during emergent situations like emergencies or disasters because information and conditions change quickly. Fortunately, the RSS technology helps to quickly and efficiently address this challenge.

The earliest internet aggregation technologies were first developed in 1999 but solidified as RSS by 2005 when the Firefox and Internet Explorer browsers adopted the orange square logo to represent the capability that is now known as RSS.[16] Since that time, the RSS technology has quickly become commonplace and actively utilized by internet content owners. Specifically, these content owners benefit from adding RSS feeds to their web content so it can be aggregated and more often read by others. The feed is a unique code that is autogenerated through secondary providers and can then be added to other websites.[17] Although RSS is somewhat of an older technology in the spectrum of Web 2.0 technologies, it is extremely beneficial to streamline the efficient and effective aggregation of multiple internet content streams.

In addition to RSS feeds and readers, there is a web application called Yahoo Pipes that allows an aggregation of various sources like RSS feeds or other output feeds through a graphical user interface. These aggregations are called pipes and allow end users to generate personalized streams of information on various issues, topics, or situations of interest.[18] For example, there is a Yahoo pipe that takes the *New York Times* RSS feed and runs it through Flickr to add tagged photos with similar categories or terms.[19] Each pipe is available to be copied and simulated for others to follow or emulate. Much like RSS, the Yahoo Pipes technology is an older social media technology (originally released in 2007) but still holds a lot of potential for dynamic information management as Web 2.0 technologies become more commonly accepted by both the general public and emergency managers.

In addition to RSS feeds and Yahoo Pipes, Facebook has a third-party integration tool that allows the Facebook interface of liking certain pages or issues to be transfered to non-Facebook web outlets. This Facebook platform integration allows an aggregation of public opinion related to web content on external sites such as media outlets and community blogs. Since over 500 million people maintain Facebook accounts, this level of integration is an extremely powerful tool, especially as third-party websites are utilizing this platform in higher numbers. Specifically, by 2011, more than 250 million people engaged with Facebook on more than 2.5 million external websites through the Facebook platform.[20]

Integration with Traditional Systems

The use of social media systems to aggregate and validate information is also being utilized through integration with traditional aggregation systems. Specifically, social media data is being collected simultaneously with traditional information intake, management, analysis, and reporting systems that have long been used by the public. Because of the long-standing use of these traditional systems, there is a high level of trust within these systems that makes their integration with social media an interesting concurrence between traditional and new public communication strategies.

Specifically, the City of San Francisco implemented an integration of their traditional phone-based 3-1-1 information system with their public Twitter account. San Francisco was the first city in the United States to utilize the Twitter application called CoTweet to allow citizens to send direct messages via Twitter 24 hours a day to the @sf311 account to report "non-emergency city-related sightings (like potholes), request street cleanings, and any other service already supported by the phone or website."[23] The only stipulation to facilitate the direct message was for local citizens to follow the @sf311 account. Upon submission of the 3-1-1 Twitter report, local citizens received a direct message confirmation with contact information or requests for additional information.[23] Within two years of San Francisco's integration of Twitter with their 3-1-1 system, they received 5 million messages utilizing this system.[24] Although more common among major corporations like Time Warner, Comcast, Whole Foods, and Home Depot, this level of integration of social media is groundbreaking in government and would be a tremendous asset for emergency managers looking to find as much information aggregation as possible before, during, and after an event.[24,25]

Since very few communities have embraced San Francisco's level of Web 2.0 integration, governmental operators and emergency managers alike need to continue to evaluate alternative models to gather information from the citizens to validate overall situational awareness about everything from current city conditions to emergencies or disasters. One example of this integration is a social awareness site called SeeClickFix. Much like the 3-1-1 integration previously discussed, the SeeClickFix website and related mobile applications center on a web-based map that displays anonymous public comments, photos, or videos about any noticed issues within the community. In addition, anyone can receive email alerts based on keyword filters in a particular geographic region. SeeClickFix was founded in 2008 and currently supports 25,000 towns and 8,000 neighborhoods in the United States. City governments in Houston, Philadelphia, and Tucson utilize SeeClickFix for work orders within their municipalities for minimal monthly charges.[26] This type of utilization, although primarily used for non-emergencies, certainly could become a powerful crowdsourcing tool for emergency information as well. This type of crowdsourcing integration is further discussed in Chapter 11.

In addition to 3-1-1 integration and other similar services, this type of complex public engagement in 9-1-1 systems is not far off. Specifically, enhanced or next-generation 9-1-1 systems that allow for the integration of publicly generated photos, videos, and text messaging will be embraced by public safety answering points (PSAPs) and dispatch centers throughout the modern world. Unfortunately, this level of public feedback into the emergency notification process is not yet fully functional and fundamentally questioned by some traditional emergency managers and communicators. The possibilities of this type of an approach are further discussed in Chapter 8.

Practitioner Profile: Lee Arning, Southern Methodist University

As the director of emergency preparedness and business continuity for Southern Methodist University, Lee Arning has seen emergencies, disasters, and community events of great complexity across his university system. Because of his experience, he has been an early adopter of social technologies with a particular focus on

Figure 7.4　Lee Arning.

its utilization for situational awareness and aggregation of information. When asked about the importance of social media adoption within the emergency management field, Mr. Arning stated that "In the information age of 2011, the act of postponing the development of a social media strategy for public safety and emergency response programs would have the same effects as a mid-19th-century fire department postponing the act to purchase the first motorized fire engines, despite the fact that by doing so they would speed their response, reducing the loss of life and property." When asked to discuss implementation challenges to social media usage, Mr. Arning blamed it on what he called a "9-1-1 system mentality." Specifically, he stressed that the development of the 9-1-1 system stressed "one mode of communication (phone) and one number (9-1-1)...which created a unified, quick access to police, fire, and EMS, but it was predicated [on] the premise that the public must reach out by phone and that phones were always working." This 9-1-1 system mentality described by Mr. Arning is challenging considering not only that there are numerous different social media information streams that are potentially valuable to give and receive information during emergencies but that phone service in most areas is often impacted during major events and threatens the integrity of the emergency call-back system long thought to be *the* way of communicating emergency information.

Chapter Terms

Aggregation: Collection and classification of social media information into manageable packets of information.

Validation: Analysis and confirmation of social media information into verifiable and actionable information.

RSS feed: Type of social media aggregation tool that exports content via a particular technology that can be read and collected for aggregation and validation. This type of feed is commonly designated by an orange square with three curved lines.

RSS reader: Type of social media technology that can aggregate and collect RSS feeds into one manageable and reviewable source. Common readers are available through Google and Microsoft.

Social validation: Sociological phenomenon where individuals seek out validation and confirmation from other individuals (or sources) to validate the information they have received. This is often witnessed during emergency warning and notifications.

Self-Correction mechanism: Social media phenomenon where the overall social media system will correct misinformation or inaccuracies before any formal correction is possible or required.

Chapter Questions

General Questions

1. True/False: RSS and Yahoo Pipes are both social media information aggregation systems.
2. True/False: Is social media information more biased than traditional information received and utilized by media?
3. Which of the following is a social media news aggregator?
   a. Reddit
   b. Digg
   c. StumbleUpon
   d. All of the above

Essay Questions

1. Discuss the importance of aggregation and validation of social media information during emergencies and disasters.
2. Discuss the impact of generational demographics on the validation of social media information.
3. Discuss the theory of social validation and how it impacts the aggregation and validation of social media information during emergencies and disasters.

Works Cited

1. "Generations 2010: What Different Generations Do Online." *Pew Internet*, December 16, 2010. http://www.pewinternet.org/Infographics/2010/Generations-2010-Summary.aspx (accessed April 3, 2011).
2. Murphy, Samantha. "Twitter Popular among Young Adults, Minorities, Urbanities." *Business News Daily*, December 9, 2010. http://www.businessnewsdaily.com/twitter-popular-among-young-adults-minorities-urbanites-0798/.
3. Washington, Jesse. "Minorities See New 'Digital Divide.'" *All Business*, 2011. http://www.allbusiness.com/population-demographics/demographic-groups/15429194-1.html.
4. Bloch, Ethan. "Social Media Demographics: Who's Using Each Site?" *Flowtown*, April 9, 2010. http://www.flowtown.com/blog/social-media-demographics-whos-using-which-sites.
5. "FEMA Administrator Fugate Addresses National Commission on Children and Disasters." *FEMA Press Release*, August 23, 2010. http://www.fema.gov/news/newsrelease.fema?id=52432.
6. "Fort Hood Shooting." Wikipedia. http://en.wikipedia.org/wiki/Fort_Hood_shooting.
7. Holdeman, Eric. "Fort Hood Shooting and Social Media Accuracy." *Emergency Management Magazine*, November 7, 2009. http://www.emergencymgmt.com/emergency-blogs/disaster-zone/Fort-Hood-Shooting-and.html

8. "Google Crisis Response." *Google*, 2010. http://www.google.com/crisisresponse/index. html.

9. "Soon to Launch: Lists." *Twitter Blog*, September 30, 2009. http://blog.twitter. com/2009/09/soon-to-launch-lists.html.

10. Kanalley, Craig. "Fort Hood Shooting Shows How Twitter, Lists Can Be Used for Breaking News." *Poynter*, November 6, 2009. http://www.poynter.org/how-tos/digital-strategies/e-media-tidbits/99282/fort-hood-shooting-shows-how -twitter-lists-can-be-used-for-breaking-news/.

11. "The Fort Hood Tragedy Highlights the Reporting Role of Social Media." *Pew Research Center's Project for Excellence in Journalism*, November 2–6, 2009. http://www.journalism.org/index_report/fort_hood_tragedy_highlights_reporting_role_social_media.

12. Akil II, Bakari. "The Theory of Social Validation." *Psychology Today*, September 13, 2009. http://www.psychologytoday.com/node/32823.

13. Sutton, Jeannette. "Twittering Tennessee: Distributed Networks and Collaboration Following a Technological Disaster." Proceedings of the seventh international ISCRAM conference, Seattle, 2010. http://www.jeannettesutton.com/uploads/Twittering_Tennessee_FINAL.pdf.

14. Wauters, Robin. "StumbleUpon Quietly Signs Up 10 Millionth User." *TechCrunch*, May 18, 2010. http://techcrunch.com/2010/05/18/stumbleupon-10-million/.

15. "Digg Has Accepted Reddit's Challenge to a Fundraising Competition for Haiti." *Direct Relief International.* http://dri.convio.net/site/TR/Events/Tributes?pg=fund&fr_id=1030&pxfid=1511&JServSessionIdr004=r7t58phav1.app245b.

16. "RSS." Wikipedia. http://en.wikipedia.org/wiki/Rss.

17. "Icons: It's Still Orange." *Microsoft Blog*, December 14, 2005. http://blogs.msdn.com/b/rssteam/archive/2005/12/14/503778.aspx

18. "Yahoo! Pipes." Wikipedia. http://en.wikipedia.org/wiki/Yahoo!_Pipes.

19. "New York Times thru Flickr." *Yahoo! Pipes.* http://pipes.yahoo.com/pipes/pipe. info?_id=vvW1cD212xGMiR9aqu51kA

20. "Pressroom." *Facebook*, 2011. http://www.facebook.com/press/info.php?statistics.

21. Shirky, Clay. *Cognitive Surplus: Creativity and Generosity in a Connected Age.* New York: Penguin Press, 2011, p. 122–123.

22. "Fundamental Attribution Error." Wikipedia. http://en.wikipedia.org/wiki/Fundamental_attribution_error

23. Van Grove, Jennifer. "San Francisco First City to Instate City-Wide 311 Twitter Program." *Mashable*, June 2, 2009. http://mashable.com/2009/06/02/san-francisco-311-twitter/.

24. Albanesius, Chloe. "San Francisco Links 311 Call Center to Twitter." *PC Magazine*, 2009. http://www.pcmag.com/article2/0,2817,2348072,00.asp.

25. "20 Ways Businesses Use Twitter." *Bloomberg Business Week,* October 8, 2009. http://images.businessweek.com/ss/09/10/1006_twitterville/15.htm.

26. "SeeClickFix." *Wikipedia.* http://en.wikipedia.org/wiki/SeeClickFix

Chapter 8

When Status Quo Becomes Obsolete: Modern Integrated Emergency Warning and Notification Strategies

A highly digitized and interconnected world is one that's rapidly democ-ratizing power. The big media originally had an upper hand in news coverage but now social media is challenging the way the traditional media has done things. The main effect...is the change in economics and the rapid speed at which social media multiplies information.

—Nik Gowing, British television journalist[1]

Chapter Objectives

- To analyze the need to incorporate social media and Web 2.0 strategies into commonly utilized emergency notification and warning systems
- To evaluate the impact of mobility and portability on mass notification
- To consider the reliability of various emerging and new emergency notifica-tion and warning systems

- To consider the components of a strategically diversified emergency notification and warning system
- To understand the foundations of the next generation 9-1-1 systems
- To consider the limitations of modernizing emergency warning and notification systems

DISASTER FOCUS—LONDON BOMBINGS

On July 7, 2005, at 8:50 a.m. (local time) in London, three separate bombs on the London Underground exploded within 50 seconds of each other. The first bomb exploded on subsurface Underground train #204 that was traveling between two stations. The second bomb exploded on subsurface Underground train #216, which had just left a local station. The third bomb exploded on deep-level Underground train #311. All three bombs caused significant primary damage to the impacted trains but also caused secondary damage to passing or nearby trains as well as the tunnels around them. Local emergency responders initially thought there had been six rather than three explosions in the underground train system. This confusion was caused by the fact that the train explosions occurred between stations, which resulted in casualties to emerge at stations both forward and to the rear of the train on each track. At 9:19 a.m., a Code Amber Alert was declared, leading to the cessation of the operations of the Underground train system. By 9:47 a.m., a fourth explosion occurred in Tavistock Square on a double-decker bus operated by the Stagecoach London Stratford depot. Earlier, the bus had traveled past train stations where crowds of people had been evacuated due to the earlier explosions. The explosion on the bus ripped the roof off the top deck and destroyed the back of the bus, causing witnesses to report seeing "half a bus flying through the air." Fortunately, the bus explosion took place near the British Medical Association building and a number of doctors in or near the building provided immediate medical attention. Four Muslim men aged 18–30 were later identified as the suicide bombers. These men were unknown as terrorist threats prior to the bombing. Ultimately, 56 people (including the four suicide bombers) were killed by the bombings and about 700 were injured. This incident was the deadliest single act of terrorism in the United Kingdom since the 1988 bombing of Pan Am Flight 103 over Lockerbie that killed 270 souls. Police forensic investigators examined about 2,500 items of closed caption television from the scenes of the bombings to determine the details surrounding the event. Interestingly, the most influential evidence was the eyewitness testimony of hundreds of witnesses who reported the event via social media.[2] In the hours immediately after the bombings, the British government put forth that the shocking damage and related casualties had been caused by some sort of localized power surge. However, within two hours of the official government story being released, there were over 1,300 blog posts identifying that the cause was actually an explosion. According to one expert, "Camera phones and sites for sharing photos globally meant that the public could see images of the subway interior and of a double-decker whose roof had been blown to pieces—evidence utterly incompatible with the official story." Consequently, due to the influence and impact of citizen journalism and the utilized social media tools, the British government had to correct the official story within two hours of the initial release.[3] (See Figure 8.1.)

Figure 8.1   British prime minister Tony Blair announcing London subway attacks at G8 summit. (From White House, Eric Draper.)

The Fallacy of Traditional Approaches

Outdoor warning sirens have long been one of the primary emergency notification systems utilized by emergency managers to warn their citizens about severe weather threats or other community hazards. (See Figure 8.2.) They are based on the infrastructure and philosophy of civil defense sirens and are often distributed throughout communities based on budgetary availability and population density. Unfortunately, technology, human behavior, and social science have reached the point where sirens may no longer be capable of serving as the primary system for emergency warnings. Dennis Mileti and John Sorensen state that effective public warnings include consideration of the warning source, message content, frequency of warning, and the need for different warnings (e.g., to address multiple languages).[18] This complexity is not solely achievable through the use of outdoor warning sirens and other traditional methods and therefore necessitates the consideration of a new approach that embraces new and emerging technologies.

Moreover, according to one Environmental Protection Agency (EPA) study, Americans spend 90% of their time inside, which severely limits the effectiveness

Figure 8.2 Outdoor warning sirens have long been a traditional public notification strategy. (From FEMA, Leif Skoogfors.)

of an outdoor warning notification system.[4] This fundamental divide represents the most basic challenge to effective public notification through outdoor sirens. Although outdoor warning sirens create a "universal" language at first blush, this "language" does not necessarily mean the same thing for everyone in a given community. For instance, some local communities activate outdoor warning sirens for high wind events and some do not (even if they are adjacent communities). This significantly challenges the current accepted social science research that indicates people are most likely to respond correctly if the warning mechanism contains directed protective information and is clear, consistent, and repeated.[5]

In addition to the need for consistent messaging from multiple sources, Dr. Dennis Mileti, former head of the Colorado Natural Hazards Center with the University of Colorado, states that citizens are driven by four criteria. First, the content of the emergency notification message is critical with particular importance on the directed actions given to the public.[30] This is particularly interesting considering that traditional outdoor warning sirens provide no protective action statements but simply provide notification of some emergency condition. Secondly, Mileti stresses that emergency warning notification messages must be repeated endlessly to facilitate effective and efficient public response.[30] He goes so far as to describe the general public as "information vampires" during emergency events, noting that there is no such thing as too much information for the general public impacted during emergencies or disasters. While outdoor warning sirens are often repeated for the duration of the event, most emergency management offices do not repeat other notification methods. However, this is correctable with the implementation of emergency technologies. Mileti's third and fourth considerations relate to the need for the general public to observe the response of others to the emergency notification and to discuss with trusted sources about the appropriate response to

**FOUR CONSIDERATIONS FOR EFFECTIVE
EMERGENCY NOTIFICATIONS**

1. Message content
2. Message repetition
3. Community observation
4. Community confirmation[30]

the message.[30] This type of peer-to-peer confirmation harkens back to the theory of social validation discussed in Chapter 7 that creates some of the foundational concepts in social media. These last considerations are perhaps the most challenging to traditional methods of emergency notification but could significantly be improved through social media and Web 2.0 systems that allow for feedback and conversational consideration of shared information.

Outdoor warning sirens and most traditional emergency notification strategies are often costly to purchase and maintain by local jurisdictions. For example, an average community might have sirens that are up to 25–40 years old that could only be replaced with costs exceeding $20,000 per siren.[6] Every community would also need multiple sirens to cover the entire municipal area (or at least areas identified as most populated or critical to the community). While newer siren systems incorporate increased technological capabilities that allow for better feedback regarding the effectiveness of the sirens, these systems are few and far between and do not often integrate with older devices that are still present in many communities. Moreover, because the sirens often stay dormant for the vast majority of the year there is always a vulnerability that the sirens may fail to operate or act unpredictably.

Mobility and Portability

Over the past decade—with specific focus on the last half of the decade—there has been an explosion in the availability and acceptance of equipment and technology that allows individual portability and mobility of information, services, and notification. This capability is based on global positioning systems (GPS) as well as wireless, infrared, Bluetooth, and social media technology. Notification systems utilizing this type of mobility and portability include National Oceanic and Atmospheric Administration (NOAA) all-hazard alert radios, cell phones, smartphones, GPS devices, and many others. These systems are not only mobile but, due to their relatively small size, are extremely portable, which means they are often close to the owner rather than geographically limited to a home, building, or area like outdoor warning sirens.

The first and perhaps most pervasive of these mobile and portable notification tools is the cell phone. As the final years of the 20th century expired and a new

Table 8.1 Rate of Household Wireless Replacement (by State)

Highest Replacement		Lowest Replacement	
Oklahoma	26.2%	Vermont	5.1%
Utah	25.5%	Connecticut	5.6%
Nebraska	23.2%	Delaware	5.7%
Arkansas	22.6%	South Dakota	6.4%
Idaho	22.1%	Rhode Island	7.9%

Source: From U.S. Centers for Disease Control and Prevention (CDC) Study. "Wireless-Only Phone Use Varies Widely across United States." *CDC Press Room*, March 11, 2009. http://www.cdc.gov/media/pressrel/2009/r090311.htm (accessed February 22, 2011).

Note: Wireless replacement refers to the rate at which homeowners have cell-phone-only households.

decade dawned, cell phone usage in the United States jumped by nearly 600%, with saturation between 75% and 82%.[7,20] Moreover, nearly one out of every five Americans—regardless of race or gender—maintains only a cell phone in their home or residence.[7,19] Interestingly, this number varies throughout the United States, with Oklahoma's wireless replacement being the highest and Vermont's being the lowest. Table 8.1 contains a breakdown of this movement at the state level. Cell phone uses has also become pervasive across all ages, genders, and racial groups, which is critical for emergency managers to consider as public expectations and realistic utilization of modern emergency public notification strategies become more common.

One of the primary functions available on cell phones is the capability to use the common transfer protocol called Short Messaging Service (SMS) texting. As of 2009, there were more than 4.1 billion texts sent daily based on this protocol.[8] At that time, U.S. cell phone users sent and received an average of 357 text messages per month while only making and receiving 204 phone calls each month. This text message rate compares to 2006 when an average cell phone user only sent and received 65 text messages per month. Interestingly, the rate of placed phone calls stayed relatively steady over that same period of time[21]; however, the average length of those calls dropped from 2.27 minutes in 2008 to 1.81 minutes in 2009.[25] These usage statistics strongly indicate that text messaging is not replacing traditional communication forms but rather has become a sustained additional form of two-way communication.

Historically, emergencies and disasters have also proven the reliability and effectiveness of SMS texting when landlines and other communication infrastructure

Figure 8.3 **Residents are lining up to get into the Superdome, which was opened as a hurricane shelter in advance of Hurricane Katrina. (From FEMA, Marty Bahamonde.)**

is damaged or overloaded. For example, after the terrorist attacks of September 11, 2001, the cellular traffic in New York City increased 1300% over peak usage, which caused about 95% of the calls to fail due to congestion.[23] However, texting has shown a far greater resiliency during the high-demand levels necessary during disasters. During Hurricane Katrina (see Figure 8.3), cellular providers released public messaging to their users in the impacted regions to strongly consider text messaging to communicate with family and friends who were otherwise unavailable on landlines.[22] Likewise, based on debriefings after the response to Hurricane Katrina was over, the Mississippi Department of Transportation announced recommendations for future response to encourage local citizens to be prepared to utilize SMS texting by pre-identifying friends and family who use texting features and to practice before another event happens.[22]

In addition to the SMS text capability that exists on cellular phones, many cell phones have added data-transfer capability such as mobile internet. These phones are typically referred to as smartphones and are common to brands such as iPhone, BlackBerry, and Android. By the end of 2010, more than 60 million Americans owned smartphones, which represents a 60% increase from the same time in 2009.[24] These smartphones are quickly becoming a primary mechanism for accessing social media systems and other internet sites. Specifically, in 2010, almost 33% of smartphone users accessed social media sites through their phones, which was an increase of 8% from 2009. Moreover, mobile access to Facebook grew 112% and Twitter 347% in the same period of time.[26] Since these systems have already been established as leading social media systems for the exchange of accurate real-time information, their availability via smartphones may profoundly impact the form and function of how emergency public notifications are received by the public in the future. These systems and the impact of mobile information are discussed in greater detail in Chapter 12.

In addition to mobile phones, the National Oceanic and Atmospheric Administration (NOAA) supports all-hazard alert radios as an auxiliary mechanism for emergency public notification (particularly indoors). (See Figure 8.4.) Depending on the complexity of the device in question, the radio can be programmed for one geographic area (e.g., county) or multiple areas by the end user. This programming is based on the National Weather Service's (NWS) Specific Area Message Encoding (SAME) code.[14] Therefore, when NOAA's National Weather Service distributes a weather notification product such as a watch, warning, advisory, or Amber Alert, they attach corresponding SAME code that limits the announcement to only those in the impacted area. Currently there are over 400 NOAA weather stations broadcasting to a coverage area of approximately 98% of the United States.[9]

Figure 8.4   FEMA assistance worker distributes weather radio to a disaster survivor living in FEMA temporary housing. (From FEMA, Jennifer Smits.)

The Emergency Alert System (EAS) is another traditional public notification system that has significant saturation and is generally accepted and understood by the public. EAS is a national public warning system that requires television, cable television, and radio broadcasters to provide the capability to issue priority messaging during local, regional, state, or national emergencies such as weather advisories or Amber Alerts. It is supported at the national level by the Federal Communications Commission (FCC) in conjunction with the Federal Emergency Management Agency (FEMA) and the National Weather Service (NWS).[36] Because it is a national system that can be activated at all levels of government, there are typically strict rules about when, where, and how the system is activated to protect its effectiveness and minimize potential abuse. Like all traditional notification systems, EAS does have some limitations, including the need for an individual to be actively engaged in the given network to receive the message. Specifically, if individuals do not have the TV or radio on, the EAS system will not be heard. This issue is further compounded by the rise in use of digital video recorders that delay broadcasts of given programming, which again delays or eliminates the receipt of the EAS message.

Although not available to everyone, these types of mobile and portable communication tools make emergency notification easier and often more effective than outdoor warning sirens, regardless of the time or location. With systems that are location static (e.g., NOAA alert radios), notifications and alerts are available inside buildings and homes where people spend the overwhelming majority of their time. Likewise, cell phones are location dynamic and are often within close reach of the individual user. Combined, the portability and mobility of these types of systems ensures the ability to provide obtrusive alerts for people asleep or otherwise distracted, which may not be possible inside homes from outdoor warning sirens.

Dynamic and Diverse Emergency Notification Strategies

The concept of creating a more dynamic and diverse emergency notification strategy that moves away from outdoor warning sirens as the primary function is not new. In 2005, in response to significant severe weather that caused the deaths of 25 residents living in a mobile home community, the State of Indiana passed a law that required all new manufactured homes to come with NOAA all-hazard alert radios.[9] Other communities have also identified funding or grants to purchase weather radios for nearly all citizens in the given area.[11] Many communities have also begun to institute various forms of social media to send out emergency notification through systems such as Facebook and Twitter to reach the growing numbers of citizens engaged in those communication streams.[12] Consequently, it is merely a matter of allowing this movement to shift from localized to industry-wide to truly be effective. For a comprehensive comparison of the various types of emergency notification systems, see Table 8.2.

Table 8.2 A Comparison of Emergency Notification Systems

System Name	Type	Mobility[b]	Portability[b]	Service Purpose	Implementer	System Established
Outdoor Warning Sirens	Siren	None	None	Outdoor Notification	Local	1950s
National Warning System (NAWAS)	Telephone	None	None	Responder Notification	State and Federal	1950s
Twitter	Social Media	Yes	Yes	Universal Notification	Local	2006
Facebook	Social Media	Yes	Yes	Universal Notification	Local	2004
SMS Text Notification Systems[a]	Text	Yes	Yes	Universal Notification	Local	1992
Public Safety Communication Systems[a]	Telephone	None	Yes	Universal Notification	Local and State	2000s
Emergency Alert System (EAS)	Alert Radio	None	Yes	Universal Notification	Local, State, and Federal	1997
Integrated Public Alert and Warning System (IPAWS)	Integrated	Yes	Yes	Universal Notification	Local, State, and Federal	N/A

[a] There are many companies that provide this messaging system for a wide range of fees.

[b] For the purpose of this comparison, the distinction between mobility and portability is related to the dissemination capability of the emergency notification system. Specifically, mobility is based on the capability to receive emergency notification regardless of geographic location. Portability allows the notification system to be moved and reprogrammed or designated for a new geographic position. This distinction is slight but critical for this comparison.

Figure 8.5 Along with the secretary of the Department of Homeland Security, FEMA administrator Fugate was specifically tasked in the GAO report to improve national emergency warning strategies. (From FEMA, Bill Koplitz.)

The need for a more robust and effective national emergency warning strategy was also established by the 2009 Governmental Accountability Office's (GAO) review report entitled "Improved Planning and Coordination Necessary for Development of Integrated Public Alert and Warning Systems" (IPAWS).[13] While the title sounds as convoluted as the problem, the report clearly identified a need for an updated overall strategy that fully implemented technology and programmatic implementations that have been undermanaged (Emergency Alert System) or underdeveloped (IPAWS). The report noticeably charged the U.S. secretary of Homeland Security and the FEMA administrator to improve emergency warning strategies through additional project development, testing, and increased project transparency.[13] (See Figure 8.5.)

The first and perhaps most promising development by the various federal agencies with responsibilities related to mass emergency public notification is the development of the Integrated Public Alert and Warning System (IPAWS). IPAWS was originally launched in 2006 in response to presidential Executive Order 13407, which required the United States to have "an effective, reliable, integrated, flexible, and comprehensive system to alert and warn the American people in situations of war, terrorist attack, natural disaster or other hazard."[27] Unfortunately, it has been plagued by setbacks over the years under the Federal Emergency Management Agency's (FEMA) control as the technological and philosophical developments necessary to replace the national Emergency Alert System (EAS) matured. However, by late 2010, under rejuvenated leadership, IPAWS made significant developmental jumps toward possible implementation.

One of the primary reasons for this progression was related to the development of the Commercial Mobile Alert System (CMAS) that allows for the sending of

IN A NUTSHELL

The United States should have "an effective, reliable, integrated, flexible, and comprehensive system to alert and warn the American people in situations of war, terrorist attack, natural disaster or other hazard."

—Presidential Executive Order 13407[27]

text-based alerts to mobile devices in selected geographic areas without subscription services or other contractual obligations.[28] The CMAS protocol was based on Federal Communications Commission orders in 2008 to begin a process to allow mobile providers to opt into a system that would allow for emergency cellular notifications to all subscribers.[29] Specifically, the CMAS protocols allow for a cell broadcast message (one-to-many) approach rather than a traditional text message (one-to-one) approach, which can be slow on cellular systems (when sent to a bulk list of contacts) and equipment already under high demand. This type of directed messaging is one of the most significant challenges to modern warnings strategies by local emergency managers who have often lacked the technology, services, equipment, and understanding to implement it. If implementable as a comprehensive system, IPAWS would solve this problem by empowering emergency managers at all levels and for all hazards to provide the necessary and timely messages needed during an emergency event. (See Figure 8.6.)

Interestingly, with all the developments in directed messaging through IPAWS and ultimately the revision of the Emergency Alert System, these systems are still based on directed rather than conversational interactions. Social media allows for

Figure 8.6 IPAWS division director Antwane Johnson demonstrates the IPAWS program to domestic and international dignitaries. (From FEMA, Bill Koplitz.)

an incorporated mechanism for the distribution of emergency notifications as well as feedback for the effectiveness and distribution frequency of the message. For example, emergency notifications distributed on Twitter can be quickly retweeted across a multitude of users who may be in need or are otherwise impacted by that warning. This allows the initial emergency notification action to be enormously magnified without any additional energy or resources from the source provider (e.g., emergency manager).

In addition to the fundamental uses of social media already discussed, many of these systems allow information to be disseminated through internal systems as well as through SMS text messaging. For example, Johnson County Emergency Management in Olathe, Kansas, created an SMS emergency notification system by automating National Weather Service (NWS) products (such as tornado warnings) to be posted to Twitter within seconds by utilizing Twitter's advanced programming interface (API). The organization promoted this program by encouraging people to follow the specified Twitter account (@JOCOAlert) by utilizing Twitter's Fast Follow SMS notification feature. Consequently, Johnson County Emergency Management utilized the free social media tools to create a voluntary mass notification system at a fraction of the cost of commercial systems currently available.[12,15] This type of efficient and cost-effective utilization is potentially a powerful tool for emergency managers to apply, especially in technology-limited or financially strapped areas.

Next Generation 9-1-1

In addition to modifications and modernization of emergency mass notification strategies, there is also a concerted effort to upgrade the 9-1-1 system throughout the United States to meet the growing use of Voice over Internet Protocol (VoIP), social media, and texting for the receiving, sharing, and distribution of information. This change is significant considering that the 9-1-1 system has conceptually remained relatively unchanged since its initial implementation by the Federal Communications Commission in partnership with AT&T in 1968.[31] Conceptually, the 9-1-1 service allowed for automated connectivity from a phone line to a central public safety answering point (PSAP) for dispatching of emergency response personnel and equipment appropriate for the information received. Technological changes to allow for caller location information were eventually integrated into the PSAP capability through the enhanced 9-1-1 (E911) systems; however, this functionality is not fully integrated for use with wireless devices. Regardless, the only integrated information available to PSAP stations and their dispatchers from mobile callers is the verbal reporting available from callers related to an event or incident. Even secondary information available from auxiliary sources (e.g., local highway cameras) is not integrated into traditional 9-1-1 systems and therefore creates an additional burden for dispatchers to perform primary job functions and monitor additional sources to make clear and effective response decisions.

Table 8.3 Comparison of Current 9-1-1 versus Next Generation 9-1-1 Systems

Current 9-1-1 Capabilities	Next Generation 9-1-1 Capabilities
Virtually all calls are voice callers via telephones over analog lines.	Voice, text, or video information from many types of communication devices, sent over internet protocol (IP) networks
Data transferred via voice	Advanced data sharing is automatically performed
Callers manually routed through legacy selective routers, limited forwarding/backup ability	Physical location of PSAP becomes immaterial, callers routed automatically based on geographic location, enhanced backup abilities
Limited ability to handle overflow situations, leading to callers potentially receiving a busy signal	PSAPs able to control call congestion treatment, including dynamically rerouting callers

Source: From "The U.S. Department of Transportation Next Generation 9-1-1- Initiative." *U.S. Department of Transportation,* 2007. http://www.its.dot.gov/ ng911/docs/NG2007.ppt (accessed February 22, 2011).

These issues have led to a large-scale commitment to begin to evaluate what is often being referred to as "Next Generation 9-1-1" (NG911).[32] Initial planning for the NG911 concept was started in 2000 with implementation beginning in 2003. According to the National Emergency Number Association (NENA), the NG911 concept continues to be a priority implementation for the future of 9-1-1 service delivery.[33] NENA states that the NG911 concept "provides location-based routing to the appropriate emergency entities" while supporting "the transfer of calls to other NG911-capable PSAPs or other authorized entities based on and including accumulated data…including non-voice (multimedia) messages."[33] Unfortunately, to date, most 9-1-1 systems are not capable of handling the text, data, images, and video that are increasingly common in personal communications and critical to the public engagement on the NG911 systems. This conversion will be guided by national and statewide emergency communication groups as well as some regional and local jurisdictions with significant resources tied to their PSAP operations and effectiveness. A comparison of the capabilities of current 9-1-1 systems versus proposed NG911 models is included in Table 8.3.

While the NG911 conversation continues, there are several communities beginning to embrace alternative forms to receive emergency information from citizens that incorporates the social media and Web 2.0 concepts of two-way information exchange and documentation. For example, the University of Maryland has released a new smartphone application (app) that allows users to call 9-1-1 and stream audio and video from the incident to emergency dispatchers. The app uses

IN A NUTSHELL

The ongoing evolution of the functionality and capabilities of digital communication devices has resulted in a technically savvy population that routinely uses communications services significantly more sophisticated than the 1960s era switched circuit analog telephone systems that are the foundation of today's 9-1-1 systems in the United States. Citizens using these digital devices have a growing expectation that they can exchange voice, data and graphic information to governmental public safety organizations as easily as they do with peers, family and businesses.

—Walt Way, State of Kansas Federal E911 Grant Project Oversight Committee Chairman (personal communication April 8, 2011)

the university's campus wireless network with an approximate transfer of 20 MB of data per minute of streamed video. Unfortunately, some students have objected to the potential use of the app in areas of campus not covered by the wireless system, which would force users to use personal data plans (if available) and be charged any corresponding charges.[34] Likewise, some communities have released 9-1-1 registries where local residents can pre-register personal and health information so dispatchers can obtain background information more efficiently and effectively during emergency response.[35] Although innovative, best practices still need to be developed for more comprehensive implementation.

Limitations to Modernization

Legal requirements must also be considered when evaluating the effectiveness of outdoor warning sirens versus other mechanisms. Unfortunately, this issue has no clarity on a national level but has been addressed in various ways at the state and local levels. For instance, in *Griffin vs. Osage County Sheriff's Office*, the Kansas State Supreme Court ruled that "the dissemination of weather information by a government agency...is generally held to be a discretionary function," which implies an unrestricted option to style and approach to emergency public notification. Conversely, entire states like New Hampshire have passed laws establishing statewide emergency notification systems.[17] Unfortunately, disorganized governmental notification often leads to citizen confusion and disorder based on the research presented earlier in this chapter.

Although sirens and traditional emergency notification systems will most likely never be eliminated as a component of public emergency notification, it may be time for communities to reevaluate their philosophies for strategic emergency public information. For instance, are sirens the most efficient and cost-effective strategy for emergency public notification or should the location and impact of sirens be modified to outdoor locations with high vulnerability (e.g., recreational parks and waterways)? Moreover, should secondary systems that allow for mobility and portability be provided (i.e., purchased) or supported (i.e., subsidized) within a selected area? This need for reevaluation is supported by research that indicates improvements in notification lead times for warnings (and therefore improvement in siren sounding times) does not show significant reduction in fatality and injury rates related to severe weather.[10] Bold action and strong leadership will be necessary to adjust this industry philosophy to become more in line with currently available technology and to continue to utilize current research and communication techniques.

Recognizing the need to diversify public emergency warning strategies to include technology based on mobility and portability will not be easy or quick. Many communities have significant commitments to the infrastructure and technology of outdoor warning sirens and other traditional strategies. However, with local economies and governmental budgets being restricted by the economic downturn, it is a pivotal time for local leadership to thoroughly evaluate warning strategies to ensure that future planning and implementation will result in the most effective strategy to keep local communities as safe as possible from severe weather and other community hazards.

In addition to the legal challenges to the implementation of modern emergency warning strategies, there are financial considerations as well. Clearly, purchasing and maintaining outdoor warning sirens is expensive, but those costs are absorbed by the community as a whole rather than by individuals or families. Because the modern strategies discussed are inherently driven by two-way or citizen-centric capabilities, any associated costs often impact the individual. For instance, the NG911 system being implemented by the University of Maryland discussed earlier potentially creates a sense of improved public safety with an unexpected cost when it is used outside their provided wireless system. In addition, according to national reports, the average local 9-1-1 service charges $0.72 per month to local users regardless of the amount of usage over time. This inherently creates a regressive tax structure where low volume users are charged a disproportionate amount, especially when compared to multiple-line users like businesses.[31]

Lastly, all emergency warning notification systems are also challenged in their effectiveness in reaching functional and accessible needs populations. These populations include those who are economically challenged, have limited language proficiency, have physical or mental handicaps, or are culturally or geographically isolated, not to mention those who represent the youngest and oldest generational demographics.[16] Both traditional and suggested modern strategies have limitations to reach these populations universally. For example, culturally and geographically isolated communities like the Amish would refuse to allow personal notification strategies available through social media because of an aversion to technology. Conversely, traditional outdoor warning sirens would be ineffective for the deaf and hard-of-hearing community. Striking a balance between traditional and modern notification strategies will be critical to effectively reach the community as a whole.

Practitioner Profile: Walt Way, Johnson County Emergency Communications Center

Walt Way has worked in the emergency communication field for more than 30 years and is nationally respected as a leader in emergency communications and the integration of emergency technologies into the next-generation 9-1-1 approach. He currently chairs the Federal E911 Grant Project Oversight Committee for the State of Kansas, which is reviewing the implementation of NG911 in that field. Mr. Way stressed that the NG911 process began after the terrorist attack of September 11 when the public safety community identified the need for improved interoperability across disciplines and jurisdictions. When asked why the integration of new technologies like text messaging and video are important, Mr. Way reported that "There is a growing interest by the public safety community to allow the public to send photos and videos to a dispatcher, showing conditions at an incident scene with more detail than a verbal description can provide," which includes "pictures of perpetrators or suspect vehicles [which] could be sent for immediate distribution to

Figure 8.7 Walt Way.

emergency responders in an area as well as for later use by investigators." However, Mr. Way pointed out that there is a concern that the "Provision of such information to a 9-1-1 center is that without suitable means of verification of the sender and of a particular event, these tools could be used to feed misinformation to emergency personnel or could introduce confusion as to which images are associated with what incident." Mr. Way continued to discuss the challenges to implementation by addressing costs and the adoption of national protocols as the primary challenges but did identify other more surprising challenges. Specifically, Mr. Way stated that "today's Short Message Service (SMS) text messages are delivered by the carriers on a best-effort basis," which means "there is no guarantee the message will be delivered at all…[or] it may be delayed by minutes or hours…[so that] multiple messages may be delivered out of sequence." Clearly, Mr. Way and other leaders in the 9-1-1 community will continue to seek improvements in these systems to address the availability of technology and the expectations associated with it to ensure maximum benefit.

Chapter Terms

Next Generation 9-1-1: Public safety movement that looks to incorporate emergency technologies such as SMS texting, steaming video, and social media into 9-1-1 dispatching centers.

Mobility: Systematic capability to receive emergency notification and/or warnings regardless of geographic location.

Portability: Systematic capability that allows emergency notification and warnings systems to be moved and reprogrammed or designated for a new geographic position.

Integrated Public Alert and Warning System (IPAWS): Proposed public notification and emergency warning system for future development that will utilize notification based on mobile device and geographic proximity to the threat.

Emergency Alert System (EAS): National public alert and notification system that has the capability to override television and radio broadcasts to provide public notification and emergency warning messages.

NOAA all-hazard radio: National public alert and notification system that provides alerting mechanisms via portable radios based on SAME codes that correspond to certain geographic areas (e.g., local counties).

SAME code: Geographic designation used in NOAA all-hazard radio system to limit the geographic range of notification.

Short messaging system (SMS) protocol: Type of text messaging that utilizes small packets of information to improve the efficiency of message distribution.

Chapter Questions

General Questions

1. True/False: IPAWS, EAS, and NG911 are all the same.
2. Which of the following would not be considered modern emergency notification strategies?
   a. IPAWS
   b. Outdoor warning sirens
   c. Twitter
   d. SMS Text Messaging
3. True/False: Mobility and portability mean the same thing when it comes to emergency notification.

Essay Questions

1. Discuss Mileti's four considerations for effective emergency notification with particular consideration of how modern tools apply.
2. Discuss the implementation challenges of next generation 9-1-1.
3. Discuss traditional public notification strategies versus the application of emerging technologies for emergency notification and warning.

Works Cited

1. Anil, Philip. "Use Social Media Responsibly: Nik Gowing." *Kerala IT News*, 2010. http://keralaitnews.com/state-scan/thiruvananthapuram/1717-mik-gowing-skyful-of-lies-social-media (accessed February 22, 2011).
2. Storm, Kevin J., and Joe Eyerman. "Interagency Coordination: Lessons Learned from the 2005 London Bombings," National Institutes of Justice, 2011. http://www.nij.gov/journals/261/coordination.htm (accessed October 30, 2011).
3. Shirky, Clay. *Cognitive Surplus: Creativity and Generosity in a Connected Age*. New York: Penguin Press, 2010, p. 62.
4. "The Inside Story: A Guide to Indoor Air Quality," *Environmental Protection Agency (EPA)*. http://www.epa.gov/iaq/pubs/insidest.html (accessed February 22, 2011).
5. Farley, John E. "Call-to-Action Statements in Tornado Warnings: Do They Reflect Recent Developments in Tornado-Safety Research?" *International Journal of Mass Emergencies and Disasters* 25, no. 1 (2007): 1–36.
6. Poston, Ben. "Some Areas Lack Tornado Sirens." *Journal Sentinel*, January 22, 2008. http://www.jsonline.com/news/milwaukee/29581894.html (accessed February 22, 2011).
7. Horrigan, John. "Mobile Access to Data and Information." *Pew Internet Study*, March 5, 2008. http://www.pewinternet.org/Reports/2008/Mobile-Access-to-Data-and-Information.aspx?r=1 (accessed February 22, 2011).

8. Van Grove, Jennifer. "Wow: 4.1 Billion SMS Messages Are Sent Daily." *Mashable. com Blog*, October 7, 2009. http://mashable.com/2009/10/07/ctia-wireless-survey/ (accessed February 22, 2011).

9. Kupec, Robert J. "Tuning In: Weather Radios for Those Most at Risk." *Journal of Emergency Management* 6, no. 4 (2008): 51–55.

10. Simmons, Kevin M., and Daniel Sutter. "Improvements in Tornado Warnings and Tornado Casualties." *International Journal of Mass Emergencies and Disasters* 24, no. 3 (2006): 351–369.

11. Lenz, Ryan. "Indiana Law Requires Weather Radios for Mobile Homes." *USA Today*, June 29, 2007. http://www.usatoday.com/weather/news/2007-06-29-ind-radios_N. htm (accessed October 30, 2011).

12. "SMS Text." *Johnson County (KS) Emergency Management and Homeland Security*, 2011. http://www.jocoem.org/CIT/jocoalert.shtml (accessed October 30, 2011).

13. "Improved Planning and Coordination Necessary for Development of Integrated Public Alert and Warning System." *Governmental Accountability Office*, September 9, 2009. http://www.gao.gov/products/GAO-09–834 (accessed February 22, 2011).

14. "Weather Radios Save Lives." *PrepareMetroKC*. www.preparemetrokc.org (accessed February 22, 2011).

15. "What Is WeatherCall." http://www.weathercall.net/wc_whatisit.html (accessed February 22, 2011).

16. Mitchel, Helena, et al. "Wireless Emergency Communications." *Rehabilitation Engineering Research Center for Wireless Technologies*, 2009. http://www.wirelessrerc. org/about-us/projects/development-projects/d3-wireless-emergency-communications. html/?searchterm=wireless%20Emergency%20Communications (accessed February 22, 2011).

17. "Governor Lynch Signs Law Creating Emergency Notification System." *State of New Hampshire*, July 7, 2010. http://www.governor.nh.gov/media/news/2010/070710-emergency-notification.htm (accessed February 22, 2011).

18. Mileti, Dennis, and John H. Sorensen. "Communication of Emergency Public Warnings." *Oak Ridge National Laboratories*, 1990, p. 3–7. http://www.emc.ornl.gov/ publications/CommunicationFinal.pdf (accessed February 22, 2011).

19. "Wireless-Only Phone Use Varies Widely across United States." *CDC Press Room*, March 11, 2009. http://www.cdc.gov/media/pressrel/2009/r090311.htm (accessed February 22, 2011).

20. Leo, Peter. "Cell Phone Statistics That May Surprise You." *Pittsburgh Gazette Online*, March 16, 2006. http://www.post-gazette.com/pg/06075/671034–294.stm (accessed February 22, 2011).

21. "Text Messaging Explodes in America." *CNET Tech News*, September 23, 2008. http:// www.cbsnews.com/stories/2008/09/23/tech/cnettechnews/main4471183.shtml (accessed February 22, 2011).

22. "Katrina—Recovery: Verizon Explains Text Messaging Is Most Efficient Use of Wireless Networks." *Wireless News Desk*, September 10, 2005. http://wireless.sys-con. com/node/128261 (accessed February 22, 2011).

23. Guernsey, Lisa (2001). "An Unimaginable Emergency Put Communications to the Test." New York Times. http://www.nytimes.com/2001/09/20/technology/ circuits/20INFR.html (accessed January 11, 2012).

24. Leggatt, Helen. "Use of Smartphones up 60%." *BizReport*, February 2011. http://www.bizreport.com/2011/02/use-of-smartphones-up-60.html (accessed February 22, 2011).

25. Wortham, Jenna. "Cellphones Now Used for Data More than Calls." *New York Times*, May 14, 2010. http://www.nytimes.com/2010/05/14/technology/personaltech/14talk.html?_r=1 (accessed February 22, 2011).

26. Gonsalves, Antone. "Social Network Use by Smartphones Jumps." *Information Week*, March 4, 2010. http://www.informationweek.com/news/hardware/handheld/show-Article.jhtml?articleID=223101506 (accessed February 22, 2011).

27. "Executive Order 13407 of June 26, 2006." *Federation of American Scientists*, 2006. http://www.fas.org/irp/offdocs/eo/eo-13407.htm (accessed February 22, 2011).

28. Bristow, Lorin. "The Impact of IPAWS on Public Alerts and Warnings." *Emergency Management Magazine*, January 17, 2011. http://www.emergencymgmt.com/disaster/Impact-IPAWS-Public-Alerts-Warnings.html (accessed February 22, 2011).

29. "Commercial Mobile Telephone Alerts." *Federal Communications Commission*, 2010. http://www.fcc.gov/pshs/services/cmas.html (accessed February 22, 2011).

30. "Dennis Mileti 'Social Media and Public Warnings.'" *Denver UASI Presents: Shared Strategies*, 2010. http://www.slideshare.net/COEmergency/warnings-social-media-rev-3 (accessed February 22, 2011).

31. "The History of 9-1-1—Basic Questions." Clark *Regional Emergency Services Agency*. http://www.cresa911.org/911/questions-history.php (accessed on October 30, 2011).

32. "The U.S. Department of Transportation Next Generation 9-1-1 Initiative." *U.S. Department of Transportation*, 2007. http://www.its.dot.gov/ng911/docs/NG2007.ppt (accessed February 22, 2011).

33. "NG9-1-1 Project." *National Emergency Number Association (NEMA)*, 2010. http://www.nena.org/?NG911_Project (accessed February 22, 2011).

34. McKenna, Corey. "Smartphone Application Will Give Campus Police a Virtual Look at an Incident." *Emergency Management Magazine*, February 2, 2011. http://www.emergencymgmt.com/safety/Smartphone-Application-V911-Maryland.html (accessed February 22, 2011).

35. Rich, Sarah. "911 Responders in Georgia Aided by Online Citizen Profiles." March 7, 2011. http://www.govtech.com/public-safety/911-Responders-in-Georgia-Aided-by-Online-Citizen-Profiles.html?elq=9c44c934d3524723b5b339e4bf3bd1b5 (accessed February 22, 2011).

36. "Emergency Alert System." *FCC—Public Safety and Homeland Security Bureau*. http://transition.fcc.gov/pshs/services/eas/ (accessed March 22, 2011).

Chapter 9

Volunteer and Donations Management 2.0: How Social Media Has Revolutionized the Management and Recruitment of People and Supplies

Put people into an open system and they'll automatically want to contribute.

—**Ori Brafman and Rod A. Beckstrom,** *Starfish and Spider: The Unstoppable Power of Leaderless Organizations*[1]

Chapter Objectives

- To understand the potential impact of social media and Web 2.0 systems on secondary emergency management functions such as volunteer and donations management

- To identify and understand the impact of social media demographics on volunteerism and donations generation
- To understand the context of national volunteerism and donations management standards within social media use and utilization
- To identify social media systems that are optimally utilized for volunteerism and donations management
- To identify measurements of success for social media use in support of donations and volunteerism management

Demographics of Volunteerism

Volunteerism has always been commonplace to address day-to-day individual, family, and community needs. Because these needs are compounded during emergencies and disasters, the need to utilize and manage both affiliated and unaffiliated volunteers has long been a necessary challenge to emergency management. Unfortunately, this process is often time consuming and resource intensive, which can be undermining to the time sensitivity of emergency response and recovery. Consequently, it is time for modern emergency managers to begin to embrace the influence and impact of social media and Web 2.0 tools on volunteer management.

For instance, according to a Pew Internet study, 75% of all American adults are active in a volunteer organization. This volunteerism increases to 80% for internet users, 82% for social networking users, and 85% for Twitter users.[5] Clearly there is a positive correlation between social media usage and interest in volunteering. Additionally, nearly 25% of those surveyed indicated that their ability to volunteer was greatly improved through the use and access to social media.[5] Along with increased participation in volunteer organizations, social media users who personally utilized Facebook and Twitter were found to be 15%–18% more involved in the volunteer organizations.[5]

This type of inherent symbiosis between volunteerism and social media was epitomized during the Alabama tornado outbreak of 2011 that left many communities throughout the state in desperate need of assistance. (See Figure 9.2.) One of these communities was the city of Tuscaloosa. As the home of the University of Alabama, one of the state's two major colleges and longtime rival to Auburn University, typically a high level of animosity exists between the fans, followers, and alumni of each school. However, this animosity was put aside during disaster recovery, which allowed a 32-year-old auto service center manager (and Auburn fan) to organize a volunteerism and donations management site called Toomers for Tuscaloosa, which played off of a local landmark in the Auburn area.[29] He quickly established Facebook and Twitter pages that exponentially fueled public support for his endeavor, with ultimately more than 86,000 people following and supporting his activities via Facebook.[30] At one point, the support operation got so large

DISASTER FOCUS—HAITI EARTHQUAKE

On January 12, 2010, a 7.0 magnitude earthquake with an epicenter near the town of Leogane struck Haiti, causing significant damage to local infrastructure. With the epicenter approximately 16 miles west of Port-au-Prince (Haiti's capitol), the Haitian government estimated 3 million people were affected with more than 316,000 associated deaths, 300,000 injuries, 1,000,000 made homeless, and 280,000 residences and commercial buildings that collapsed or were severely damaged. The leaders of Leogane reported nearly 90% of all local buildings destroyed. (See Figure 9.1.) Many countries provided immediate humanitarian aid through pledged funds and the provision of emergency response teams, engineers, and additional support personnel. Local Haitian infrastructure systems supporting communications systems, facilities, hospitals, and electrical networks were significantly damaged by the earthquake, which created additional confusion over lines of authority, air traffic congestion, and traditional communication systems. By January 22, the Haiti government officially called off the search for survivors and the United Nations noted that the emergency phase of relief operation was complete. The neighboring Dominican Republic was the first country to give aid by sending water, food, and heavy machinery. Additional emergency search and rescue teams from Iceland, China, Qatar, South Korea, Israel, the United States, and many other countries were in Haiti within a few days of the event to provide emergency support and resources. Clearly, there was a significant need for monies and resources to help Haiti recover from the devastation of this earthquake.[2] This disaster event marked the first time that social media and Web 2.0 technologies were significantly utilized to aid in the recruitment and management of public donations and volunteerism. For example, the American Red Cross created a donations management system that allowed users of any cellular carrier to text "Haiti" to 90999 and automatically donate $10 to Haiti earthquake relief. This process generated $5 million in the first 24 hours and ultimately more than $32 million.[3] In addition to the donations management, other social media volunteers from throughout the world extracted incident-related information from Twitter feeds, translated messages from Creole (spoken in Haiti) to English, and helped utilize geographic tools to identify locations of response needs or similar issues. Or as Jaroslav Valuch said, "It was an incredible symbiosis between humans and machines, because no matter how advanced the technology...it could never have performed without the human manpower behind it."[4] This type of modern volunteer and donations management will continue to define how future emergency managers coordinate response to emergencies and disasters.

Figure 9.1   Hundreds of Haitian survivors on crowded boat awaiting transportation. (From U.S. Navy, Mass Communication Specialist 2nd Class Candice Villarrea.)

that the Toomers for Tuscaloosa ad hoc system was not only managing local donations but donation sites in 23 different states as well.[31] This type of emergence was not necessarily new but had never reached this level of impact before.

Most communities maintain local affiliates with well-known volunteer organizations such as the American Red Cross, the Salvation Army, Community Emergency Response Teams, or Medical Reserve Corps. Not surprisingly, because of the strong cultural and community reaction to disasters and the corresponding desire

Figure 9.2   Modern volunteerism transcends pre-existing limitations particularly through the use and utilization of social media. (From FEMA. Tim Burkitt.)

STANDARDIZED COMPONENTS FOR THE MANAGEMENT OF UNAFFILIATED AND SPONTANEOUS VOLUNTEERS

1. Volunteering and community life
2. Volunteering and the emergency management framework
3. Value of affiliation
4. Volunteer involvement in the four phases
5. Management systems
6. Shared responsibility
7. Volunteer expectations
8. Impact on volunteers
9. Build on existing capacity
10. Information management
11. Consistent terminology[6]

to provide support through volunteerism, individuals unaffiliated with traditional volunteer organizations seek out ways to volunteer as well. These unaffiliated and spontaneous volunteers can often be extremely challenging considering their lack of pre-event training or prescreened status. The National Volunteer Organizations Active in Disasters (NVOAD) established 11 national principles to observe in the management of unaffiliated volunteers. These national principles include the promotion of volunteerism in the community and within the emergency management framework, affiliation with known volunteer organizations, management systems, reasonable expectations, capacity building, and consistent terminology.[6]

Contemporary Volunteer Management

Volunteer management in modern emergency management will continue to be challenged by the administration of affiliated volunteers and unaffiliated volunteers. However, the multitude of social media and Web 2.0 tools available can either further hinder the process or magnify the capability of recruitment for volunteer agencies active in emergency response. The difference lies in the use and utilization of the various tools that are available. Interestingly, in many ways social media tools allow for the bridging between affiliated and nonaffiliated groups. The use of social media nearly eliminates the concept of a stranger appearing at a response scene desiring to help in any way possible. Rather, individuals now show up at disaster scenes driven by information and knowledge acquired through trusted social media sources to respond to specific needs in definitive ways rather than generic ways. Specifically, blogs, microblogs, social networks, and Web 2.0 technologies such as crowdsourcing are being used in contemporary volunteer management during emergencies and disasters.

For instance, in March 2009, the city of Fargo, North Dakota, was fighting flooding on their portion of the Red River and experienced insufficient human resources necessary to create sandbag dikes fast enough to significantly mitigate the risk. When a local man named Kevin Tobosa was notified that a friend needed help filling sandbags, he immediately posted to Facebook his intention to respond. Additionally, he recommended that local city planners utilize Facebook to create additional volunteers for further support of flood response. Upon approval from city leaders, Tobosa created the Fargo-Moorhead Flood Volunteer Network, which generated more than 4,550 members within a week.[7] (See Figure 9.3.) This type of utilization of social networking magnified the volunteer response in the community due to the connectivity of shared interest—in this case, the flooding.

Facebook was also utilized as an effective volunteer recruitment tool during the 2011 Christchurch earthquake in New Zealand. The earthquake caused significant infrastructure damage and quickly required supplemental volunteer workers to

Figure 9.3 **Members of the North Dakota National Guard and civilian volunteers filling sandbags at the Fargodome in Fargo, North Dakota. (From U.S. Air Force Senior Master Sgt. David H. Lipp.)**

support search and rescue, debris management, and other response-related activities. To help address this need, the University of Canterbury Student Association created a Facebook page called the UC Volunteer Army to help recruit and manage volunteers interested in responding to recovery efforts. Within two days of the earthquake, the UC Volunteer Army claimed 10,000 fans on Facebook and by later that month that number had jumped to 25,000 individuals.[10,11] Interestingly, the organizers of the UC Volunteer Army were so committed to Facebook as its primary tool that they posted messages on Facebook indicating that alternative communications (e.g., phone or email) about volunteer opportunities would not be responded to because all available information was posted on Facebook.[11] Much like the volunteer sandbagging efforts in Fargo, Facebook clearly amplified the interest in response and therefore the number of individuals willing to become a volunteer in the response.

Similarly, the use of blogs in modern volunteer recruitment and management for emergencies and disasters also provides unique opportunities. Specifically, because blogs utilize unlimited space for text, photos, and videos, the content and purpose of blog postings about volunteerism can be strongly framed to focus on the issues of greatest importance to the response. As blogs are the most time-consuming social media form to update and maintain, they are inherently most often utilized by formal volunteer agencies working before, during, and after an event to recruit, train, and maintain a strong volunteer base. For instance, on the fifth anniversary of Hurricane Katrina, the HandsOn Volunteer Network utilized their blog to post 39 roles for volunteers in disaster response that were divided by functions that could be performed during preparedness, response, recovery, and mitigation.[8] This type of multiphased approach to blog usage meets several of the national principles of disaster volunteerism and effectively controls the need for clear and concise information to current and prospective volunteers.

Voluntweeters and Other Crowdsourcing Opportunities

In addition to social networks and blogging, a variety of social media tools have been used organically during emergencies and disasters to allow volunteer behaviors and/or capabilities to be magnified through technology. Because social media is inherently built on connections between individuals or groups of people, crowdsourcing for disaster volunteerism is often based on group dynamics for a common purpose. Sociologists refer to organizations of people who previously did not exist or had no standing structure or defined tasks during a crisis as emergency organizations. These emergency groups usually self-organize during emergencies or disasters (of various scales) to meet those unmet needs generated because of consequences of the event.[9]

For example, during the 2010 Haiti earthquake, researchers from the University of Colorado-Boulder in conjunction with CrisisCommons established Twitter accounts to redistribute disaster-related information from sources like Ushahidi and from firsthand accounts. (Note: More information about Ushahidi is available in Chapter 12.) Interestingly, Twitter users from around the world emerged as "translators" who converted the earthquake-related information from the multiple sources into terminology that could be followed throughout the system. Specifically, these self-proclaimed "Voluntweeters" added significant value to disaster response without direction or affiliation other than what organically existed through social media to help support an international disaster.[9]

In addition to the Voluntweeters utilized during the Haiti earthquake, there are additional crowdsourcing opportunities for disaster volunteers. For instance, there is a volunteer recruitment and connection site called VolunteerMatch that helps facilitate positive matches between interests and skills of prospective volunteers to the needs and functions of volunteer agencies. For disaster volunteerism, VolunteerMatch created a mapping site that allows a prospective volunteer to review agencies located in their geographic area. For instance, the website contained 87 different volunteer opportunities for South Carolina from dozens of different organizations, including local American Red Cross chapters, church ministries, youth services, and Habitat for Humanity. The characteristics of each volunteer opportunity were defined by the posting agency to include categorical tags for targeted demographics (e.g., teens or 55+) and interest areas (e.g., child services or disaster services). According to the website, volunteers are allowed to rate the posting organization, which is an effective feedback mechanism for other volunteers to have an indicator about the quality and reliability of the volunteer agency.[12]

Perhaps the most well-known use of crowdsourcing in support of disaster victims is CrisisCommons. According to their own website, this loosely affiliated group is a "concept that is being explored to define how a commons-based approach can provide long-term sustainability for the CrisisCamp community as well as other volunteer technology communities and support shared knowledge, collaborative tools, open development, project management and data to crisis response organizations."[13] Fundamentally, CrisisCommons and the closely related CrisisCamps are focused on the use of emergent communities of technologically savvy volunteers to support disaster response. This crowdsourcing of volunteered skills is based on a combination of surveys available to both prospective volunteers and organizations in need of support. For instance, the prospective volunteer survey asks for information about knowledge of wiki functions, mapping, and various other functions like language translation.[14] Because crowdsourcing allows for the collective knowledge and capabilities of volunteers from throughout the world, locally impacted communities in both developed and third-world countries can utilize these resources immediately to restore local infrastructure and increase situational awareness without any dedication of limited local resources. The benefits of CrisisCommons and the broader concept of crowdsourcing are further expanded in Chapter 11.

Donations Management 2.0

Much like disaster volunteerism, the management of donations after an emergency or disaster has long been a significant challenge to emergency managers. Clearly, nonimpacted citizens from throughout the world see the effect of localized disasters and want to help but are unable to volunteer for a variety of reasons. Consequently, they often feel they must provide donations for the "good of the cause." These donations can be in the form of direct financial support or can be given as donated goods. Regardless of the form, there are social, physical, psychological, political, and administrative challenges. For instance, in the aftermath of Hurricane Katrina, the British government donated MREs (Meals Ready to Eat) that were ultimately redirected to other countries in need because of American fears of bovine spongiform encephalitis (mad cow disease) potentially present in the food from previous outbreaks in England. Additionally, more than $60 million was donated to the Federal Emergency Management Agency (FEMA) in support of Hurricane Katrina relief that ultimately had to be funneled down to voluntary response and recovery agencies fairly and effectively to ensure the needs of local victims were met.[15] These two examples just begin to address the complexity of the management and administration necessary to store, manage, distribute, and maintain accountability of donated goods and funds. (See Figure 9.4.) These types of challenges are always present at some scale regardless of the size and complexity of the event. Fortunately, as was seen during the American Red Cross's fund-raising efforts during the Haiti earthquake of 2010, the use of social media and Web 2.0 tools is beginning to make the process of donations management far more efficient and effective.

Figure 9.4   Donations management is often a resource-intensive effort for emergency managers and nongovernmental organizations. (From FEMA, George Armstrong.)

Nearly all affiliated volunteer organizations like the American Red Cross and the Salvation Army must simultaneously manage donations before, during, and after events. This process can be divided between fund-raising and event-driven donations management. In both cases, social media is beginning to strongly impact the execution and facilitation of this process. For instance, the Salvation Army's traditional holiday bell ringers and their hanging red kettles have long been physical representations of the Salvation Army's purpose and fund-raising. However, since 2010, the Salvation Army has mirrored its physical recruitment by offering an Online Red Kettle that is linked to Facebook, Twitter, YouTube, and Flickr to maximize the fund-raising capabilities of social media systems.[16] Additionally, according to a 2009 study of nonprofit fund-raising trends from the previous two years, there were sharp increases in the number of nonprofit organizations using blogs, videos, social networking sites, and microblogs as well as nearly universal application of basic monitoring of social media to determine public perception and opinion about the various organizations.[17]

Perhaps the most profound change in the donations management structure was the use of donations by SMS text message that was implemented by the American Red Cross in early 2010 in response to the earthquake in Haiti. The donations via text messaging allowed individuals on any cellular system to text "Haiti" to 90999, which initiated a donation of $10 to the American Red Cross Haiti response and relief fund. (See Figure 9.5.) Within hours of the news of the disaster spreading throughout the globe, the American Red Cross quickly initiated the text-messaging donation method in partnership with the U.S. State Department and leveraged participation in online systems like Facebook and Twitter to propel the need for donations as well as the simple venue for its execution.[3] Within 4 days of its initiation, the donate-by-text campaign generated $5 million.[23] Within 30 days, the campaign generated $32 million.[24] The positive value of this type of availability was supported by the 4.2 million tweets that mentioned the concept.[32] Although this type of electronic transfer typically takes 30–60 days to complete, all major cell phone carriers agreed to expedite requests to ensure the donations were instituted in a timely manner.[25]

At that time, the $32 million donated by text messaging constituted 41% of the $78 million spent or committed to short-term relief and long-term recovery in Haiti.[24] By far, this was the largest texting donation campaign that had ever occurred for disaster relief. Specifically, previous donating-via-text-message efforts raised $400,000 after Hurricane Katrina and $200,000 after the Indian Ocean tsunami, and in 2009 donations by text message to all charities totaled slightly less than $4 million.[25] Because of this tremendous response to the texting campaign, this model of fund-raising and support has become commonplace and was used in the 2010 Chile earthquake, Deepwater Horizon oil spill, and the 2011 Japan earthquake as well as many other significant domestic and/or international disasters since that time. This utilization is a continued fund-raising tool by not only the American Red Cross but also by additional nonprofit and disaster response agencies including the Salvation Army and World Wildlife Fund.

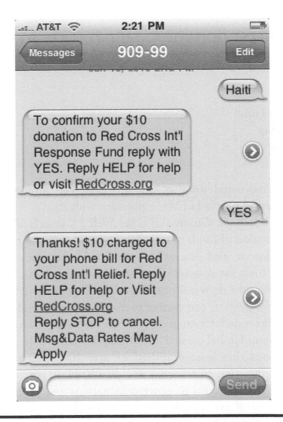

Figure 9.5 A screenshot of the text-for-donation campaign utilized by the American Red Cross during the 2010 Haiti earthquake response.

In addition to simple emulation of traditional fund-raising mechanisms, several different social media systems have also been established to allow social media activity and engagement to magnify the results. For example, sites like HelpAttack!, FirstGiving, and Facebook Causes allow individuals or organizations to set up sites that can accept donations for a particular organization, issue, or event from the general public. For instance, within 30 days of the 2011 earthquake in Japan, donations management sites on FirstGiving and Facebook Causes had generated more than $480,000 and $280,000, respectively. Not only is the total amount impressive, the systems allow for cost-effective generation and management of those donations at little to no cost. Unlike traditional fund-raising strategies, no staffing or physical resources are necessary and financial accountability for the donated funds is handled and processed by those social media systems providing the interface. Similarly, some nonprofits and fund-raising organizations have begun to connect PayPal and Google Checkout widgets to their traditional websites to facilitate the quick, efficient, and accountable collection of donated funds. Much like PayPal and Google Checkout, FirstGiving and Facebook Causes are both available for

ONLINE DONATIONS FACILITATION SITES

Facebook Causes
FirstGiving
HelpAttack!
Network for Good
Global Giving
WhatGives!?

integration with traditional websites through advanced programming interface (API) connectivity and simple HTML-embedded widgets.

In addition to Facebook Causes and other Web 2.0 interface sites built strictly to facilitate the donation of funds to certain causes, other social media systems like Second Life, FourSquare, and Twitter have also quickly become effective fund-raising magnification tools for disaster-related fund-raising efforts. For example, the virtual world of Second Life is built on the establishment of virtual islands where Second Life users (or avatars) can engage each other socially and within the island environment that is created. Consequently, a San Francisco–based technology provider called TechSoup Global created a four-island Second Life community called Nonprofit Commons that was comprised of over 100 charitable organizations from 10 different countries. In response to the 2010 Haiti earthquake, Nonprofit Commons hosted virtual events to generate donations and revenue in support of response and recovery efforts in Haiti. These events included virtual goods auctions, virtual arts and music festivals, expert speakers, and virtual dances to raise awareness and donations. In addition, this Second Life island hosted a three-dimensional exhibit area where avatars could visit a depicted image of the devastation of Haiti, including a map showing impacted areas and local infrastructure damage.[18] The usefulness of Second Life as a training and support tool is further discussed in Chapter 14.

Additionally, there is a social media user-driven fund-raising strategy referred to as "Checkins for Charity." This concept utilizes a person's application of location-based social networking systems like Google Latitude, FourSquare, GoWalla, and Facebook Places as well as several other mobile applications. For instance, a free mobile application for iPhones and Android called CauseWorld allows individuals to earn "karma points" by checking in to certain locations. These "karma points" can be donated to support certain causes based on predetermined transaction rates (e.g., 100 karma points = $1).[19] Likewise, FourSquare supported a Checkin for Charity campaign at the SXSW 2010 event where PayPal and Microsoft pledged $0.25 for each check-in at the event up to $15,000 that would go to the Save the Children Haiti Relief Fund. Because the campaign was heavily promoted, attendees logged over 135,000 check-ins on FourSquare and met the maximum match of

$15,000 within 48 hours.[20] The impact of location-based social networks such as FourSquare is further discussed in Chapter 13.

Additional Web 2.0 concepts that are being utilized to facilitate the active donations of monies in support of disaster response and recovery in efficient and effective ways include embedded links, transactions of virtual goods, and virtual "upselling." Specifically, the "Hello Bar" places a simple message (e.g., A disaster has occurred. Please donate to the Red Cross) at the top of a website with only a few lines of HTML code. This Web 2.0 tool was widely used during response and recovery to the 2011 Japan earthquake and related tsunami.[21] Similarly, online social gaming company Zynga allowed for the purchase of virtual goods in online games like CityVille, FrontierVille, and FarmVille in support of response and recovery efforts to the 2011 Japan earthquake and tsunami. This facilitation was a partnership with Save the Children's Japan Earthquake Tsunami Emergency Fund and ultimately raised more than $2 million for the relief efforts. Zynga provided a similar effort for the 2010 Haiti earthquake.[21] Finally, online retailers such as iTunes who are not typically considered social media or Web 2.0 systems helped facilitate donations through online upselling by allowing users who were already purchasing products to make additional donations of various denominations to the American Red Cross in support of their various disaster responses.[21]

Measurements of Success

Clearly any donated funds generated to support emergency or disaster response and recovery efforts would be deemed a success. However, it is critical to look at that process analytically with the hope of ascertaining a fair and reasonable measurement of success, particularly when compared to traditional fund-raising mechanisms. Traditional fund-raising processes would be evaluated through a variety of mechanisms, such as cost-versus-benefit analysis, total money generated, programmatic implementation, and percentage of funds retained by the organization. However, these measurements may not be adequate measurements for donations management in a Web 2.0 world.

For example, some have suggested that the principle measuring tool for online fund-raising through social media and Web 2.0 systems should be the average donation per user. However, in many cases this number is relatively low as compared to traditional fund-raising efforts.[26] This type of analytical measurement is not comprehensive enough to generate a true picture of the effectiveness of online fund-raising. Specifically, the use of social media and Web 2.0 tools is about the engagement between individuals or, in this case, the engagement between individuals and a cause. For example, even though the number of individuals who donate may be relatively low, there may be hundreds or thousands of more followers or fans

> **IN A NUTSHELL**
>
> People are much more altruistic if they get social credit for it.... [Specifically] the social incentive is to show on your profile how many volunteers you've recruited or how much money you've raised."
>
> **—Joe Green, founder of Facebook Causes**[28]

of that cause who are learning more about the issues and becoming knowledgeable about the challenge.[26]

For example, several social media sites have seen significant increases in activity or online participation during online fund-raising campaigns. For instance, Loopt (a location-based social networking system) sponsored a Checkins for Charity event for Haiti earthquake efforts where Loopt donated $1 for every check-in at Whole Foods, Chipotle Grill, and Panera Bread locations for a set period of time. During that time, check-ins increased by an average of 200% for those sites.[19] Likewise, during a similar campaign for Haiti relief, Zynga stated that 60,000 FishVille players visited sites related to the response and recovery effort, which constituted 10 times the normal number of visitors generated from playing the online game.[27] Although still difficult to measure, these types of measurements of success do indicate a trend of strong return on investment (ROI) for online campaigning and the continued use of technology to bridge the gap for traditional nonprofit fund-raising intended to generate funds for emergencies and disasters. Interestingly, this phenomenon was summarized by Joe Green, one of the founders of Facebook Causes (which has raised $7 million overall), who said, "People are much more altruistic if they get social credit for it....[Specifically] the social incentive is to show on your profile how many volunteers you've recruited or how much money you've raised."[28]

These nonprofit fundraising examples have thus far all been for significant large-scale domestic or international disasters that have required donations to support voluntary agency activations. The challenge to this model is to determine how—if at all—it translates to local emergency managers trying to generate support for emergencies or disasters impacting their area. For instance, would major telecommunication carriers like AT&T, Verizon, or Sprint initiate a donate-by-text campaign for a local community that is overwhelmed, or is this type of Web 2.0 implementation only available through state agencies, federal agencies, or national voluntary organizations active in disasters? Likewise, local communities are most likely not going to be able to engage large social media outlets or system developers like Zynga without significant attention or intervention. Unfortunately, bridging this connectivity and mind-set to local communities will be a critical future step in the development and full integration of donations management into modern emergency management strategies.

Practitioner Profile: Heather Blanchard, Co-Founder of CrisisCommons

In March 2009, Heather Blanchard, in partnership with dozens of resourceful and inventive volunteers, held the first CrisisCamp to facilitate a virtual partnership between emergency managers and the global technology community. This positive relationship resulted in the Alfred P. Sloan Foundation in association with the Woodrow Wilson International Center for Scholars providing a planning trustee grant to support CrisisCommons under the direction and leadership of Ms. Blanchard to "curate a new body of knowledge, document lessons learned from volunteer response and to convene communities to support the growth of CrisisCamps...and other volunteer technology communities."[13] During her 2011 testimony before the U.S. Senate's Ad Hoc Subcommittee on Disaster Recovery and Intergovernmental Affairs, Ms. Blanchard stated, "One challenge we often see is that government agencies simplify the use of social media as a public affairs function when in fact, during a crisis, access to citizen-generated information is an operational necessity."[33] When asked about local implementation challenges for emergency management, Ms. Blanchard stated that in "local Emergency Operations Centers the connection between social media information and operations is largely absent...[due to] some centers lacking high bandwidth Internet, technical skills or collaborative tools." She stressed that this connectivity was critical due to the fact that during a crisis, emergency management continuously finds itself overwhelmed

Figure 9.6 Congressional testimony provided by Heather Blanchard is helping shape national policy on the use of social media in disasters. (From FEMA, Bill Koplitz.)

with information. In the conclusion to her testimony, Ms. Blanchard recommended to the Senate committee to "devote [resources] toward helping emergency managers with data preparedness and filtering, increasing the level of digital literacy of the emergency management workforce and empowering their ability to connect with technology support."[33] Ms. Blanchard's leadership and the continued impact of CrisisCommons and other volunteer groups will continue to impact how, when, and where social media can be leveraged to improve disaster response.

Chapter Terms

Voluntweeters: Term to describe volunteers who utilize social media skills and resources in disaster response and recovery efforts.

CrisisCommons: Nongovernmental organization that is helping leverage social media and Web 2.0 systems to maximize the impact of volunteerism and donations management during emergency and disaster response and recovery.

Donate-by-text: Fund-raising technique used by several nongovernmental organizations during emergency and disaster response and recovery that leverages the capability and popularity of SMS text messaging to allow for quick and efficient donations.

Checkins-for-Charity: Fund-raising technique used by several nongovernmental organizations to leverage location-based social networking systems to allow for sponsored system engagement by the social media system or interested third parties.

Upselling: Fund-raising technique used by social gaming systems to allow for natural, in-game purchases to be applied for third-party disaster recovery and relief efforts.

NVOAD: National Voluntary Organizations Active in Disasters, a national group of nongovernmental organizations active in disaster response and recovery.

Chapter Questions

General Questions

1. Which of the following terms describe the process of utilizing location-based social networking sites to receive money for system engagement?
   a. Upselling
   b. Checkins-for-Charity
   c. Donations 2.0
   d. Texting
2. True/False: Social media has not yet been thoroughly utilized during disaster donations management.

3. The following considerations should be considered during disaster volunteer management:
   a. Emergency management framework
   b. Value of affiliation
   c. Volunteer involvement in the four phases of emergency management
   d. All of the above

Essay Questions

1. Discuss the impact of social media use on the likelihood to volunteer for disaster response.
2. Discuss how social media impacts national principles for successful volunteerism.
3. Discuss the impact of Checkins for Charity, upselling, donations by texting, and other emergency technologies on disaster donations management.

Works Cited

1. Brafman, Ori, and Rod A. Beckstrom. *The Starfish and the Spider: The Unstoppable Power of Leaderless Organizations.* New York: Penguin Group, 2008.
2. "Haiti Earthquake Facts and Figures." *Disasters Emergency Committee.* http://www.dec.org.uk/haiti-earthquake-facts-and-figures (accessed October 30, 2011).
3. Van Grove, Jennifer. "Red Cross Raises $5,000,000+ for Haiti through Text Message Campaign." *Mashable,* January 13, 2010. http://mashable.com/2010/01/13/haiti-red-cross-donations/ (accessed March 3, 2011).
4. Valuch, Jaroslav. "Haiti's Viral Volunteers: How Social Media Is Changing the Face of Crisis Response." *Washington Post,* http://views.washingtonpost.com/leadership/guestinsights/2011/01/viral-volunteers-for-haiti-how-social-media-is-changing-the-face-of-crisis-response.html (accessed March 3, 2011).
5. Rainie, Lee, Kristin Purcell, and Aaron Smith. "The Social Side of the Internet." *Pew Internet,* January 18, 2011. http://pewinternet.org/Reports/2011/The-Social-Side-of-the-Internet/Summary.aspx (accessed March 3, 2011).
6. "Managing Spontaneous Volunteers in Times of Disasters: The Synergy of Structure and Good Intentions." *National Volunteer Organizations Active in Disasters,* 2004. http://www.citizencorps.gov/downloads/pdf/ManagingSpontaneousVolunteers.pdf (accessed March 3, 2011).
7. Condon, Patrick. "Fargo Uses Social Networks to Fight Floodwaters." *MSNBC,* March 26, 2009. http://www.msnbc.msn.com/id/29901184/ns/technology_and_science-tech_and_gadgets/ (accessed March 3, 2011).
8. "39 Roles for Disaster Volunteers." *HandsOn Network,* August 25, 2010. http://handsonblog.org/2010/08/25/volunteer-disaster-relief-3/ (accessed March 3, 2011).
9. Starbird, Kate, and Leysia Palen. "'Voluntweeters': Self-Organizing by Digital Volunteers in Times of Crisis." *University of Colorado at Boulder,* 2010. http://www.cs.colorado.edu/~palen/voluntweetersStarbirdPalen.pdf (accessed March 3, 2011).

10. "Student Volunteer Army Mobilizes." *Stuff.co.nz*, February 24, 2011. http://www.stuff. co.nz/national/christchurch-earthquake/what-you-need-to-know/4698056/Student-volunteer-army-mobilises (accessed March 3, 2011).

11. "UC Student Volunteer Army." *Facebook*, 2011. http://www.facebook.com/ StudentVolunteerArmy.

12. "South Carolina Volunteer Agencies." VolunteerMatch, 2011. http://www.volunteer-match.org/search/index.jsp?r=region&aff=&categories=42&1 =South+Carolina%2C+ USA&o=recency&s=21 (accessed March 3, 2011).

13. "CrisisCommons." CrisisCommons, 2010. http://crisiscommons.org/about/ (accessed March 3, 2011).

14. "CrisisCommons Volunteer Form." Crisis Commons. https://spreadsheets.google. com/viewform?hl=en&formkey=dHA2YkJvSjZxeE9oYkhNR0MtVTgyY1E6MQ# gid=0 (accessed March 3, 2011).

15. Edwards, Frances L. "The Challenges of Donations Management." *Public Management, Emergency Management Forum*, 2009. http://www.docstoc.com/docs/45007600/The-Challenges-of-Donation-Management (accessed March 3, 2011).

16. Morris, Nomi. "Salvation Army Takes Bell Ringing Online." *Los Angeles Times*, December 25, 2010. http://articles.latimes.com/2010/dec/25/local/la-me-1225-be-liefs-salvation-army-20101225 (accessed March 3, 2011).

17. "Best Practices of Social Media Implemented by the Top 200 U.S. Charities." *Social Media for Non-Profits: Who's Doing It and What Works. Red Rooster Group*. http://redro-ostergroup.com/wp-content/uploads/2010/11/SocialMediaCaseStudies.pdf (accessed March 3, 2011).

18. "Avatars Raise Money for Haiti through Virtual Events, Goods, Campaigns." *Social Media for Non-Profits: Who's Doing It and What Works. Red Rooster Group*. http://redro-ostergroup.com/wp-content/uploads/2010/11/SocialMediaCaseStudies.pdf (accessed March 3, 2011).

19. Elliot, Amy Mae. "Checkins for Charity: The Rise of Geo-Social Good." *Mashable*, November 16, 2010 http://mashable.com/2010/11/16/charity-checkins/ (accessed March 3, 2011).

20. "Foursquare 'Checkin for Charity' Hits 135k Checkins, Raises $15k." *Selfish Giving Blog*, March 18, 2010. http://selfishgiving.com/location-based-cause-marketing/four-square-at-sxsw (accessed March 3, 2011).

21. Parr, Ben. "Japan Earthquake & Tsunami: 7 Simple Ways to Help." *Mashable,* March 13, 2011. http://mashable.com/2011/03/13/japan-earthquake-tsunami-help-donate/ (accessed March 3, 2011).

22. Van Grove, Jennifer. "Red Cross Raises $5,000,000+ for Haiti through Text Message Campaign." *Mashable*, January 13, 2010. http://mashable.com/2010/01/13/haiti-red-cross-donations/ (accessed March 3, 2011).

23. Cashmore, Pete. "Help the Haiti Text Message Campaign Raise $20 Million by Midnight." *Mashable*, January 17, 2010. http://mashable.com/2010/01/17/haiti-20-million/ (accessed March 3, 2011).

24. "Red Cross Raises More Than $32 Million in Mobile Giving Program." *American Red Cross Press Release*, February 11, 2010. http://www.redcross.org/portal/site/en/menuite m.94aae335470e233f6cf911df43181aa0/?vgnextoid=43ffe0b8da8b6210VgnVCM10 000089f0870aRCRD (accessed March 3, 2011).

25. Choney, Suzanne. "Mobile Giving to Help Haiti Exceeds $30 Million." *MSNBC*, January 21, 2010. http://today.msnbc.msn.com/id/34850532/ns/today-today_tech/ (accessed March 3, 2011).
26. Kanter, Beth. "Beth's Blog: How Nonprofit Organizations Can Use Social Media to Power Social Networks for Change. *Beth Kanter's Blog*, April 22, 2009. http://beth.typepad.com/beths_blog/2009/04/hello-washington-post-dollars-per-facebook-donor-is-not-the-right-metric-for-success.html (accessed March 3, 2011).
27. O'Dell, Jolie. "Mafia Wars and FishVille Players Raise Money for Charities." *Mashable*, April 22, 2010. http://mashable.com/2010/04/22/zynga-social-good/ (accessed March 3, 2011).
28. Hart, Kim, and Megan Greenwell. "To Nonprofits Seeking Cash, Facebook App Isn't So Green." *Washington Post*, April 21, 2009. http://www.washingtonpost.com/wp-dyn/content/article/2009/04/21/AR2009042103786.html?sub=AR (accessed March 3, 2011).
29. Henderson, Jeremy. "Toomers for Tuscaloosa on NBC Nightly News." *War Eagle Reader*, April 30, 2011. http://www.thewareaglereader.com/2011/04/toomers-for-tuscaloosa-featured-on-nbc-nightly-news-organizer-says-iron-bowl-rivalry-forever-changed/ (accessed May 3, 2011).
30. "Toomers for Tuscaloosa." *Facebook*. http://www.facebook.com/toomersfortuscaloosa (accessed March 3, 2011).
31. "Out of State Donations." *Toomers for Tuscaloosa*, 2011. http://toomersfortuscaloosa.com/out-of-state-donations/
32. Harman, Wendy. "Social Media and Volunteerism." Presentation at NVOAD conference, 2011.
33. Blanchard, Heather. Testimony of Heather Blanchard, Co-Founder of CrisisCommons before the Ad Hoc Subcommittee on Disaster Recovery and Intergovernmental Affairs, U.S. Senate Homeland Security and Government Affairs Committee, May 5, 2011.

Chapter 10

The Elephant in the Emergency Operations Center: The Fundamental Flaw within Formal Response Systems

If you want to succeed in social media you've got to be okay to just lose control.

Alexis Ohanian, Co-Founder of Reddit.com[1a]

Chapter Objectives

- To address foundational considerations of national response and preparedness models for emergency management and response
- To analyze the challenges of implementation and integration of social media into national models of emergency management and response
- To consider the implementation of social media into intelligence processes utilized by incident commanders and Emergency Operations Center management

- To apply social media concept into the understanding of modern review and approval of public information processes
- To consider the potential impact of using social media during emergency exercises and trainings

National Preparedness and Response Systems

Emergency management disciplines throughout the United States have long been defined by national response systems based on best practices, disaster experiences, and political motivations and direction. Such systems include the Incident Command System (ICS), National Incident Management System (NIMS), and the Homeland Security Exercise and Evaluation Program (HSEEP). In each case, these systems have had positive and negative impacts related to their application before, during, and after emergencies and/or disasters and are significantly impacted by the use and implementation of social media and Web 2.0 technologies. To understand these effects, it is critical to understand the structures and intended purposes of the national response systems first.

In February 2003, President George W. Bush issued Homeland Security Presidential Directive 5 (HSPD-5) which directed the U.S. Department of Homeland Security to develop and administer a National Incident Management System (NIMS). (See Figure 10.2.) This system was in response to the management and communication disorder and chaos that was noted during and after action reports for the terrorist attacks on September 11, 2011. The intention of NIMS was to provide a nationwide template to enable all government, private-sector, and nongovernmental organizations to work together in a coordinated and efficient way during all types of emergencies and disasters regardless of size, scope, or complexity.[6] Specifically, NIMS created a "framework for interoperability and compatibility by balancing flexibility and standardization."[6] Specific components of NIMS included command and management, preparedness, resource management, communications and information management, supporting technologies, and ongoing management and maintenance.

The command and management structure within the NIMS framework is divided into three major organizational systems: Incident Command System, Multiagency Coordination Systems, and Public Information Systems. The Incident

---

IN A NUTSHELL

NIMS created a "framework for interoperability and compatibility by balancing flexibility and standardization."

—Introduction to the National Incident Management System[6]

DISASTER PROFILE—INDIAN GULCH FIRE

On Monday, March 21, 2011, a large fire in the Indian Gulch area of Colorado was started by arsonists. This area, which comprises a large part of rural Colorado to the west of Colorado Springs and south of Denver, quickly became a blazing wildfire; nearly 1,570 acres burned by the time fire responders had contained the fire by the end of the week.[8] (See Figure 10.1.) Rowdy Muir, the incident commander for the response, indicated that the operation was extremely difficult to deal with due to steep slopes and challenging footholds, especially considering the smoky atmosphere. During the response, Colorado governor John Hickenlooper issued an emergency disaster declaration that authorized $1.5 million in state money to help cover firefighting costs and opened up the possibility of additional federal support. A total of 401 firefighters from more than 40 different local, state, and federal agencies were ultimately involved in response to the wildfire.[8] Those responders utilized a plethora of resources, including numerous National Incident Management System (NIMS) types of resources, such as one type 1 helicopter, one type 2 helicopter, one type 3 helicopter, two single-engine air tankers, and one fixed-wing heavy tanker.[8] American Red Cross shelters as well as large animal shelters were established in nearby communities that were not impacted by the fire. Jacob Smith, mayor of nearby Golden, stated on his blog that the emergency response plan was quickly initiated and "relied primarily on a traditional communications model: the emergency operations team would compile and verify information about the fire and they would provide it to our public information office." Mayor Smith continued by stating that the public information officer "could periodically brief the news media…relying largely on the media to then broadcast that information via television, radio, and print media."[9,10] Mayor Smith and local councilman Bill Fisher expanded this formal communication by disseminating periodic email updates, newsletters, and updates to personal Twitter and Facebook pages. Mayor Smith even noted on his blog that "a very large number of folks expressed their gratitude for the communication efforts often especially referring to the Facebook or Twitter."[10] This particular disaster presents a dichotomy of application of communications and intelligence tools between formal response systems and social media and Web 2.0 technologies. Was one system more effective than the other? Did the mayor's use of social media violate traditional command and control structures utilized in emergency response and public information for the dissemination of event-related information? Is there a clear and consistent message being disseminated across these multiple new media platforms? These are the types of questions that challenge emergency managers as they consider how to apply social media in modern emergency management.

Figure 10.1   Wildfire response near Loveland, Colorado, in the Indian Gulch region. (From FEMA, Michael Rieger.)

Command System (ICS) is the paramount component of these organization systems and not only is it the most traditional but it is also fundamental to the other two sections. According to NIMS training materials, ICS "defines the operating characteristics, management components, and structure of incident management organizations throughout the life cycle of an incident."[6] Interestingly, the national commitment to ICS as part of the NIMS is based strongly on nearly 40 years of best practices by various first responder disciplines, but particularly fire services throughout the United States. The best-practice features included common terminology, organizational resources, manageable span of control, organizational facilities, position titles, use of incident action plans, integrated communications, and systematic accountability.[6]

These systematic characterizations of ICS are critical to understanding further evaluation regarding how NIMS and ICS integrate with social media. Specifically,

Figure 10.2   In February 2003, President George W. Bush issued Homeland Security Presidential Directive 5 (HSPD-5), which directed the establishment of NIMS. (From U.S. Coast Guard, Telfair H. Brown Sr.)

Figure 10.3 FEMA representatives provide briefing in Greensburg (Kansas) Emergency Operations Center. (From Greg Henshall. With permission.)

the ICS characteristics of manageable span of control, position titles and accountability, and common terminology, among others, create an inherent command and control structure that is dictated by a hierarchal structural dependent on review and approval at all levels within the ICS structure. Even under ideal circumstances, this type of structure creates an innate elongation in the time required to initiate response actions, receive approval, and execute the direction. Unfortunately, this typical timeframe from start to finish is often incompatible with public expectations and the natural pace of social media exchanges.

An additional command and management component of the National Incident Management System is the utilization of multiagency coordination systems. While Emergency Operations Centers (EOCs) are the most common example of multiagency coordination systems, Joint Information Centers (JICs) are also important examples to consider, especially when evaluating the potential interaction with social media. (See Figure 10.3.) Originally, the JIC was created out of ICS best practices. It functions as the communication and public information element at all levels ranging from localized incident commanders to unified command, EOC managers, and other governmental response entities. Much like its ICS cohort, the fundamental rule in all Joint Information Centers is that no information can be released by public information officers or other response personnel to anyone outside the formal response hierarchy without the preapproval of the highest ranking official (e.g., incident commander or EOC manager). Additionally, this type of structure facilitates the need for multiple organizations and/or jurisdictions to coordinate message dissemination and public "voice."[7] Although this system has been shown to be capable of distributing information in a timely manner, much like ICS it would be challenged to distribute information quickly enough to help manage the reception and distribution of information via social media systems during emergencies and disasters.

As mentioned previously, the other multiagency coordination system that must be considered is the Emergency Operations Center (EOC). In many ways, the structure established by the National Incident Management System for the use of the Incident Command System is mirrored in most Emergency Operations Centers. Typically, EOCs are based on a structured hierarchal environment that often utilizes similar functions like span of control, unity of command, incident action planning, and many others. Consequently, some of the same challenges exist for the use of social media in EOC and ICS structures. Both command and management systems require a high level of situational awareness at all times to initiate proper responses to ensure efficient and effective protection of life, property, and community resources. Unfortunately, like the JIC challenge, the pace of situational awareness is exponentially shorter when the public is capable of receiving and distributing incident information in a nearly instantaneous manner via social media and Web 2.0 systems.

In addition to the National Incident Management System and the Incident Command System, emergency managers are encouraged (and mandated when receiving federal funds) to utilize the Homeland Security Exercise and Evaluation Program (HSEEP) when creating and executing various exercise scenarios. This includes the spectrum of exercise activities that includes seminars, workshops, tabletop exercises, drills, games, functional exercises, and full-scale exercises. In all cases, a scenario is developed and utilized to test and evaluate certain predetermined exercise goals and objectives. As such, it is necessary to utilize real responders, equipment, and resources, which is potentially not only expensive and time consuming but also confusing to the general public. For instance, if a local community was testing a large mass casualty scenario via a full-scale exercise, it would require the colocations of multiple emergency response personnel, vehicles, and equipment. Because it is critical to ensure the effectiveness of operational plans, most organizations routinely pull equipment and resources off of actual responses to perform the exercise and support primary operations through backfilled or mutual aid support. Unfortunately, this is not possible to do when testing plans and response related to the incorporation of social media because real social media channels are difficult to take out of active commission. Consequently, exercises based on the HSEEP model can sometimes be extremely ineffective at safely and effectively testing plans and response protocols related to social media for public information and situational awareness.

Conflicts and Contradictions

Formalized emergency response systems like the National Incident Management System (NIMS) and the Incident Command System (ICS) are quickly becoming conflicting entities within the realm of emergency public information as social media becomes more commonly utilized. NIMS was built on the foundation of formally organized command, control, and approval of all emergency actions, including public dissemination of information, while social media was built on open, organic, and informal responses. NIMS is also based on best practices and is accepted as the national model for disaster response, including public information. Unfortunately, it does not address the impact of social media forms such as social networking, microblogs, blogs, and video sharing, which have quickly become pervasive in emergencies and disasters. These two entities (the formal command structure and social media) are fundamentally in conflict and must be reconciled to ensure the dissemination of future emergency public information is efficient and effective.

NIMS calls for all information released to the public during an emergency or disaster to be reviewed and approved by the incident commander (or EOC director in larger events). However, it is difficult for public information staff to continue to be timely and efficient when getting approval for traditional outreach strategies such as television, radio, and print (often online) media considering the time constraints and universal responsibilities of the incident commander during an emergency or disaster. If NIMS does not properly establish protocols for situational analysis by planning, operations, and logistics components, there may be significant disaster-related information that is missed or unincorporated due to the incompatibility of the NIMS structure with social media. These incompatibilities create significant gaps in emergency readiness.

As the need to use and monitor social media increases during emergencies, this time challenge is further exacerbated by the intrinsic and demanded brevity of time related to the various forms of social media. Press releases to traditional media outlets such as television and radio can be adequately handled from creation to approval within a few hours so the media outlets are satisfied and have information to use during the next broadcast or publication. On the other hand, social media outlets (e.g., Twitter and Facebook) desire information nearly instantaneously with virtually complete transparency. This means social media works in the realm of minutes, not hours like traditional communications. Therefore, it is fairly self-evident that the incident commander's approval of messages and/or information disseminated through social media outlets in a similar timeframe is extraordinarily difficult, if not impossible. Regardless, social media (like traditional media) must be provided information (aka "fed") to reduce the distribution of misinformation and minimize public discord related to the emergency or disaster.

This was no more evident than during the 2007 Virginia Tech shooting (see Chapter 5). During this event, students inside and around the impacted buildings were providing a steady flow of information related to the incident through Facebook and other social media sources. The traditional communication streams such as press releases and press conferences were (relatively speaking) slow to react and took several hours to release information related to the event, including the number and names of the student fatalities. For example, although the shootings occurred at approximately 7:00 a.m. and again at 9:30 a.m., the Virginia Tech administration did not formally announce a death toll (without names) until 2:13

IN A NUTSHELL

In the simplest form, social media benefits emergency response by providing ears and mouths. In other words, using it can help the responders listen in to the conversation going on and glean valuable information that can help inform response priorities, help understand public sentiment, and help identify emerging issues, misinformation, and rumors.

—Gerald Baron, founder of PIER Systems

p.m. Meanwhile, social media sites and online communities such as the "I'm ok at VT" Facebook group were actively confirming the identities of those victims. Although researchers found that no single online social media list contained all 32 victims' names, they were routinely accurate and preceded the formal partial release of names at 4:00 p.m. and the full list at 5:15 p.m.[11] Clearly, the social media communication sought out and acquired accurate, event-related information significantly faster than traditional media outreach.

The Virginia Tech example is significant because the community of Facebook users and other social media systems successfully identified all casualties without ever posting a name erroneously.[1] Moreover, because of the speed and accuracy of public information via social media during the event, traditional media outlets began to reference social media content rather than wait for the formally released information from the university. (See Figure 10.4.) Ultimately, as discussed in Chapter 3, this event as well as other similar major disasters led to the exponential growth of citizen journalism and the use of social media systems for primary news tracking, documentation, and sourcing. Some experts have even suggested that social media sources such as Twitter are the new press release systems and will ultimately replace the current news distribution structure.[2] Managers of traditional response systems that oversee the distribution of public information would be foolhardy to not directly address how social media can be adopted to optimize the best practices established along practical application of modern communication systems.

Figure 10.4 Students at Virginia Tech hold a candlelight vigil after the Virginia Tech shooting.

Figure 10.5 Cars rest on the collapsed portion of I-35W Mississippi River bridge in Minneapolis, after the August 2007 collapse. (From U.S. Coast Guard, Kevin Rofidal.)

Another challenge for emergency public information within the NIMS framework is the style and structure of released messages. Specifically, the most common form of message distribution is a press release. The message contained within the press release is generally crafted in a very structured way using formalized language and polished contextual placement. They often contain generalized and nonspecific quotes from decision makers (e.g., the incident commander) or other local authority figures (e.g., the mayor or governor) that are intended to personalize, empathize, and validate the emergency situation in support of classical crisis communication models.[12] Unfortunately, this model is wholly contradictory to the expected style of social media. For instance, Twitter only allows posts of 140 characters or less to provide status updates. Because the limited space available for status updates is inherently a relaxed response, most users are very informal, casual, and brief.

Facebook adds further complication due to its multifaceted approach. It adds microblog-like status updates as well as links to photos, videos, and websites. Within social media systems, both written and visual context to emergency situations can be distributed via preexisting, trusted networks. This phenomenon was evident by the usage of social photo-sharing capabilities during the London bombings (2005), Hurricane Katrina (2005), Virginia Tech shootings (2007), Minneapolis I-35 bridge collapse (2007) (see Figure 10.5), and the Southern California wildfires (2007).[3] The style and substance of these social media sites are very different from the standard press release and make their combination delicate at best. Again, some sort of additional version of the press release such as pre-identified and preapproved social media messages is vital for the successful management of public information but is not currently explicitly allowable under the NIMS structure.

Lastly, part of the formalized NIMS structure is to ensure unified messages that support overall incident priorities. This unified message construction is particularly designed to increase the credibility of the message and to increase the public's ability to validate the released information. The challenge facing emergency public information is that the trustworthiness of governmental communications is often low. Government communications are particularly challenged within certain cultural and ethnic sectors of the population. For instance, the University of Michigan's Institute for Social Research has long noted that some demographic groups such as African Americans typically show higher levels of governmental distrust than other community groups.[14] Additional research has indicated that predictors of trust in government include race, gender, and individual social capital such as civic engagement or interpersonal trust.[15] Overcoming these preestablished hurdles is one of the many challenges that must be overcome during formal emergency public information activities. Interestingly, there is some thought that social media may help bridge these trust gaps as the online communities of Facebook, Twitter, and others are not based on forced relationships (e.g., traditional government–citizen relationships) but rather on trusted sources and associations.

Take the Filter Off

Due to preexisting space or time restrictions, traditional media outlets get the opportunity to filter the formally approved government message, which can result in a biased or distorted presentation or further fracture an already challenged message. Conversely, social media sites address both of these issues. Social media sites such as Facebook and Twitter are fundamentally built on the foundation of trusted networks and open community. Specifically, these social media outlets are established by being "friends" or "fans" of someone or something. As such, the social networks provide a local community an opportunity to validate additionally released messages about the emergency event. Secondly, social media sites allow for direct messaging to the impacted community by cutting out the traditional media and thus their interpretation and presentation. Although social media is not free of bias, one of its core principles is self-correction.[4] It is extremely likely that any misinformation presented intentionally or unintentionally via social media channels would be quickly corrected by members of the shared community. Consequently, these two components support the potential effectiveness of using social media during an emergency event at least in support of traditional formalized communications (e.g., press releases).

In conclusion, the application of NIMS guidelines and social media for emergency public information is currently antagonistic and counterproductive. The structured review and approval process greatly reduces the effectiveness of social media, which is ultimately detrimental to the overall success of the emergency public information and situational awareness process. The NIMS process was well vetted, nationally practiced, and based on best practices, but the rise of social media has been quick and fierce, which leaves emergency managers and public information officers in an unenviable and challenging situation. Identifying and implementing a resolution to this conflict will be critical to the future of emergency management for all disciplines.

Contrasting Opinions

Some emergency managers have suggested that the integration of national response systems (like NIMS) and social media is not as challenging as it appears in its most fundamental sense. A common argument put forth is one that suggests social media is merely a communications tool similar to email and cell phones that are commonly used by disaster responders. This argument continues by stressing that NIMS does not explicitly address how, when, and where these communication systems should be utilized but that they are important. Therefore, based on this argument, social media should also not be specifically addressed as long as NIMS maintains its flexibility for technology and application. Unfortunately, this argument is fundamentally flawed. While social media is a communication tool similar to email and cellular phones, the scope and application of social media is much greater than those systems. The time, application, and systematic expectations associated with social media usage are much more complicated.

Additional counterarguments against adjusting national response systems to better incorporate social media and Web 2.0 technologies are based in foundational interpretations of these response systems. For instance, Hal Grieb, a prominent emergency manager utilizing social media (see Chapter 2 Practitioner Profile), references the ongoing management and maintenance components of NIMS, which states that the "ongoing development of science and technology is integral to the continual improvement and refinement of NIMS."[13] In other words, Mr. Grieb is presenting a view that NIMS was inherently built with flexibility to absorb new technologies and systems that impact the systems and structure of national response to emergencies and disasters. He goes on to say that ICS has "flexible guidance that allows information and intelligence pulled in via multiple positions...[so that] the incident command can either pull information and intelligence themselves, designate a person as Information/Intelligence command staff officer, create an Information/Intelligence General Staff Branch, create a position within the Planning Section, or for more tactical decision information put a unit directly under the incident's operations section."[13] The question is whether system organizers ever envisioned emerging technologies as dynamic and complex as social media when NIMS was initially established.

Clearly, Mr. Grieb is well versed in the systematic components of NIMS and ICS and has thoroughly analyzed the application of how a social media branch might be established during an emergency or disaster. The problem is that typical responders in most communities who may serve as incident commanders have not had the opportunity to review and/or are not as comfortable with NIMS or social media beyond basic trainings available in the local community. Moreover, if they can only basically and fundamentally apply the NIMS concepts, they are most likely to focus on the command and control and review and approval processes that are not only critical components of NIMS but also parallel to many responder organizations' day-to-day function and structure rather than the flexibility and adaptation inherent to social media.

It is this gap between knowledge and application for the average user that justifies not necessarily more training but rather modification of the system and/or training that is available to the majority of responders. If the NIMS and ICS courses do not specifically provide examples for implementation such as what Mr. Grieb suggests, it is unlikely that responding agencies will correctly utilize social media within their response structures. Moreover, the lack of clear application may lead to underutilization or the complete disregard of social media intelligence and information related to the disaster. This type of avoidance could significantly affect the effectiveness of the response and the safety of the responders and impacted citizens.

One possible modification to the NIMS model in regard to the use, review, and approval of social media would be to specifically allow the incident commander or Emergency Operations Center (EOC) manager to establish a spectrum of information that can be disseminated via social media without approval every time. This type of preapproval could be accomplished through pre-event topical reviews similar in nature to message mapping or press release templates that are utilized in traditional crisis communication models. Similarly, there can be a spoken or written understanding established between the incident commander or EOC manager and the public information officer to agree on what limitations and context should be established in regard to how and when social media should be utilized. It is this second option that was utilized by the State of Alabama in 2011 during their response to the tornado outbreak where they utilized nontraditional staff (e.g., Emergency Management Assistance Compact [EMAC] deployed public information officers) and new social media systems to share critical public information.

Challenges to Social Media and Exercise Management

Similar challenges exist to the integration of social media into the Homeland Security Exercise and Evaluation Program (HSEEP) but may be overcome through the creative use of certain social media systems. HSEEP was mandated by the U.S. Department of Homeland Security (DHS) as the method to create, execute, and evaluate emergency management exercises for all disciplines. Much like the National Incident Management System, part of this mandate is connected to preparedness funding provided by DHS to emergency management organizations.

For instance, support funds provided through national grant programs like the State Homeland Security Program (SHSP), Urban Area Security Initiative (UASI), Metropolitan Medical Response System (MMRS), Port Security Grant Program (PSGP), and many others allow utilization of funding for exercise only if the HSEEP model is maintained. Moreover, HSEEP was designed to encourage the testing and evaluation of the capabilities of a given jurisdiction or discipline. Since these capabilities are often independent of the type of event suggested, scenarios are often simply used as vehicles to test those identified capabilities that need testing.

As established earlier, the challenge of this type of mandate is that a resource has to be identified (e.g., fire truck) that can execute the tested function (e.g., fire suppression), which often takes that particular resource, equipment, or personnel away from regular duties to ensure the capability can be tested in full without distraction or division. Unfortunately, this type of testing and exercise modeling cannot be achieved when incorporating social media systems into the mock-up. It is far too great a risk for public information or intelligence officers to put exercise and/or training material on real and legitimate social media sites due to the potential confusion with real information and potential risk of eroding the trusted communication system already established. For instance, many local emergency management offices routinely utilize social media systems like Twitter and Facebook to distribute preparedness information about tornadoes, including standard messaging about emergency sheltering and storm mitigation activities. If these same social media channels were then used to distribute simulated messages about tornadoes in the area, there is a significant risk that system users (fans or followers) could be confused or misled unintentionally. This confusion would ultimately negatively impact the effectiveness of the system. Traditional exercise simulations and the HSEEP model just cannot accommodate for this issue and therefore are not suitable options in the strictest sense for how to efficiently and effectively test social media in modern emergency management.

However, there are some creative applications within social media systems that might help bridge this gap. For instance, most public microblogs like Twitter allow for accounts to be protected where the general public cannot see posted content unless approved by the account holder. Given this format, it would be possible to create several protected accounts that would only share information with each other. This would then simulate the interest and public response of local citizens without the general public seeing or potentially misunderstanding the exercise content. Although technically possible, this type of artificial account creation would be frowned upon, if not completely prohibited by, the social media system and its user agreement.

Perhaps a more successful alternative to artificially created private microblogging accounts would be the use of Yammer. Yammer was started in 2008 as an enterprise microblogging service that, contrary to other microblogs like Twitter, was only accessible through private networks of people such as might exist at a business or organization.[16] Although originally started as an enterprise microblogging site, it quickly expanded into a full-fledged enterprise social network that included the capability to support enterprise microblogging, profiles, groups, direct messaging, communities, application development, and mobile interfaces.[17] In addition, Yammer is already utilized by more than 1 million users at more than 80,000 companies worldwide.[16] Although still a different format and structure from major social media sites like Facebook and Twitter, Yammer would successfully allow for the conceptual testing of response and engagement protocols that could be used during an emergency or disaster for both public information and situational awareness activities without any risk to real social media information sources.

Ultimately the U.S. Department of Homeland Security under the direction of Federal Emergency Management Agency (FEMA) personnel will need to restructure either the formal configuration or related training of response systems like the National Incident Management System (NIMS) or Homeland Security Exercise and Evaluation Program (HSEEP) to better address the poor application of social media through these systems. While some interpretation and application can successfully combine these two conflicting platforms, it is not being done uniformly and consistently across all jurisdictions and disciplines (if at all). If this divergence is not corrected, the national progression toward building response systems that are flexible, dynamic, available to all jurisdictions and disciplines, and fundamentally utilized the same way throughout the response system would become eroded, if not unusable.

Practitioner Profile: Gerald Baron, Public Relations and Crisis Communications Consultant

Gerald Baron (Figure 10.6) has served as a university professor, publisher, and candidate for state elected office, and is a self-declared "serial entrepreneur." He is also the founder and creator of PIER Systems, which was acquired by O'Brien's Response Management in late 2009 and used by various local, state, and federal agencies such as the City of Houston and the U.S. Coast Guard. Since then he has served as the executive vice president of communications for O'Brien's and now is a senior advisor to the company. He has written several books, including *Now Is Too Late: Survival in an Era of Instant News*, and recently published *Unending Flow: Case Study on Gulf Spill Communications* about the crisis communication challenges related to the 2010 Deepwater Horizon oil spill.

As a national leader in crisis communications and an avid observer of the rise of social media and its impact on emergency management, Mr. Baron was asked to provide commentary on how well social media is integrating with national response systems. He stated, "ICS [and NIMS] does not present major obstacles

Figure 10.6 Gerald Baron.

to effectively integrating social media….[H]owever, there are some elements, particularly in the public information structures that clearly present a hindrance…in light of the internet, social media, and more advanced communication technology." Mr. Baron continued by stating that one particular challenge is the need to have social media monitoring and observation in both the intelligence and public information areas, which are often separated. Specifically, he stated, "To separate these functions creates a barrier to efficient and effective communication with all stakeholders and audiences with high interest in the event." When asked why social media is so effective in large disasters, Mr. Baron stated that "In the simplest form, social media benefits the response by providing ears and mouths…[for] the responders to listen in to the conversation going on and glean valuable information that can help inform response priorities, help understand public sentiment, and help identify emerging issues, misinformation, and rumors." When asked why social media was so difficult to embrace via national response models, Mr. Baron stated, "Perception, public sentiment, and understanding of the facts surrounding the event and response cannot be manipulated and controlled….[Formal response] can participate in the conversation or not, but participation only means that the response is one voice among many." He also stated that "To ignore this new reality or fight against it is to put at risk those who are impacted by an event or those citizens who are responding on their own…[which] puts at risk public trust and confidence." Clearly, Mr. Baron is passionate and expresses his belief that social media is challenging to traditional response mechanisms but can be overcome through dedication and purposeful decision making.

Chapter Terms

National Incident Management System (NIMS): National model of emergency and disaster response that is based on best practices, flexibility of response, and modularity of organization. NIMS includes other management systems such as the Joint Information Center (JIC), Incident Command Structure (ICS), and Emergency Operations Center (EOC) management.

Homeland Security Exercise Evaluation Program (HSEEP): National model of emergency and disaster exercise development and management that is required for utilization by all emergency management and response disciplines.

Incident Command System (ICS): Fundamental component of NIMS that is based on a command and control structure limited by span of control and functional divisions. All decisions are reviewed and approved by a predetermined hierarchal structure before they are performed. There is one incident commander who serves as the executive decision maker under this management structure.

Joint Information Center (JIC): Physical location where public information activities occur during an emergency or disaster. The lead public information officer often oversees this function under the supervision of the incident commander or EOC manager.

Emergency Operations Center (EOC): Physical location where disaster response coordination is conducted. It is typically organized in a command and control structure with similar features to an Incident Command Structure (ICS).

Chapter Questions

General Questions

1. True/False: National response systems like NIMS and ICS maintain flexibility clauses that allow for the integration and acceptance of new technology like social media.
2. Social media can be utilized by the following ICS sections:
   a. Public Information
   b. Intelligence
   c. Planning
   d. All of the above
3. Which of the following could be utilized during exercises to protect real social media information outlets?
   a. Yammer
   b. Facebook
   c. YouTube
   d. None of the above

Essay Questions

1. Discuss the complications of utilizing social media within traditional response systems like NIMS and ICS.
2. Discuss the complications of testing social media plans and procedures during HSEEP-formatted exercises.
3. Suggest methods to effectively merge social media and Web 2.0 technologies into traditional response systems (e.g., NIMS).

Works Cited

1a. Ohanian, Alexis. (2010). "You've Lost Control and that's Okay!" TedX Talks. http://www.youtube.com/watch?v=Gdr1jgGjxV0 (accessed January 8, 2012).
1. Palen, Leysia, et al. "Crisis Informatics: Studying Crisis in a Networked World." Third international conference on e-Social Science, Ann Arbor, Michigan, October 7–9, 2007.
2. Baron, Gerald. "Emergency Management and Social Media." Kansas Emergency Managers Association (KEMA) annual conference, Topeka, Kansas, September 17, 2009.
3. Liu, Sophia B., et al. "In Search of the Bigger Picture: The Emergent Role of Online Photo Sharing in Times of Disaster." Fifth international ISCRAM conference, Washington, D.C., May 2008.
4. Sutton, Jeannette. "Social Media and the Democratic Convention: What Happens When Web 2.0 Meets the 'Official Version'?" *Natural Hazards Observer*, November 2008.
5. Schaefer, Mark. "Five Mega-Trends: How Social Media Is Transforming Government." *Grow Blog*, April 4, 2011. http://www.businessesgrow.com/2011/04/04/five-mega-trends-how-social-media-is-transforming-government/ (accessed April 10, 2011).
6. "NIMS: Frequently Asked Questions." (n.d) FEMA Bulletin. http://www.fema.gov/pdf/emergency/nims/NIMSFAQs.pdf (accessed January 9, 2012).
7. Baron, Gerald. "National Incident Management System and Social Media." *PIER Systems, Inc. White Paper*, April 2009. http://www.piersystems.com/go/doc/1533/269904/National-Incident-Management-System-NIMS-and-Social-Media (accessed March 10, 2011).
8. "Indian Gulch Fire 100 Percent Contained." *KDVR Denver*, March 25, 2011. http://www.kdvr.com/news/kdvr-golden-fire-text,0,1837279.story (accessed May 10, 2011).
9. Baron, Gerald. "Golden, Colorado Indian Gulch Fire Provides Key Lessons for Emergency Communications." *Emergency Management Magazine*, April 7, 2011. http://www.emergencymgmt.com/emergency-blogs/crisis-comm/Golden-Colorado-Indian-Gulch-040711.html (accessed April 10, 2011).
10. Smith, Jacob. "Communication during a Crisis: Lessons from Golden's Indian Gulch Fire." *Jacob Smith for Golden Blog*, April 5, 2011. http://smithforgolden.com/lessons-from-the-indian-gulch-fire/ (accessed April 10, 2011).
11. Vieweg, Sarah, et al. "Collective Intelligence in Disaster: An Examination of the Phenomenon in the Aftermath of the 2007 Virginia Tech Shooting." Proceedings of the fifth international ISCRAM conference, Washington, D.C., May 2008. http://www.jeannettesutton.com/uploads/CollectiveIntelligenceISCRAM08.pdf (accessed March 10, 2011).

12. Lukaszewski, James E. "Seven Dimensions of Crisis Communication Management: A Strategic Analysis and Planning Model." *Ragan's Communications Journal*, January/February 1999. http://www.e911.com/monos/A001.html (accessed March 10, 2011).

13. Grieb, Hal. "Social Media/Web 2.0 & NIMS." *iDisaster 2.0 Blog*, December 20, 2010. https://idisaster.wordpress.com/category/nims/ (accessed March 10, 2011).

14. Howell, Susan E., and Deborah Fagan. "Race and Trust in Government." *JSTOR*, 1988 http://www.jstor.org/pss/2749076 (accessed March 10, 2011).

15. Perrin, Andrew J., and Sondra J. Smolek. "Who Trusts? Race, Gender, and the September 11 Rally Effect among Young Adults." *NIHPA Author Manuscripts*, March 2009. http://www.ncbi.nlm.nih.gov/pmc/articles/PMC2662604/ (accessed March 10, 2011).

16. Hall, Aneta. "Yammer Pros and Cons." *Aneta Hall's Blog*, February 22, 2009. http://anetahall.wordpress.com/2009/02/22/yammer-pros-cons/ (accessed October 30, 2011).

17. "What Is Yammer?" *Yammer*. https://www.yammer.com/about/product (accessed March 10, 2011).

SOCIAL MEDIA TOOLS AND THE POWER OF VIRTUAL COMMUNITY

Collaborative production, where people have to coordinate with one another to get anything done, is considerably harder than simply sharing, but the results can be more profound. New tools allow large groups to collaborate, by taking advantage of nonfinancial motivations and by allowing for wildly differing levels of contribution.

—**Clay Snarky,** *Here Comes Everybody*
The Power of Organizing Without Organizations[1]

Chapter 11

It Takes a Village to Raise a Prepared Community: The Power and Purpose of Crowdsourcing

[A] fundamental truth about humans that had gone largely unnoticed until the connectivity of the Internet brought it into high relief...[is that] labor can often be organized more efficiently in the context of community than it can in the context of a corporation.

—**Jeff Howe,** *Crowdsourcing: Why the Power of the Crowd Is Driving the Future of Business*[2]

Chapter Objectives

- To analyze the challenges of implementation and integration of social media into national models of emergency management and response
- To define crowdsourcing within the context of its application to emergency and disaster response
- To analyze the impact of virtual volunteers in disaster crowdsourcing
- To evaluate the impact of organizational and citizen crowdsourcing during emergencies and disasters
- To understand the use of geospatial display systems with crowdsourcing

DISASTER FOCUS—CHRISTCHURCH EARTHQUAKE

At 12:51 p.m. (local time) on February 22, 2011, a 6.3 magnitude earthquake struck the Canterbury region of New Zealand's South Island. The earthquake was centered approximately one mile west of the town of Lyttelton and six miles southeast of the center of Christchurch (New Zealand's second-largest city). The earthquake caused 181 deaths, making it the second-deadliest natural disaster on record for New Zealand (after the 1931 Hawke's Bay earthquake). Insurance experts estimated that the earthquake resulted in $12 million (NZ $16 million) in damage. (See Figure 11.1) Moreover, this earthquake came six months after the 7.1 magnitude 2010 Canterbury earthquake that impacted the region but had no related fatalities. The February 2011 earthquake was different from the previous earthquake because it occurred during lunchtime when local commerce was high and many buildings had increased occupancy. In addition, many buildings were already weakened from the 2010 earthquake and were significantly impacted by the high liquefaction of local soils that caused significant ground movement. This geological phenomenon resulted in damage to 80% of local water and sewer systems as well as approximately 200,000 tons of upturned silt.[3] Because of the widespread impact to localized infrastructure, crowdsourcing played a significant role in supplementing resources, personnel, and situational awareness. Specifically, within one hour of the disaster, a CrisisCommons Community Working Group established a collaborative editing site and launched an event instance on Crowdmap.com in partnership with local emergency managers. Crowdsourcing volunteers quickly divided themselves into four simultaneous functional groups: situational awareness, crisis coordination and emergency response, technical migration (to more robust systems), and volunteer plan and management. The number of volunteers and the complexity of their available tools grew exponentially, with a fully integrated crowdsourcing disaster map (eq.org.nz) being launched within six hours of the earthquake.[4] The site received feedback on a plethora of disaster-related issues, including disaster survivor assistance in acquiring maintenance medications and identification of places to purchase food and gasoline.[4]

What Is Crowdsourcing?

In the simplest terms, crowdsourcing is the utilization of a collection of individuals to address a problem or challenge that would not be possible by the individual parts. The collection of individuals constituting the "crowd" can provide a superior collection of various capabilities, including knowledge, skills, abilities, equipment, resources, time, and infrastructure. These capabilities exist as physical, social, and economic collectives that far exceed individual or common capabilities and thus add

Figure 11.1 FEMA Deputy Administrator Tim Manning visits Christchurch after the 2011 earthquake. (From U.S. Embassy in New Zealand, Janine Burns.)

a benefit to the overall issue at hand. Moreover, the contribution of capabilities by individuals is often provided at minimal cost, if not free. Consequently, the crowdsourcing concept is an extremely efficient as well as cost-effective option for organizations or community groups looking for more robust operational considerations.

While crowdsourcing may initially seem like an inherent quality of all social media systems, this would be incorrect. There is great value in monitoring, analyzing, and surveying the social media spectrum of activity to get a general and aggregated sense of issues and needs as well as positive attributes, but this activity is not asking for anything specific in return from the end user. End users may engage or converse, but there is no assumption or guarantee that any quantifiable value will be returned. On the other hand, the crowdsourcing concepts presented in this chapter are action oriented and require clearly defined tasks to be accomplished due to the inherently magnified capabilities of the knowledge, skills, and abilities that exist within the groups. These action steps go much farther than traditional systems in becoming dynamic tools of emergency management and response due to the potential for extremely efficient and effective response.

The efficacy of crowdsourcing is potentially very important to emergency managers of all disciplines. Emergency managers, like many other disciplines, are often burdened by such a wide spectrum of job duties that it is often difficult to achieve any truly positive preparedness or planning within the communities because of a lack of time and resources. Even when volunteers are effectively utilized, there is often a realistic and legal limitation to the responsibilities that can be officially bestowed upon volunteers and/or a similar time or resource limitation to what the volunteer is willing to contribute in support of emergency management. Consequently, the potential benefit of crowdsourcing during emergency and disaster response is nearly endless and has already been effectively deployed during several domestic and international disasters like the Christchurch earthquake discussed in the disaster profile. Much like many of the other social media and new Web 2.0 technology systems already discussed, the challenge for emergency managers is to address how crowdsourcing should be integrated into traditional response mechanisms since it is predominately organically initiated, managed, and deployed by networks without formal supervision.

How Crowdsourcing Works

To begin to consider this implementation challenge, it is important to establish a formalized definition of crowdsourcing. For instance, Jeff Howe in his book *Crowdsourcing: Why the Power of the Crowd Is Driving the Future of Business* states that there are nine fundamental concepts of crowdsourcing. Howe suggests that effective crowdsourcing is based on identifying the right model and crowd as well as addressing how the collective application will be incentivized and integrated into established frameworks. Howe describes five models: collective intelligence, crowd wisdom, crowd creation, crowd voting, and crowd funding. The presented challenge is that simply identifying the right number of individuals is not sufficient; identifying the correct individuals is required as well. For example, asking scientists to discuss fantasy baseball might result in a collection of smart individuals with poor collective knowledge of the assigned task. In contrast, asking a group of fantasy baseball fanatics about fantasy baseball would quickly generate a great collective knowledge about the assigned issue.[2]

Howe also notes that crowdsourcing requires simple tasks, organic group leadership, and self-correction to be efficient and effective.[2] He refers to the need for "benevolent dictators" to lead crowds who often want to help but lack the collective capability to aggregate their combined knowledge and skills. This type of leadership leverage might also be thought of as the catalyst to facilitate the reaction among the crowd to facilitate the beneficial response that generates efficient and effective activities particularly during emergencies and disasters. Lastly, the tasks and expectations of the crowd must be controlled prior to implementation.[2] For instance, crowd leaders must quickly ascertain either from formal emergency management representatives or from identified community needs what issues must be addressed and then should implement strategies within the crowd to establish a limitation of activities to hyper-focus the collected knowledge on the issue at hand. However, the activities of the crowd can and will self-correct its activities as event priorities change or specific needs become clear. This self-correction is a fundamental concept of most social media systems, and crowdsourcing is no exception to the rule.

Conceptually, crowdsourcing is very common through commerce-based websites and in support of some online commerce sites. For instance, there are numerous photo sites such as iStockPhoto.com that allow for individual users to contribute royalty-free photos (and other multimedia sources) that can be downloaded for free or for a basic fee (typically fairly low).[5] These sites generate a myriad of content available to others. Much like the disaster uses that are discussed later in this chapter, these kinds of common-use sites exponentially magnify the skills, resources, and abilities of the individual photographers with little additional effort by the individual and at an extremely affordable cost. Similarly, online commerce sites such as Amazon, TigerDirect, and others like them utilize the collective feedback of users and customers to create ratings and evaluations for sold products. The opinion of individual users and customers of these commercial products lack any validity regarding its accuracy or truthfulness; however, when many of the unvalidated opinions are collected together into a crowd of opinions, the opinion of the group now has verification, accuracy, and precision and thereby removes the risk of individual truthfulness because it is overcome by the collective.

Interestingly, this phenomenon of crowdsourcing has quickly bled over into emergency management and disaster response throughout the world. Crowdsourcing platforms such as Ushahidi were quickly modified from their origins as political monitoring tools to geographic-based collectors of disaster information that are managed by a group of spontaneous disaster volunteers. Traditional social media sites like Facebook, Twitter, and YouTube have also been utilized to facilitate crowdsourcing opportunities. Disaster response crowdsourcing can be categorized into four groups based on past utilization: virtual volunteers, businesses and nongovernmental organizations, traditional media, and local volunteers.

Witnessing Disaster

The single most impactful crowdsourcing tool used by virtual volunteers throughout the world is Ushahidi. Ushahidi is a nonprofit company that developed a free and open-sourced software for information collection, visualization, and interactive mapping.[6] Ushahidi (which is Swahili for "witness") first created a crowdsourcing website after Kenya's disputed 2007 presidential election that included electoral manipulation by both candidates' parties and ultimately lead to widespread hostility and ethnic violence.[7] In response to this violence, the operators of Ushahidi created a website that collected eyewitness reports of violence that were sent in via email and text messaging and then plotted via Google Maps. Since that time, Ushahidi has been used to track anti-immigration violence in South Africa, public discord in Congo, and election monitoring in Mexico and India, as well as eyewitness reporting during the 2008–2009 Gaza War.[7] Ushahidi has continued to provide crowdsourcing capability for social activism, political observing, and ultimately disaster response and management by utilization of citizen journalism and geospatial information and context.

Ushahidi has created three components for its crowdsourcing capabilities: the original Ushahidi platform, SwiftRiver platform, and Crowdmap. Each of these components can be utilized to varying degrees to facilitate the capturing of real-time information from witnesses. The major differences have to do with time, hosting resources, and management source of the crowdsourced information. The Ushahidi platform is the most robust version available from Ushahidi and is a free server-based software available through a GNU Lesser General Public License. It provides the capability to create interactive mapping via multiple sources of public input such as text messaging, email, Twitter, and web forms, and provides detailed timelines of crowdsourced information.[8] Similarly, SwiftRiver allows for the filtering and verification of crowdsourced data from the same types of input as the Ushahidi platform. This filtering is particularly important by adding "context to content using semantic analysis" by helping categorize seemingly unrelated information from email, Twitter, text messages, and other web content based on keywords and other classification tags.[9] The final Ushahidi tool available for use is the Crowdmap. The Crowdmap tool provides similar functionality to the Ushahidi platform, including the collection of crowdsourced information about large-scale events, emergencies, or disasters, but does not require a local server to host and process the data. Rather, the Crowdmap platform is hosted on Ushahidi servers.[10] These three Ushahidi platforms create a powerfully dynamic tool for crowdsourcing activities.

Since 2010, various Ushahidi deployments have been developed for use during several international emergencies and/or disasters. Specifically, response and recovery efforts for the Haiti earthquake (2010) (see Figure 11.2), Chile earthquake

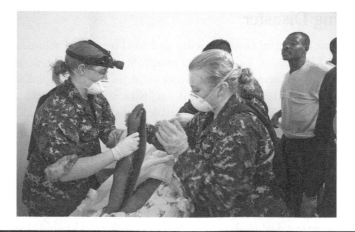

Figure 11.2 Treatment of Haiti earthquake victim. (From U.S. Navy Mass Communication Specialist 2nd Class Adrian White.)

(2010), Washington, D.C., winter storms (2010), Christchurch earthquake (2011), Alabama tornadoes (2011), and the Japan earthquake and tsunami (2011) were all significantly impacted by the use of Ushahidi as a facilitation tool for disaster crowdsourcing.[6] While Ushahidi is an extremely powerful crowdsourcing tool, it is not the only tool utilized during emergency management and response. Conversely, it is critical to evaluate the methods by which crowdsourcing has been implemented.

Crowdsourcing by Virtual Volunteers

Perhaps the most common use of disaster crowdsourcing is by virtual volunteers who are not located in the impacted area. These virtual volunteers often are collectives of people in unaffected areas who can bring to bear human knowledge, technology, and connectivity interfaces without strain on the infrastructure of the impacted area. Additionally, these collected groups of people often bring superior capabilities from those that existed in the disaster zone prior to the event, much less after the disaster struck the area. In many ways, the basis for this virtual volunteerism was a perceived need for a better exchange of information and technology to the impacted areas. This perceived need was particularly evident during international disasters where the infrastructure, governmental response, and local quality of life were already low (e.g., Haiti earthquake) or the disaster was so impactful that even robust systems were overcome by the effect of the disaster (e.g., Japan earthquake and tsunami). (See Figure 11.3.)

In the broadest sense, these collections of virtual volunteers are self-referred to as BarCamps. These BarCamps are informal and impromptu gatherings driven by a desire for people to share and learn in an open environment, which often leads to intense discussions and interactions between participants.[11] Most BarCamps adopt

Figure 11.3   Impact at the Sendei Airport in Japan from the 2011 earthquake and tsunami. (From U.S. Air Force, Samuel Morse.)

rules that do not allow spectators (either physically or virtually) to participate to ensure all energy related to the event is focused on addressing the exchange of information about the topic on hand. These BarCamps are held throughout the world as workshop-style events open to anyone who wants to participate and is willing to share content and information on the BarCamp wiki site. The earliest BarCamps focused on web applications through open-sourced technologies and open data formats.[12] Although the first BarCamp was held in Palo Alto, California, in August 2005, for approximately 200 attendees, BarCamps have since been held in over 350 cities in North America, South America, Africa, Europe, the Middle East, Australia, and Asia with one event generating more than 4,700 participants![12]

Over the past few years, the concept of a disaster BarCamp quickly grew and has become known as a CrisisCamp. Like the broader focused BarCamps, the CrisisCamps similarly gather information technology professionals, software developers, application programmers, Web 2.0 users, and other volunteers. This organic gathering of volunteers focuses on providing vision and guidance to the response efforts to help provide the coordination of targeted relief efforts and disaster aid to areas impacted by various hazards such as earthquakes, floods, hurricanes, and tsunamis.[13,14] For example, CrisisCamps have helped set up social networks for people to help locate missing friends and relatives or create inventories of needed items in disaster areas. These systems are almost universally anchored by geographic considerations in the disaster-affected area or disaster zone.[13]

Although extremely beneficial in support of large-scale disasters, these CrisisCamps still require significant oversight and organization. For instance, according to Clay Shirky in his book *Here Comes Everybody: The Power of Organizing without Organization*, "collaborative production, where people have to coordinate with one another to get anything done, is considerably harder than simply sharing, but the results can be more profound...[because] new tools allow large groups to collaborate, by taking advantage of nonfinancial motivations and by allowing for wildly differing levels of contribution."[15] For example, since 2009, an organization called CrisisCommons has helped provide oversight and coordination for CrisisCamps to a variety of disasters such as the Haiti earthquake (2010), Chile earthquake (2010),

IN A NUTSHELL

The best person to do a job is the one who most wants to do that job; and the best people to evaluate their performance are their friends and peers who, by the way, will enthusiastically pitch in to improve the final product, simply for the sheer pleasure of helping one another and creating something beautiful from which they all will benefit.

—**Jeff Howe,** *Crowdsourcing: Why the Power of the Crowd Is Driving the Future of Business*[2]

Figure 11.4 CrisisCommons helped support a CrisisCamp for Pakistan flooding in 2010 that helped address localized issues like complications from this washed-out bridge. (From U.S. Army, Horace Murray.)

Japan earthquake (2011), and flooding events in Thailand, Nashville, and Pakistan, with over 3,000 people having participated in CrisisCamps in over 30 cities in 10 different countries.[14] (See Figure 11.4.) As a strong indicator of the success of CrisisCamps and the oversight and management of CrisisCommons, the Alfred P. Sloan Foundation in partnership with the Woodrow Wilson International Center for Scholars established a planning grant for $124,000 and a trustee grant for $1.2 million in 2010 to support a repository of lessons learned from CrisisCommons and to continue the support of CrisisCamps at all levels of government.[14]

As CrisisCommons states on their blog,[14] the crowdsourcing support of the January 2010 Haiti earthquake was a watershed moment in disaster virtual volunteer support. The Ushahidi site established for the response to Haiti (http://haiti.ushahidi.com/) was multifaceted facilitation of information from the crowd. Specifically, the site allowed for public reporting via SMS text, international SMS text, email, and web submissions on topics such as local emergencies, public health issues, security risks, natural hazards and aid stations, as well as a generic category for other issues that needed reporting.[16] Moreover, it used embedded Twitter and Google Person Finder widgets to provide dynamic content that was filtered to the specific incident in Haiti. Additionally, it provided embedded lists of locally reported incidents, mainstream news reports, and citizen news reports. In addition to the content functionality, the entire site was also presentable in a selection of four different languages. All of this publicly generated content was geographically mapped and filtered based on categories, including photos, videos, and reports, which ultimately lead to a clear visual indicator of incident patterns that needed additional management, resources, or direct response. Utilizing this type of single-source aggregation tool is a powerful outlet of information for professional responders, victims' families, and potentially the victims themselves without any formal government control or intervention.

This particular application of the Ushahidi system was strongly supported by volunteers at Tufts University who helped train hundreds of volunteers on the use and implementation of the system in "situation rooms" established in Washington, D.C., Geneva, London, and Portland.[17] The facilitation of this service through an international virtual volunteer network helped to map more than 3,000 urgent and actionable reports from the Haiti Ushahidi site, which ultimately helped guide local emergency responders on the ground in Haiti to provide services and support that were directed to the areas of most need.[17] Once the activities in Haiti shifted from response to long-term recovery, Tufts continued to utilize Ushahidi in partnership with local government to ensure there continues to be accountability during this process.[17] These kinds of functions are phenomenal tools for emergency managers to measure how well Ushahidi and other crowdsourcing tools can be used not only in support of disaster response but in all phases of emergency management as well.

Organizational Implementation of Crowdsourcing

In addition to the earthquake in Haiti, there are numerous other regional and international emergencies and disasters where crowdsourcing was uniquely implemented during emergency management activities. This is particularly the case when third parties such as businesses, public organizations, and nongovernmental organizations are involved. The involvement can be as a direct response agency or an impacted party from the disaster event. In other words, these organizations can use crowdsourcing techniques to observe and engage in the event or be held accountable due to actions or mis-actions related to event response. Specifically, crowdsourcing expert Jeff Howe summarizes that organizations "employing crowdsourcing [don't] get a free ride…[and] those that view the crowd as a cheap labor force are doomed to fail…[because] what unites all successful crowdsourcing efforts is a deep commitment to the community."[2] This is the critical issue for organizations to decipher risk and benefits; however, crowdsourcing often has an impact, with or without formalized input.

IN A NUTSHELL

Those that view the crowd as a cheap labor force are doomed to fail…[because] what unites all successful crowdsourcing efforts is a deep commitment to the community.

—**Jeff Howe,** *Crowdsourcing: Why the Power of the Crowd is Driving the Future of Business*[2]

Perhaps the best example of this phenomenon was during the Deepwater Horizon oil spill in the summer of 2010. (See Figure 11.5.) In early 2010, an environmental activist group called the Louisiana Bucket Brigade was working with a Tulane University geographic information system (GIS) class that was using Ushahidi to establish an interactive map about Louisiana's repeated oil refinery accidents.[18] Coincidentally, on the day of the final exam for the class, the Deepwater Horizon oil rig exploded, which led to an immediate launch of the Oil Spill Crisis Map built on the Ushahidi model by the Bucket Brigade. The focus of this new map was to track, verify, and validate how the oil spill was affecting residents and the environment of the Gulf Coast. Community reports to the Oil Spill Crisis Map included a variety of environmental and humanitarian issues, including reports of large dead turtles (Bay St. Louis, Mississippi), chemical smells in the air (Dunedin, Florida), and oil-contaminated storm water discharge (Meraux, Louisiana). While the Oil Spill Crisis Map functioned similarly to the Haiti earthquake application of Ushahidi, the categorical breakdowns differed significantly. Specifically, the Oil Spill Crisis Map was more focused on immediate situational awareness of the threat (i.e., spill conditions) than the appropriate emergency response. Consequently, the categories were related to infrastructure such as schools, daycares, refineries, and hazardous materials plants that might have been impacted as well as oil spill exposure reports throughout the Gulf Coast region.[19] Within one month of the explosion, the Oil Spill Crisis Map had received more than 300 field reports (via text

Figure 11.5   Oil spill crisis map screenshot during the Deepwater Horizon oil spill.

message, email, Twitter, photos, mobile application, or web report)—80% of which were ultimately verified by project personnel to be accurate.[18]

Unfortunately, not all crowdsourcing was as successfully utilized as during the Deepwater Horizon oil spill response and recovery. (See Figure 11.6.) Some local jurisdictions in the Gulf Coast area chose to utilize commercial products for information and collection instead of open-sourced crowdsourcing sites like Ushahidi. This type of structure allowed for the collection and feedback of data from approved responders that were deployed into the field for collection.[20] Although the data collected by approved responders is certainly valid, it is limited to the time and space at which they were at the moment of response. The limitations of this practice are particularly exposed when the data are not compared and/or considered in concert with other situational awareness provided by traditional review and open-sourced sites such as the Oil Spill Crisis Map. This represents one of the most significant challenges for emergency managers to adopt social media and apply it in modern management and response tactics. Rather than utilize free information that is validated by the collected response of others, many emergency managers simply ignore these types of sources with the mind-set that the public is not trustworthy or dependable for information. However, clearly that type of philosophy is devalued by social media in general and crowdsourcing in particular.

In addition to the virtual volunteers utilizing crowdsourcing systems to identify needs of the impacted communities, media outlets have also begun to utilize systems like Ushahidi to gather information about events in their communities. For instance, the Australian Broadcasting Company (ABC) experimented using

Figure 11.6 Commercial crowdsourcing systems were utilized to respond to the Deepwater Horizon oil spill but were not utilized in parallel with open systems. (From NASA satellite.)

Ushahidi's Crowdmap functionality to gather information about the impacts of a significant flooding event in the Queensland area. Specifically, ABC acknowledged that since their correspondents and reporters were covering a variety of news angles about the event but could not be everywhere, there was a strong need to utilizing crowdsourcing to fill information gaps about the event. In other words, according to the created site, "the Crowdmap [aimed] to combine verified reports from government agencies and media outlets including ABC but potentially invaluable information supplied by people…who simply see, hear or record incidents or situations due to the floodwaters."[21] Similar to the previously discussed Ushahidi sites, ABC's Crowdmap accepted public reports by email, text message, Twitter, or through a website report.[21] Although mainstream media has quickly embraced publicly generated photos and videos, this type of utilization is a new trend and must be closely watched by emergency managers of all disciplines for both situational intelligence and public information.

Crowdsourcing by Impacted Citizens

Virtual volunteers from throughout the world and local media are not the only groups engaging in crowdsourcing activities during emergencies or disasters. Specifically, citizens and visitors in the impacted areas are utilizing crowdsourcing concepts to personally prepare for, respond to, and recover from the event in an attempt to stabilize and/or sustain their current circumstances. This crowdsourcing support may also be applied to the assistance of neighbors, friends, and family in the impacted area. This is perhaps the most amazing utilization of crowdsourcing since it requires an entirely different level of personal commitment and capability than is necessary for virtual volunteers at CrisisCamps or external organizations. Moreover, it attempts to facilitate the phases of emergency management without the direct support or intervention of formal response agencies.

For instance, there are several occasions where local residents in impacted areas have offered transportation and housing to those individuals (both residents and visitors) who were impacted and/or displaced due to the emergency or disaster. For instance, a website called OzDisasterHelp that professes to "opening hearts and homes to Australians affected by natural disasters" was created by an independent community advocacy organization called GetUp Austrailian.[22] This website very simply presented two options: find a place to stay or offer a place to stay. This type of module quickly aggregates individuals in need of housing with those who can provide this type of mass care support. This classic example of crowdsourcing yet again occurred without formal governmental activation or intervention.

Likewise the 2010 volcanic eruption of the Icelandic volcano Eyjafjallajökull caused significant delays in air travel throughout most of Europe for several weeks. In response, impacted travelers quickly utilized Facebook and Twitter to post messages using organic hashtags such as #getmehome, #putmeup, #ashtag, or #stranded. Because of the classification and aggregation capability through these terms, individuals were able to quickly post messages asking for and/or offering carpooling or lodging to and from various forms of alternative transportation such as buses, trains, and personal vehicles.[23] Much like the Australian example, real citizens self-collected available resources to address regionally identified challenges due to an emergency or disaster without any formal initiation or control from governmental response managers. This volcanic example is unique in that it utilized a traditional social media system rather than a freestanding crowdsourcing system like Ushahidi. As discussed earlier, such use is not inherent in these systems but is possible when organized around certain classifications and/or categories.

Crowdsourcing help by local citizens does not stop at the direct basic care of others in the impacted region. Specifically, there are some disaster scenarios that have led to the use of crowdsourcing tools to provide secondary support to those in need. For instance, during the Queensland flooding previously mentioned, a registered charity called Animal Rescue QLD identified that the existing animal shelters and rescue organizations in the Queensland area were overwhelmed with animal rescues and were not able to fully meet the animal health and rescue needs from the event.[24] To help address this issue, Animal Rescue QLD established a Facebook page called "Animals lost and found in QLD floods" to help facilitate the reunification of impacted families and their displaced animals.[25] Likewise, during the 2011 tornado outbreak that impacted much of the southeast United States and killed several hundred individuals, a Facebook page called "Pictures and Documents found after the April 27, 2011 Tornadoes" was established. (See Figure 11.7.) This Facebook page was intended to aggregate the displaced individual pictures and documents that were discovered during local recovery efforts.[26] This particular effort ultimately ended up with more than 100,000 followers. In both examples, these organically created crowdsourcing mechanisms provided genuine solutions to real issues of disaster response and recovery that are either overly complicated or underaddressed by formal governmental response.

Crowdsourcing Usage by Governmental Response

While there has been significant application of crowdsourcing by virtual volunteers, media, and impacted citizens, formal governmental agencies have been reluctant to utilize this social media concept. Although there have been some examples of military use of crowdsourcing to allow soldiers facing field challenges to learn best practices from other soldiers, these activities are predominately classified and hidden from the review and application by domestic emergency management agencies.[27] One exception to this application is the U.S. Geological Survey (USGS), which has utilized a program called "Did You Feel It?" designed to gather and collect the locations where people felt measured

Figure 11.7 A wedding picture found in tornado debris and ultimately returned to the couple through the use of a crowdsourcing Facebook page.

earthquakes. Specifically, electronic monitors throughout the United States measure earthquakes, the results of which are then posted to the USGS website and then confirmed by residents in those areas.[28] The USGS crowdsourcing system provides a powerful tool for the organization to provide awareness to local hazards and begin to measure and map how earthquakes are felt. This collected information allows USGS operators to move forward in planning and preparedness efforts in various parts of the country that are susceptible to certain fault lines. Additionally, the federal government has utilized crowdsourcing through its Challenge.gov campaign, but very few of these suggestions were focused on emergency management or preparedness issues and no actionable items have yet resulted from the process.

Consequently, it is extremely rare for crowdsourcing during emergencies or disasters to be formally utilized by government emergency management agencies regardless of discipline. Emergency managers at all levels of government have been reluctant to formally embrace the collection of information from the crowd for a variety of reasons. In many ways, there is a high level of distrust among emergency managers as crowdsourcing utilizes sources that are unvetted, unapproved, and often anonymous to the entire operation. Unfortunately, this detachment from traditional emergency management and response makes it difficult to overcome by most governmental organizations and jurisdictions, particularly as a primary source for response and recovery activities. However, it is clear that crowdsourcing is significantly impacting how citizens, media, and concerned individuals engage disaster response and recovery. Perhaps more amazingly, these organic crowdsourcing examples are in many ways more efficiently and effectively responding to the needs of the given incident than traditional response mechanisms.

Practitioner Profile: Jim Garrow, Philadelphia Department of Public Health

Jim Garrow (Figure 11.8) works with the Philadelphia Department of Public Health coordinating emergency and risk communication with a particular focus on social media. As a self-described "disaster planner with an eye to the future," Mr. Garrow spends his free time writing about emergency public information on his "Face of the Matter" blog (http://jgarrow.posterous.com). As an active member of the #SMEM Twitter initiative, the U.S. Department of Homeland Security's Virtual Social Media Working Group, and the CrisisCommons Communications

Figure 11.8   Jim Garrow.

workgroup, Mr. Garrow has presented to national groups on how social media can be a successful component of emergency public information campaigning. When asked why social media was important to emergency management and preparedness, Mr. Garrow talked about the importance of customer service, particularly in support of disaster victims. Specifically, he stated that "Our product [life safety] depends on the successful transfer of information and if we can't make that connection, we have no product...[and] if we have no product, in whose best interest are we working?" When asked about current levels of social media implementation within the emergency preparedness community, Mr. Garrow stated that social media is beginning to be implemented into day-to-day operations and that "This process will likely continue for a long time and that the timeline will be punctuated by rousing successes and critical failures, both in operations and from a public relations perspective." Moreover, Mr. Garrow indicated that this movement toward social media and Web 2.0 systems is forcing "emergency managers...to see their customers not as helpless folks, but instead as valuable partners who can help inform a response." In regard to emergency management and preparedness professionals who continue to fight against embracing social media, Mr. Garrow indicated that local offices who strive to be trusted sources of information will instead be marginalized as "fewer and fewer people will seek them out for information in normal or emergency situations." Mr. Garrow continued by stressing that "Empty space needs to be filled and into the void created by non-communicative government officials are thousands of others who desire that megaphone" and will become the trusted source that most emergency managers seek to be within their communities. Mr. Garrow is passionate about social media and creates a clearly envisioned metaphorical line in the sand that has been drawn by the public for emergency managers—one side leads to success and one to failure.

Chapter Terms

Crowdsourcing: Concept of utilizing the collected knowledge, skills, and abilities of individual internet users to increase the information and infrastructure exchange during emergencies and/or disasters.

CrisisCamps: Physical colocation of internet users who share a common interest to address a particular challenge related to emergencies or disasters through crowdsourcing activities.

BarCamps: Physical colocation of internet users who share a common interest to address particular challenges through crowdsourcing activities, including election monitoring and public violence.

Ushahidi: Crowdsourcing system leveraged by CrisisCamps and BarCamps to leverage publicly reported information that is associated and plotted on a map.

Chapter Questions

General Questions

1. True/False: Crowdsourcing must be initiated by formal emergency managers to be utilized effectively.
2. True/False: Government agencies are reluctant to embrace crowdsourcing.
3. When a group of individuals gathers to virtually access and set up resources for a disaster it is called:
   a. BarCamp
   b. CrisisCamp
   c. Crowdmapping
   d. Ushahidi

Essay Questions

1. Discuss the impact of crowdsourcing on disasters.
2. Discuss the use of Ushahidi's Crowdmap system in disasters.
3. Discuss the use of disaster crowdsourcing by citizens and third parties.

Works Cited

1. Shirky, Clay. *Here Comes Everybody: The Power of Organizing without Organizations.* New York: Penguin Press, 2008, p. 109.
2. Howe, Jeff. *Crowdsourcing: Why the Power of the Crowd Is Driving the Future of Business.* New York: Crown Business, 2008, pp. 7, 15.
3. Szamborski, Marie. "Basic Facts about the Christchurch Earthquake." *Matador Change* February 23, 2011. http://matadornetwork.com/change/basic-facts-on-the-christ-church-earthquake (accessed on October 30, 2011).
4. "Launching Eq.org.nz for the New Zealand Earthquake." *Ushahidi Blog*, February 24, 2011. http://blog.ushahidi.com/index.php/2011/02/24/launching-eq-org-nz-for-the-new-zealand-earthquake/.
5. "iStockPhoto." *iStockPhoto*. www.istockphoto.com (accessed March 13, 2011).
6. Meier, Patrick. "Think You Know What Ushahidi Is? Think Again." *iRevolution*, June 16, 2010. http://irevolution.net/2010/06/16/think-again (accessed October 30, 2011).
7. "2007–2008 Kenyan Crisis." *Wikipedia*. http://en.wikipedia.org/wiki/2007%E2%80%932008_Kenyan_crisis (accessed March 13, 2011).
8. "The Ushahidi Platform." *Ushahidi*, 2011. http://www.ushahidi.com/products/usha-hidi-platform (accessed March 13, 2011).
9. "The SwiftRiver Platform." *Ushahidi*, 2011. http://www.ushahidi.com/products/swift-river-platform (accessed March 13, 2011).
10. "Crowdmap" *Ushahidi*, 2011. http://www.ushahidi.com/products/crowdmap (accessed March 13, 2011).

11. "BarCamp." *BarCamp*, 2011. http://barcamp.org/w/page/402984/FrontPage (accessed March 13, 2011).
12. Forrester, Ian. "What Is a BarCamp: Introduction." *Slideshow Presentation*. http://www. slideshare.net/cubicgarden/what-is-a-barcamp-introduction (accessed October 30, 2011).
13. King, Rachel. "CrisisCamp Bringing Together Developers, Programs for Haiti Relief." *ZDNet*, January 19, 2010. http://www.zdnet.com/blog/gadgetreviews/crisiscamp-bringing-together-developers-programmers-for-haiti-relief-efforts/11348 (accessed October 30, 2011).
14. "CrisisCommons—About." *CrisisCommons*, 2011. http://crisiscommons.org/about/ (accessed March 13, 2011).
15. Shirky, Clay. *Here Comes Everybody: The Power of Organizing without Organizations*. New York: Penguin Press, 2008, p. 109.
16. "Haiti." *Ushahidi*, 2010. http://haiti.ushahidi.com/ (accessed March 13, 2011).
17. "Taking the Lead: Ushahidi." *Ushahidi*, February 19, 2010. http://blog.ushahidi.com/index.php/2010/02/19/taking-the-lead-ushahidi-haiti-tufts/ (accessed March 13, 2011).
18. Gahran, Amy. "BP Oil Spill: Ushahidi-Powered Crowdsourced Map." *Knight Digital Media Center*, May 17, 2010. http://www.knightdigitalmediacenter.org/news_blog/comments/20100517_crowdsourced_maps_dont_wait_for_a_crisis_to_experiment/ (accessed March 13, 2011).
19. "Oil Spill Crisis Map." *Louisiana Bucket Brigade*, 2010. http://oilspill.labucketbrigade.org/main (accessed March 13, 2011).
20. Stephens, Kim. (2011). "Crisis Mapping, Crisis Crowdsourcing, and Southern Storms." iDisaster Blog. http://idisaster.wordpress.com/2011/05/08/crisis-mapping-crisis-crowdsouring-and-southern-storms/ (accessed January 9, 2012).
21. "ABC Qld Flood Crisis and Recovery Map." *Ushahidi*, 2010. http://queenslandfloods.crowdmap.com/page/index/1
22. "FAQ." OzDisasterHelp, 2010. https://www.ozdisasterhelp.org/faq (accessed March 13, 2011).
23. "Iceland Volcano: How Twitter and Facebook Are Helping Stranded Travellers." *UK Telegraph*, April 20, 2010. http://www.telegraph.co.uk/technology/social-media/7610734/Iceland-volcano-How-Twitter-and-Facebook-are-helping-stranded-travellers.html (accessed March 13, 2011).
24. "Welcome." *Animal Rescue Queensland*. http://animalrescueqld.vpweb.com.au/ (accessed March 13, 2011).
25. "Animals Lost and Found in QLD Floods." *Facebook*. http://www.facebook.com/animalslostfoundqldfloods#!/animalslostfoundqldfloods?sk=info (accessed March 13, 2011).
26. "Pictures and Documents Found after the April 27, 2011 Tornadoes." *Facebook*. https://www.facebook.com/pages/Pictures-and-Documents-found-after-the-April-27–2011-Tornadoes/162443980482277 (accessed March 13, 2011).
27. Adler, Eric. "Social Media Quickly Alters Diplomacy and Tactics." 2011. http://www.kansascity.com/2011/04/23/2821024/social-media-make-inroads-on-battlefield.html#ixzz1KXvxkAV4 (accessed March 13, 2011).
28. "Did You Feel It?" North County Times. http://www.nctimes.com/news/local/military/article_890feac6-b19c-53ac-ac2e-3c9e82265792.html (accessed January 9, 2012).

Chapter 12

The Beaten Browser: The Rise of Video, Voice, and Information on the Go

---

The web [browser] is not the culmination of the digital revolution.

—Chris Anderson and Michael Wolff, "The Web Is Dead: Long Live the Internet"[6]

Chapter Objectives

- To understand the history and relevance of browser-accessed internet usage
- To analyze the impact of cellular phones and mobile devices on mobile-accessed internet usage
- To comprehend the impact of mobile devices on social media and Web 2.0 systems
- To analyze the impact of mobile devices on the use of social media during emergencies and disasters
- To understand the rise of user-controlled video information and systems
- To comprehend the impact of video storage and streaming video on emergencies and disasters

221

DISASTER FOCUS—TUSCALOOSA TORNADO

At approximately 5 p.m. on April 27, 2011, the city of Tuscaloosa, Alabama, was hit by a half-mile-wide tornado[3] that resulted in 36 deaths, 990 injuries, and significant devastation.[1] The tornado's path went close to a local high school and the campus of the University of Alabama, causing near total destruction of many homes, buildings, and businesses in the area.[3] (See Figure 12.1.) The damage from the tornado was exacerbated by earlier storms that had saturated the ground, causing the heavy tornadic winds to uproot trees rather than just snapping them, which contributed to the nearly 335,000 customers who were without power in the region. Representatives from the Alabama Power Company stated that the number of outages was comparable to those effects seen from Hurricane Ivan or Hurricane Katrina.[3] Officials at the local hospital reported treating more than 600 injuries, with more than 50 children arriving at the facility unaccompanied. Upon visiting the disaster scene, President Obama stated, "I have never seen devastation like this."[1] The tornado that struck Tuscaloosa was part of a significant tornado outbreak that struck the southeastern United States from April 25 to April 28, 2011, and killed 339 people in seven different states.[2] The exchange of incident-related information was significant on the various social media streams. For instance, ultra-popular (20,000+ Twitter followers and 42,000+ Facebook followers) Birmingham meteorologist James Spann was utilizing Facebook, Twitter, and uStream to both post weather-related content and receive storm reports from the general public. During the Tuscaloosa tornado, the local cable television provider signal failed, leaving only Spann's uStream feed for people to watch the developments of the storm. Likewise, when Spann's television station radar temporarily became unavailable during the storm, he simply utilized his personal computer (that had been previously wired to broadcast Facebook and Twitter) to bring up an online radar system.[4] It is this type of pervasive utilization of mobile and portable technologies that will continue to define emergency and disaster response and recovery for responders of all types.

■ To analyze the impact of voice-based systems and other social media systems that allow for the creation and distribution of mobile information

The Web Is Changing

According to Google's executive chairman and former CEO Eric Schmidt, every two days the world is creating as much information as it did from the beginning

Figure 12.1   American flag placed on debris pile from 2011 Alabama tornadoes. (From Adam Crowe.)

of civilization up to 2003. He attributes this to not only the rise of user-generated content (e.g., videos) but also the exponential growth in the availability and functionality of mobile devices.[5] To this end, some technology experts are estimating that there will be 1 trillion mobile devices with internet capability by the year 2013.[5] There is clearly a significant change in how people engage in the connection available through the information stream known as the internet.

The first description of what became the internet was in August 1962 when J. C. R. Licklider of the Massachusetts Institute of Technology (MIT) referenced a "galactic network" that would globally connect sets of computers so that people could quickly exchange information and programming. Through the next decade, Licklider and other visionaries at the Defense Advanced Research Projects Agency (DARPA) began experimenting with utilizing packets to network information rather than circuits. This led to the establishment of the first network in 1966 called ARPANET.[8] The next two decades were dominated by continued improvements in the networking capability present to support the internet. By late 1990, British software engineer Tim Berners-Lee invented transfer protocols and an internet language (HTML) that could be presented in a shared interface (e.g., browser), which was ultimately called the World Wide Web. Ironically, the first web page presented information about the project Berners-Lee was working on to establish an interface for the internet.[9]

The turning point for the internet was the continued development of web browsers that allowed for more direct engagement of the shared information. For instance, the introduction of the Mosaic web browser in 1993 utilized for the first

Figure 12.2 Disaster survivor shows her use of Facebook via her mobile phone. (From FEMA, David Fine.)

time a graphical interface for information exchange. The Mosaic web browser was supported through a program that had received funding from then-senator Al Gore's High Performance Computing and Communication Act of 1991. By 1994, the developers of the Mosaic browser had reorganized and released an updated browser called Netscape Navigator.[9] Later Microsoft released the Microsoft Explorer browser that became the dominant web interface for many years. The development and release of these robust internet browsers helped improve the quality of information exchanged on the internet and ultimately led to exponential commercialization of the internet and the "dot com" boom of the late 1990s.

However, the functionality of internet browsers has limitations. Unlike the social media and Web 2.0 concepts that have been discussed throughout this book, internet access via browsers was unidirectional. Businesses, organizations, and governmental entities were empowered to provide robust outlets of information through visual, graphical, and text formats aimed at the individual. Although it was a groundbreaking change in how people received comprehensive information about topics of interest, the browser-based engagement of the internet lacked feedback mechanisms for the end user. This flaw was initially identified by social media visionaries during the first few years of the 21st century. Social media and Web 2.0 sites began to reinvent how the internet was structured and utilized by allowing mechanisms such as RSS feeds and comment boxes to be embedded in browser-based internet pages. As these tools became increasingly pervasive, additional mechanisms began to be developed that allowed the internet infrastructure to be utilized in new ways without necessarily utilizing the traditional internet browser concept. (See Figure 12.2.) This shift in how people receive information from the internet has also unlocked the mobility and portability of information.

The Rise of Mobile Engagement

Even though the World Wide Web interface to the internet is only about 20 years old, engagement and use of the internet through the browser portal is on the decline. *Wired* magazine went so far in 2010 as to state in a long review of internet usage that "The Web is dead."[6] According to that assessment, "One of the most important shifts in the digital world has been the move from the wide-open Web to semi-closed platforms that use the Internet for transport but not the browser for display."[6] Additionally, experts with Morgan Stanley project that by 2015 internet traffic via non-browser-based interfaces will exceed traditional web traffic.[6] (See Figure 12.3.) For example, Yelp (a location-based social network) maintains a mobile application that only generates 10% of the number of users at its website, but 33% of the actual searches on Yelp. Without a doubt, mobile users are increasingly more engaged than traditional web surfers.[7]

By the end of 2009, there were more than 4.6 billion cell phone subscriptions throughout the world.[10] This vast number of cell phone subscribers has been seen in both developed and developing countries in individuals who are seeking access to mobile banking, healthcare options, and other mobile engagement opportunities. These secondary applications are important to consider, as some communication experts have projected that more than 50% of Americans will have smartphones by the end of 2011.[11] Interestingly, smartphone adoption is slightly higher for males and among Hispanic Americans and Asians, which is a trend seen in other early new technology adoptions as well. Moreover, while smartphones were initially targeted to the business world, more than two thirds of buyers are now utilizing

Figure 12.3 Yelp application on mobile phone. (From Adam Crowe.)

smartphones for personal uses only.[11] Although only 27% of all U.S. households solely utilized cell phones in 2010 (i.e., no landlines), this figure has been steadily growing from 2007 when it was only 14%. According to one study, only 13% of households only had landlines and no cell phone, which was also significantly dropped from 24% in 2007.[13] The use of mobile phones is not only on the rise, it is also significantly impacting how people communicate via traditional phone pathways and modern communication systems.

Fundamentally, smartphones are mobile telephones wrapped in computer software and functionality. Only 3% of smartphone users limit use of their device for voice communications. Likewise, the use of built-in camera and video capability is 20% higher for smartphone users due to the better quality and ease of use of the multimedia features often available. Moreover, the use of Wi-Fi internet signals increases to nearly 50% for smartphone users.[12] Additional smartphone features include a variety of software applications (apps) such as geospatial programs, office productivity tools, file sharing, social media, and multimedia systems that help improve an individual's functionality and facilitate communication through a variety of methods and mechanisms. These open and improved communication pathways allow smartphone users (and basic cell phone users as well) to document the world around them on a day-to-day basis and during emergency situations.

In April 2011, Shawna Redden was a passenger on Southwest Flight 812 from Phoenix, Arizona, to Sacramento, California, that was diverted during flight due to a six-foot hole that was ripped in the top of the plane five rows behind where she sat. Rather than simply have the harrowing experience of a tragic incident as a personal memory, Ms. Redden utilized her cell phone throughout the incident to document the scene, including photos of the hole in the plane, deployed air masks, and response activities from airline personnel. Once arriving on the ground after an emergency landing in Yuma, Arizona, she also posted these pictures to her Twitter account using the Twitter and Twitpic mobile applications.[14] As discussed in Chapter 3, this type of citizen journalism quickly reported—verbally and visually—an incident that in the past might have simply gone unreported by media and local citizens and handled as a controlled incident by the airline.

In the most basic sense, Ms. Redden utilized social media apps to post and share the information she had gathered from her cell phone. In almost every case, social media systems utilize mobile applications to broaden and magnify their use and impact. Social media apps for social networks and microblogs are particularly powerful as they now allow the robustness of receiving and distributing information to be possible at almost any time of day and in any location considering that cell phones are mobile and therefore almost always within arm's reach of the owner. For instance, according to Facebook's internal statistics, more than 250 million users actively engage Facebook through mobile devices, and Facebook users on their mobile devices are twice as active within the system than are nonmobile users.[15]

Cory Booker, the mayor of Newark, New Jersey, utilized Twitter (predominately via his mobile phone) to communicate with thousands of local citizens who were stranded during the December 2010 blizzard that was termed "Snowmageddon." This storm event generated five-foot-high snow drifts, high winds, and a rare "thundersnow" that all ultimately led to the immobilization of much of the northeast United States. Because he successfully engaged Twitter, Booker was able to personally oversee or participate in addressing local needs such as delivery of diapers to stranded mothers, providing aid to women in labor, and personally shoveling snow for local citizens. He repeatedly engaged in online conversations and requested that impacted citizens direct-message him with needs and concerns.[36] His high level of social media engagement led to significant media attention and tremendous public affirmation.

In addition to social media systems, there are numerous utility and personal safety mobile apps that have already been developed and are widely available for use. Emergency managers have long been proponents of local citizens having flashlights and batteries to encourage personal and family preparedness for local emergencies. However, several different mobile app developers have created "flashlight" apps that produce enough light for basic functions necessary for preparedness activities. Likewise, there are some mobile apps that allow for notification procedures such as emergency contacts and allergies to appear on the startup screen for cell phones and smartphones rather than having this information contained in other places that are only known to the phone owner. (See Figure 12.4.) Other apps will provide verbal commands and visual guides for individuals to execute cardiopulmonary

Figure 12.4   Screenshot of personal preparedness mobile app.

resuscitation (CPR) and the Heimlich maneuver effectively and safely.[16] These types of personal mobile apps provide tremendous support for the preparedness and safety of the individual phone user for emergencies that need direct care or advocacy of information to care providers.

Mobile Apps in Disaster Response

In addition to their utilization in disaster preparedness, mobile applications are beginning to be utilized in disaster response as well. During the 2011 Queensland flooding a nongovernmental-sanctioned mobile app was developed for iPhones and iPads that would allow for users to watch local media broadcasts about the event, read the latest news about the disaster, review road closures and power outages, and view all tweets that used the corresponding hashtag (i.e., #qldfloods).[17] Likewise geographic information system (GIS) experts from Austin Peay State University worked with local emergency managers to develop a damage assessment mobile application called the Disaster Mitigation and Recovery Kit (DMARK). According to the university, the main function of the mobile app was to "assist with the collection of damage assessment data via mobile phones, which can then be transmitted back to the Emergency Operations Center in almost real-time (if wireless connectivity is available)." The reported damage data could be tied together with property assessor data so the specific property assessment could be utilized to provide collective damage estimations. The DMARK system also allowed trained damage assessors to photograph and make digital voice records for each assessed property for further consideration in the Emergency Operations Center and long-term recovery activities.[18] Uniquely, this particular app is not just theoretical but was used during the 1000-year-flood event of 2010 that impacted Nashville and other parts of central Tennessee.[19] (See Figure 12.5.) This type of practical utilization of mobile application technology along with corresponding actual field verification will have a tremendous impact on modern emergency management as there continues to be a push to get accurate disaster information as quickly and efficiently as possible.

In addition to the DMARK project, there have also been several examples of creative uses and/or modifications of social media systems via mobile applications. For instance, in 2010, international airlines (including British Airways and Virgin Atlantic) were estimated to have lost $1.7 billion in revenue in less than one week due to the impacts of the Icelandic volcano that erupted and significantly interrupted air travel throughout Europe due to the ash cloud cover.[20] Immediately after the incident, the call centers for the airlines were overwhelmed with frantic passengers trying to gather information about delayed and/or cancelled flights. Unfortunately, in most cases, the airlines were not able to keep up with the call volume or the information available on their websites to keep impacted passengers informed. However, as described in Chapter 11, this situation was remedied when European Twitter users began to organically adopt hashtags such as #ashtag and #ashcloud to build

Figure 12.5   Aerial view of 2010 Nashville flooding. (From FEMA, David Fine.)

conversation around the impacted travel. (See Figure 12.6.) As these were impacted travelers, it can be presumed that the vast majority of the use of Twitter was facilitated through mobile devices and cell phones. Because there was an organically created community, KLM and Lufthansa (and later Air Baltic and British Airways) started communicating with their customers through the hashtags. During that first week, there were over 55,000 mentions of the Twitter hashtag #ashtag. This particular disaster allowed for the use of mobile applications of social media systems like Twitter to vastly improve the response activities related to the event.[20]

Figure 12.6   Although planes like this may have been grounded by the Icelandic volcano, the use of social media via mobile devices rose to address the needs of stranded passengers. (From FEMA, Michael Rieger.)

Another excellent utilization of mobile applications is to ensure appropriate and correct response techniques. Specifically, local emergency medical service providers in the Pittsburgh area have developed the EMS Field Partner mobile app that is targeted to emergency medical technicians, paramedics, and ambulance operations. The EMS Field Partner app contains information on medical protocols and state-mandated checklists for care as well as geospatial information for emergency air transports and the proximity of nearby system hospitals. In this particular case, the mobile application replaces the printed documentation and protocols that have traditionally been carried by emergency medical operators or contained on their vehicles.[21] Improving efficiency and effectiveness during any time of emergency management response is an extremely beneficial component to mobile apps.

In the wake of the 2010 earthquake in Haiti, a free phone number (4636) was established to allow locally impacted residents to SMS text requests for medical care, food, water, security, and shelter needs to local emergency responders. Through the "Mission 4636" service, more than 80,000 messages were received from Haitian residents primarily in the Haitian Kreyol language. Crowdsourced volunteers translated and mapped these messages into managed categories based on need and priority. This information was utilized to provide focused response from emergency responders. The creation of a system to maximize the potential of the available mobile platforms had a tremendous benefit on the Haiti response. Although seemingly paradoxical that technologically advanced mobile devices would be effective in an economically suppressed area, it is evident that these presupposed lines are being eradicated by the continued impact of social media on emergencies and disasters.

The only significant challenge to the use of mobile technology through phones and other portable devices (i.e., tablet computers) is the operating platform of each device. Much like traditional computers that might run from the Windows, Apple, or Linux platforms, mobile phones operate on various platforms and therefore are potentially only compatible with certain applications or functionality. Within cell phones—particularly smartphones—the operating platforms are most commonly provided by Apple, BlackBerry, Windows Mobile, or Google Android. Each of these operating systems has unique considerations that must be addressed when considering mobile applications during emergencies and disasters. For instance, if the EMS Field Partner app discussed earlier was only available on the Apple platform, it would necessitate the equipment and availability of its implementation. Likewise, the number of users on each platform may drive consideration of mobile application development as well as its institution. Apple and Android are currently the most successful providers of operating systems that process a wide range of functionality and maintain the greatest market share; however, as technology changes and adapts, so will current and future providers of mobile operating systems.

The Rise of User-Controlled Video Information

The growing availability and use of cellular phones is not the only mobile medium that is beginning to impact emergency management. The use and distribution of video has changed dramatically over the past few years. Video production has shifted away from professional applications and is now often created, controlled, and distributed by individuals based on their interests and motives. Social media video sites such as YouTube, Vimeo, Skype, UStream, and many others have created open platforms where messages can be presented for a variety of issues ranging from personal to professional and silly to serious. This emergency technology has already had a tremendous impact on citizen journalism (see Chapter 3) and source preservation. For instance, after the Boston Bruins defeated the Vancouver Canucks in the 2011 NHL Stanley Cup, riots broke out in various parts of Vancouver. Fortunately, quick-thinking (and law-abiding) citizens took photos and videos of those participating in the riot, which were later posted to a Tumblr blog and used by local law enforcement to have physical evidence of an extremely dynamic scene.[35]

The first and perhaps most common video system utilized by both the general public and emergency managers is an online video storage site, such as YouTube or Vimeo. These sites allow users to create video channels where videos can be posted and shared with the general public or a private audience via a unique web address. These systems allow for posted videos of relatively short length or size that can be rated, shared, commented on, and embedded in other websites. Because these systems also have mobile applications and most modern cellular phones have built-in cameras capable of capturing video, there has been an exponential growth in the content posted via these systems. Specifically, as of 2010, YouTube users were uploading more than 48 hours of video per minute![36] The capability of firsthand video recordings of witnessed events has grown exponentially. For example, after the 2011 Japan earthquake, there were dozens of videos of eyewitness experiences, including scenes from trains, parking lots, skyscrapers, and malls.[22] Consequently, the capability of mobile devices and the format of online video-storage social media systems has profoundly increased the opportunity of citizen journalism and the various risks associated with it that were discussed in greater detail in Chapter 3.

IN A NUTSHELL

I guarantee that five years from now TV as we know it will be gone. It will have been a 60-year-old experiment that will be followed by something else.

—Doc Searls, Fellow at Berman Center for Internet and Society at Harvard University

Figure 12.7 Preparedness Piggy, part of a video preparedness campaign for community awareness. (From Matt Smith and Adam Crowe.)

In addition to the opportunities of event documentation, online video-storage systems like YouTube and Vimeo also open up many public education and community outreach opportunities for emergency managers in every discipline and across all levels of government. Because of the video-recording capability of most mobile devices and the affordability of traditional photo and video equipment that will record excellent audio and video, many emergency management organizations have begun to develop self-produced public service announcements and other educational messages. For instance, Philadelphia's Office of Emergency Management routinely posts produced videos to its YouTube channel that emphasize preparedness themes, provide incident-related information, or post other personal and family preparedness tips.[23] Likewise, smaller jurisdictions like Johnson County (Kansas) Emergency Management and Homeland Security have created a video series based on common preparedness efforts. Johnson County even created a series of videos around a mascot called Preparedness Piggy.[24] (See Figure 12.7.) Previous to the rise of social media, this type of innovative outreach through videos was cost prohibitive and difficult to sustain over the long term.

An additional type of video-based social media is streaming video. This technology allows live video streams to be broadcasted or streamed to the internet via various mechanisms. Streaming video providers such as LiveStream, uStream.tv, and Justin.tv all allow users to create channels where video streams are provided with opportunities to embed the streaming video player into secondary websites through system-generated HTML coding. The source of the video stream is most often web cameras or connected traditional video cameras, but most streaming video systems also provide mobile apps that allow streaming video from cellular devices and smartphones. Much like other mobile systems, this latter capability greatly enhances the possibility that streaming video could be used to capture and record dynamic events such as emergencies and disasters.

For example, during the 2010 Deepwater Horizon oil spill, BP maintained video feeds of the source of the oil spill from more than 5,000 feet beneath the surface of the ocean. Although initially instituted as an internal BP video feed for monitoring and situational analysis, its availability was quickly made public through political pressure from U.S. lawmakers such as Representative Ed Markey (Massachusetts). As chairman of the U.S. House Energy and Environment Subcommittee within the Energy and Commerce Committee, Markey stated that "This may be BP's footage, but it's America's ocean" and continued, "We will triumph over this tragedy through technology and transparency, so our best minds can bring all resources to bear to end this spill."[25] Markey's last words about technology and transparency were perhaps the most insightful, as that BP video stream became one of the defining moments of that disaster when it was added to thousands of websites throughout the world and was streamed live in almost every newsroom in the country.

In addition to the BP video feed from the Deepwater Horizon oil spill, the earlier-discussed April 2011 response to the Alabama tornado outbreak was impacted by the use of streaming video. Specifically, Birmingham's ABC 33/40 television meteorologist James Spann utilized uStream in conjunction with Facebook and Twitter to provide dedicated information about the weather threats as they entered various portions of his viewing area. At one point during the weather outbreak, ABC 33/40's radar stopped functioning, but Spann quickly shifted to an online web-based radar to continue to provide emergency notifications and warning. Moreover, a regional television provider serving 5,000–9,000 homes also went offline during the outbreak, but because Spann's forecasting was simulcast via streaming video on uStream, many were able to continue to receive his weather reports.[26] Spann's quick use of mobile technologies and the station's continued commitment to robust support of their weather programming may have saved hundreds of lives, as it ensured that timely and accurate protective action statements continued to be available to as many individuals and families as possible.

The last major type of user-controlled video is the capability that exists to make video calls over the internet. Just like traditional phone calls, video-calling services allow for users in two different locations to be connected over the internet in a one-on-one video conversation. Although some emergency management organizations utilize commercial video-calling systems, there are limitations to this type of implementation due to the fact that end users of the commercial systems must have the specific proprietary equipment and internet connectivity necessary for it to work. On the other hand, video-calling systems like Skype and ooVoo do not require that level of functionality. Internet access and web-camera capabilities are the only required features to initiate and complete a video call via a Web 2.0 system.

Much like the video-storage and -streaming capabilities discussed earlier, online video calling also has numerous applications for the emergency management community. First, it allows emergency management experts throughout the world to get together for discussions, trainings, and presentations on critical topics for the professional community. This capability was used during the 2011 Texas Emergency

Management Association Conference, the 2011 Kansas Association of Public Information Officers, and the 2011 Midwest Disasters 2.0 Social Media Workshop to connect experts with other emergency managers in Missouri, Washington, D.C., and Texas, respectively. In addition to the added connectivity, video-calling services have also begun to be utilized by traditional media outlets as impromptu interview formats. For instance, experts from the National Weather Service have often been interviewed by local television stations during a severe weather event impacting the area. Rather than utilize a traditional phone interview, Skype is often identified as a more personal connection with the audience and therefore a more effective tool at disseminating weather-related information.

Information via Voice Systems

Communication via voice is perhaps the most fundamental form of communication. It certainly is the foundation of many historical records and cultural traditions. Interestingly, starting with the invention of the printing press in about 1440, the spoken word became significantly less important to how people communicated on a global scale. However, with the rise of complex communications technologies in the 20th century, the number of communication streams became so great that mass communications—particularly during emergencies and disasters—was difficult to accomplish in a unified format. This issue was further brought into focus by disasters like Hurricane Katrina that disproportionately impacted communities with unique functional and accessible needs and challenges regarding how, when, where, and from who they received their communications. Unfortunately, even as leaders in the emergency management community such as FEMA administrator Craig Fugate have called for planning and response for the "whole community," most emergency management organizations lack the resources to change their message to provide directed focus to meet these unique needs of accessibility or functional needs group within their jurisdiction. (See Figure 12.8.)

It is this messaging gap that may be overcome through the use of Web 2.0 tools available now and those on the horizon. For instance, Google has begun the development process of a speech-to-speech automated translator for its Android mobile phone operating system. This mobile voice translator would combine Google's existing online Translate capability with its voice recognition system with the intention of building the capability to translate passages rather than word-for-word conversions from one language to another.[27] Even if imperfect, this type of technology will provide a powerful tool to emergency managers working to disseminate protective action statements, community messaging, and other necessary statements to the impacted accessible and functional needs communities that may not otherwise receive the complete message.

Voice-to-text translation is already available through many mobile application providers, including Google, Jott, Vlingo, and Dragon Dictation. Although

Figure 12.8   FEMA administrator Craig Fugate listening to first responders after the Joplin (Missouri) tornado. (From FEMA, Leo "Jace" Anderson.)

primarily marketed as a hands-free method to generate text messages, these systems also present numerous opportunities for emergency managers as ways to streamline operational processes. For instance, many of these apps contain advanced programming interfaces (APIs) that could be utilized to allow emergency managers to use their phones to autopopulate incident management reporting systems (e.g., WebEOC) or even incident command system (ICS) forms during operational response. Not only could this potentially greatly reduce the time to complete these documentation mechanisms, a voice-to-text feature may also increase the accuracy of the report as it could be done closer to the time of the event rather than much later after the emergency when time allows for the actual reporting.

Another valuable Web 2.0 tool that utilizes speech technologies is Google Voice. Fundamentally, Google Voice is a telecommunications system that provides free computer-to-computer voice and video calling built on contact groups (e.g., friends, family, or work) or time of day. Google Voice assigns the user a local number that can then be attached to multiple other lines (e.g., desk phone, cell phone, and home phone) as a redirection mechanism. Much like a receptionist, Google Voice allows the user to filter incoming calls and then reroute them to the most appropriate source. For example, the Google Voice routing might push the call from a spouse or family member to all attached phone lines to ensure that the call is taken. On the other hand, Google might reroute known solicitation calls into only one limited line or automatically to voice mail.[28]

Considering that most emergency managers are attached to multiple phone numbers such as personal home and cell phones as well as work office and cell phone numbers, it is extremely practical for emergency managers to consider using Google Voice to filter and direct known numbers or groups of contacts. Situational awareness during emergencies and disasters as well as ensuring political astuteness for elected officials and executive management are valuable but difficult for most emergency managers to handle effectively while still facilitating the coordination of other issues necessary to ensure that the preparedness, response, recovery, and mitigation activities are being successfully implemented. While there are fewer than 1 million active users of Google Voice, this type of Web 2.0 technology will influence and shape how emergency managers interface with technology well into the future.[29]

Information on the Go

Regardless of the type of mobile media discussed, the concept of information on the go is becoming increasingly impactful. People are quickly finding ways to send and receive information not only at work or at home but in vehicles, buses, airplanes, trains, or any other public transportation mechanism. Moreover, because of the mobility of the technology, coffee shops, libraries, fast food restaurants, airports, hotels, and other communal areas or transportation mechanisms are building the infrastructure to allow internet access at minimal to no cost. As was previously discussed, this type of availability, access, and infrastructure creates a tremendous opportunity for the exchange of information about the emergency or disaster via mobile devices and related social media systems. Consequently, emergency managers must consider this impact as they prepare for how to disseminate and monitor information from the general public.

The use and availability of wireless internet (Wi-Fi) has had a tremendous impact on the exchange of mobile information. Although not a technical term, Wi-Fi generally describes a narrow range of connective technologies including wireless local area networks (WLAN) that are based on the IEEE 802.11 standards of device to device connectivity.[30] So-called hotspots to limited or open access to connected wireless internet signals have become pervasive in governmental buildings, schools, community centers, libraries, fast delivery restaurants, and businesses of all sizes. According to the Wi-Fi Alliance, this type of internet connectivity is utilized by over 700 million people worldwide, with millions of new Wi-Fi devices installed each year.[30] Because Wi-Fi connectivity inherently allows for mobility and portability of the devices accessing the internet, there is a tremendous opportunity for information to be reportable or captured via photo, video, or text and posted to the internet within seconds.

Because of the availability of Wi-Fi connectivity and the increasing number of internet-capable mobile phones, there has also been a rise in the use of mobile internet browsing. Much like a traditional computer, this type of internet access engages a browser on the mobile device (or mobile tablet computer) to visit certain web addresses to review the available information. However, given the small screen size and reduction in internet speed on mobile devices, there is a push to design mobile internet sites in a certain way that minimizes the photos, video, and text that have to initially load. This simplification of the look and feel of the website allows for load times to drop significantly and to make the information available through those sites more quickly accessible. For instance, the Federal Emergency Management Agency (FEMA) maintains a mobile internet site that contains a simplified format that focuses only on the most important points available on their traditional internet page. Mobile internet pages are often designated with an "m" before the web address (www.fema.gov compared to www.m.fema.gov).

Interestingly, as stated earlier, Morgan Stanley released a study in 2010 that predicted that mobile web use would outgrow "stationary browsing" by the year 2015. Morgan Stanley identified the implementation of 3G and later 4G mobile technologies in conjunction with Wi-Fi availability as the primary facilitators of this projected change in how people engage the internet. For instance, in Japan, Western Europe, and the United States, there is already a 3G penetration of 96%, 54%, and 46% respectively, with worldwide penetration around 21%. Moreover, videos already account for 69% of all mobile browsing and will continue to grow.[31] These trends are strong indicators that there is a significant shift toward mobile browsing and information exchange. Other than FEMA, most emergency management organizations have yet to adopt truly mobile internet websites. Consequently, emergency managers and disaster responders must be keenly aware of this moving toward the future in consideration of how and where information is distributed related to emergent events.

Another component of mobile information is the technology known as podcasting. (See Figure 12.9.) Podcasting is the aggregation of digital media files (audio or video) that are episodically released and can be downloaded through

Figure 12.9 FEMA personnel record a podcast for distribution via the internet. (From FEMA, Mike Moore.)

various internet outlets. Unlike the streaming video mentioned earlier in the chapter, these types of files are not presented live but are recorded and available after the event for streaming or downloading.[32] Although sometimes available directly from an internet site or through a mobile application, the most common distribution of podcasts is through distributors such as the iTunes Store or Google Marketplace that directly support mobile devices. These types of distribution centers collect the podcasted programs and make individual podcasts available for download to the individual devices. These podcasts are inherently based on the spoken word but can also incorporate musical and video elements, which adds to the structure and purpose of the message.

There are secondary sites that support the capability to create and disseminate podcasts. For instance, there are secondary systems like Odiogo that support the conversion of written text on blogs and websites into spoken words automatically. This type of connectivity creates a significant bridge in the method and dissemination of text-based messaging from traditional blog sites into dynamic audio content. Creating podcasts from text allows for the creation of new information streams that can directly target not only technologically savvy populations who heavily listen to podcasts but limited-language-proficiency members of the population as well who may have difficulty reading (for various reasons) but who may be capable of hearing a presented message. This type of outreach is particularly important as there has continued to be a push to ensure a diversity of messages that reach the whole community rather than just the majority components.

The final type of voice system is online radios networks such as BlogTalkRadio. BlogTalkRadio is an online system that allows users to generate online shows similar in nature to traditional terrestrial radio shows that are hosted with supporting sound files (e.g., opening music) and the capability to allow callers to call in live to the show and engage the host. However, unlike traditional radio stations, anyone can host this type of show on any topic of interest for up to 30 minutes under their free service. Moreover, each show regardless of length and date is permanently stored as a podcast available on the online radio channel. Although not yet widely utilized by emergency managers, it is utilized by individuals, volunteers, and emergency preparedness enthusiasts throughout the world to talk about readiness for various events that may happen in their communities.[33] Some local jurisdictions like Johnson County (Kansas) have created online programming focused on public safety issues in the local community as a partnership between emergency management and law enforcement. They have aired episodes on topics including emergency preparedness, severe weather preparedness, earthquake readiness, fireworks safety, and many other issues.[34] Shows that can provide critical emergency preparedness messaging without the filters of traditional media outreach at no cost to the provider are potentially extremely valuable tools for emergency managers to consider.

Practitioner Profile: Lach Mullin, Benton County Emergency Management

As the regional emergency public information systems administrator for Benton County (Texas) Emergency Management and with his previous work with PIER Systems, Mr. Mullin (Figure 12.10) is an expert at the local and regional application of information management systems. He is also a strong user and proponent of social media's integration into the formal emergency public information process. Specifically, when asked to discuss the impact of emergency managers utilizing social media, Mr. Mullin stressed that "citizens have communication channels deeper into the population" that can help emergency managers address important community subgroups such as politically radical populations, functional needs citizens, and non-native-language speakers. When asked how well emergency managers were applying social media, he stated that "One of the problems in emergency management is that social media is viewed as a 'Joint Information Center (JIC) thing'…[however] public information [is often] a rag-tag team of overworked individuals not integrated into command." He went on to say that "Intelligence gathered through social media isn't being properly vetted or integrated into the planning or operations section, let alone the PIO/JIC." When asked what social

Figure 12.10   Lach Mullin.

technologies on the horizon would be the most impactful to emergency management, Mr. Mullin talked about virtual donations, streaming video, and "smart" systems but indicated that "Community mapping combined with augmented reality is going to give emergency managers immersive, 3D views of incident scenes within two years," which will help "gain better situational awareness from anywhere." In closing, Mr. Mullin emphatically stated, "If emergency managers choose to ignore the impacts of the social web on incident management, they will become (or more likely are already) obsolete."

Chapter Terms

Internet: Worldwide network of computers that utilizes packets of information to send and receive information that can be accessed via a browser interface.

Web browsing: Graphical user interface that provides access to the internet from networked computers.

Mobile browsing: Graphical user interface that provides access to the internet from mobile devices through a reduction in the number and size of images as well as a reduction in extraneous text.

Streaming video: Web 2.0 video system that allows for a live video stream to be published to the internet via a system channel or embedded into other websites.

Whole community: Emergency management planning and preparedness concept that focuses on activities in all phases of emergency management and on incorporating everyone in the community during all phases of emergency management.

Wi-Fi: Wireless signals available from certain transmission "hot spots" that provide internet access to all electronic or mobile devices that have the appropriate receiver.

Chapter Questions

General Questions

1. True/False: The internet was originally created to share information through networked computers via small packets of information.
2. Which of the following social media systems allows for a flow of live information via a primary website or secondary integration?
   a. Google Voice
   b. Mobile browsing
   c. Streaming video
   d. Online video storage

3. Which of the following social media tools does not maintain strong mobile access and engagement?
   a. YouTube
   b. BlogTalkRadio
   c. UStream.tv
   d. None of the above

Essay Questions

1. Discuss how the rise of Wi-Fi availability in conjunction with 3G and 4G services have impacted the rise in mobile internet accessibility.
2. Discuss how various social media systems that utilize mobile information access have benefited outreach to the "whole community."
3. Discuss the potential uses of mobile internet and information-on-the-go systems on emergency preparedness, response, and recovery activities.

Works Cited

1. Samenow, James. "Alabama Tornado Outbreak Visuals: Jaw-Dropping Radar and Satellite Images." *Washington Post*, April 29, 2011. http://www.washingtonpost.com/blogs/capital-weather-gang/post/alabama-tornado-outbreak-visuals-jaw-dropping-radar-and-satellite-imagery/2011/04/29/AFg1C5YF_blog.html (accessed October 30, 2011).
2. Freedman, Andrew. "Tornado Outbreak for the Record Books: How Did Deadly, Destructive Event Happen." *Washington Post*, April 28, 2011. http://www.washington-post.com/blogs/capital-weather-gang/post/tornado-outbreak-for-the-record-books-how-did-deadly-destructive-event-happen-and-what-does-it-mean/2011/04/28/AFLQ942E_blog.html (accessed October 30, 2011).
3. O'Conner, Anahad, and Timothy Williams. "Scores Die in Storms across South; Tornado Ravages City." *New York Times*, April 28, 2011. http://www.nytimes.com/2011/04/28/us/28storm.html?_r=1&hp (accessed March 30, 2011).
4. Bergman, Cory. "TV Meteorologist Thrives in Social Media Tornado." *LostRemote*, April 15, 2011. http://www.lostremote.com/2011/04/15/popular-tv-meteorologist-in-eye-of-social-media-tornado/ (accessed March 30, 2011).
5. Golden, Bernard. "The Web Is Dead: Long Live the Cloud." *Reuters*, August 19, 2010. http://www.reuters.com/article/2010/08/19/urnidgns002570f3005978d8002577840055b1fa-idUS2893680720100819 (accessed March 30, 2011).
6. Anderson, Chris, and Michael Wolff. "The Web Is Dead: Long Live the Internet." *Wired*, August 17, 2010. http://www.wired.com/magazine/2010/08/ff_webrip/all/1 (accessed March 30, 2011).
7. Rosoff, Matt. "Square COO Explains Why the Web Is Dead." *Business Insider*, April 26, 2011. http://www.businessinsider.com/square-coo-explains-why-the-web-is-dead-2011-4 (accessed March 30, 2011).
8. Leiner, Barry M., et al. "A Brief History of the Internet." *Internet Society*, 2011. http://www.isoc.org/internet/history/brief.shtml (accessed March 30, 2011).

9. Zeltser, Lenny. "The World-Wide Web: Origins and Beyond." *Lenny Zeltser*, 2011. http://zeltser.com/web-history/ (accessed October 30, 2011).

10. Whitney, Lance. "Cell Phone Subscriptions to Hit $5 Million Globally." *CNET Reviews*, February 16, 2010. http://reviews.cnet.com/8301-13970_7-10454065-78.html (accessed March 30, 2011).

11. Tofel, Kevin C. "1 in 2 Americans Will Have Smartphone by Christmas 2011." *Gigaom*, March 26, 2010. http://gigaom.com/2010/03/26/1-in-2-americans-will-have-a-smartphone-by-christmas-2011/ (accessed March 30, 2011).

12. Entner, Roger. "Smartphones to Overtake Feature Phones by 2011." *Nielsen Wire*, March 26, 2010. http://blog.nielsen.com/nielsenwire/consumer/smartphones-to-overtake-feature-phones-in-u-s-by-2011/ (accessed March 30, 2011).

13. Fram, Alan. "More Than Half Age 25–29 Have Cell Phones." *MSNBC*, December 21, 2010. http://www.msnbc.msn.com/id/40766705/ns/technology_and_science-wireless/ (accessed March 30, 2011).

14. O'Dell, Jolie. "Hole in Plane Leads to Emergency Landing, Twitpic Shops Details." *Mashable*, April 2, 2011. http://mashable.com/2011/04/02/twitpic-plane-flight-emergency/#12201Southwest-Pilot (accessed March 30, 2011).

15. "Facebook Statistics." *Facebook*, 2011. http://www.facebook.com/press/info.php?statistics (accessed March 30, 2011).

16. Parr, Ben. "Seven Apps That Can Save Lives." *Mashable*, July 11, 2009. http://mashable.com/2009/07/11/iphone-save-lives/ (accessed March 30, 2011).

17. "Queensland Flooding 2001 for iPhone, iPad, and iPod Touch." *Apple iTunes Store*, 2011. http://itunes.apple.com/us/app/queensland-floods-2011/id412831365?mt=8# (accessed March 30, 2011).

18. Stephens, Kim. "Mobile App to Help with Damage Assessment Data Collection." *iDisaster Blog*, April 14, 2011. http://idisaster.wordpress.com/2011/04/14/mobile-app-to-help-with-damage-assessment-data-collection (accessed March 30, 2011).

19. "Damage Mitigation and Recovery Kit." *AP GIS Center*, 2010. http://gisweb.apsu.edu/dmark (accessed March 30, 2011).

20. Nigam, Shashank. "Iceland Volcano Eruption: How Social Media Helped Travelers." *Mashable.com*, April 22, 2010. http://mashable.com/2010/04/22/social-media-iceland-volcano/ (accessed March 30, 2011).

21. Harding, Margaret. "Phones Provide Medical Advice to Area's First Responders." *Pittsburgh Tribune-Review*, 2011. http://www.pittsburghlive.com/x/pittsburghtrib/news/pittsburgh/s_723985.html (accessed March 30, 2011).

22. "On the Scene Footage: Japanese Earthquake and Tsunami." *YouTube Trends*, 2011. http://youtube-trends.blogspot.com/2011/03/on-scene-footage-japan-earthquake.html (accessed March 30, 2011).

23. "PhilaOEM Channel." *YouTube*. http://www.youtube.com/philaOEM (accessed March 30, 2011).

24. "Johnson County Emergency Management & Homeland Security Channel." *YouTube*. www.youtube.com/jocoemergencymgmt (accessed March 30, 2011).

25. "Live Video Feed from BP Is Placed Online." *MSNBC.com*, 2010. http://www.msnbc.msn.com/id/37257629/ns/disaster_in_the_gulf/t/live-video-bp-spill-placed-online/ (accessed March 30, 2011).

26. Bergman, Cory. "TV Meteorologist Thrives in Social Media Tornado." *Lost Remote*, April 15, 2011. http://www.lostremote.com/2011/04/15/popular-tv-meteorologist-in-eye-of-social-media-tornado/ (accessed March 30, 2011).

27. Schroeder, Stan. "Google Is Working on Speech-to-Speech Translator for Android." *Mashable*, February 8, 2010. http://mashable.com/2010/02/08/speech-to-speech/ (accessed March 30, 2011).

28. Pepper, Chris. "What Is Google Voice?" *MacWorld*, December 9, 2009. http://www.macworld.com/article/144921/2009/12/googlevoiceexplainer.html (accessed on October 30, 2011).

29. Buchanan, Matt. "1.4 Million People Have Google Voice, but Not That Many Actually Use It." *Gizmodo*, November 2, 2009. http://gizmodo.com/5395151/14-million-people-have-google-voice-but-not-that-many-actually-use-it (accessed March 30, 2011).

30. "What Is Wifi? A Guide to WiFi for Beginners." *Squidoo*. http://www.squidoo.com/what-is-wifi (accessed October 30, 2011).

31. Zykova, Alisa. "Mobile Surfing May Surpass Desktop in 2015." *SFN Blog*, April 14, 2010. http://www.sfnblog.com/mobile/2010/04/mobile_surfing_may_surpass_desktop_by_20.php (accessed March 30, 2011).

32. Starak, Yaro. "What Is a Podcast and How Can I Use One?" *Entrepreneur's Journey*, August 15, 2005. http://www.entrepreneurs-journey.com/230/what-is-a-podcast (accessed October 30, 2011).

33. "Top 'Emergency' Talk Radio Podcasts." *BlogTalkRadio*. http://www.blogtalkradio.com/search/emergency/profiles/mostrelevent/_/_/_/_ (accessed March 30, 2011).

34. "Johnson County Radio Network." *BlogTalkRadio*. http://www.blogtalkradio.com/jocoprepared (accessed March 30, 2011).

35. "Vancouver 2011 Riot Criminal List." *Tumblr*, 2011. http://vancityriotcriminals.tumblr.com/page/3 (accessed March 30, 2011).

36. Gustin, Sam. "Mayor Hacks Snowmaggeddon with Epic Tweets." *Wired*, December 28, 2010. http://www.wired.com/epicenter/2010/12/hacking-snowmageddon/ (accessed March 30, 2011).

37. "Statistics." *YouTube*, 2011. http://www.youtube.com/t/press_statistics (accessed March 30, 2011).

Chapter 13

Location, Location, Location: The Power of Geospatial Technologies and the Environment on Social Systems

There's no need to re-create everything from scratch....Look at some of the early adopters, see what they've done and see if it makes sense for your organization. And then think about what you need to do to customize it.

—Dave Fletcher, Utah Chief Technology Officer

Chapter Objectives

- To establish the systematic structure of location-based social networking, quick response (QR) codes, and augmented reality
- To assess the application of location-based social networking on emergency management and disaster response
- To consider the possible applications of QR codes and augmented reality in the field of emergency management and disaster response

- To evaluate the use of geospatial technologies in disaster recovery activities
- To evaluate the impact of location-based social networking, geospatial technologies, and QR codes on public perception and engagement of disaster-related information.

DISASTER FOCUS—TORNADO OUTBREAK IN NORTH CAROLINA ON APRIL 16, 2011

One of the largest single-system tornado outbreaks in the United States occurred from April 14 to April 16 resulting in more than 200 confirmed tornadoes across 16 states with a total of 43 people killed from tornadoes and straight-line winds. (See Figure 13.1.) On April 16, the National Weather Service (NWS) issued a moderate risk of severe weather for North Carolina and Virginia as a cold front tracked eastward and a squall line developed across the Appalachian Mountains. As storms moved into strong atmospheric instability in North Carolina, NWS issued a Potentially Dangerous Situation (PDS) Tornado Watch just after midday for central and eastern North Carolina and immediately adjacent areas in South Carolina and Virginia. Quickly, the squall line descended along the Blue Ridge Mountains and intensified along the Interstate 77 corridor north of Charlotte and west of Greensboro. As the storm moved east, tornadoes were confirmed near Salisbury (EF-1), Monroe (EF-0), and Burlington (EF-1). Around 3:15 p.m., another tornado developed in the Raleigh-Durham metropolitan area. The estimated one-mile-wide tornado tracked through the southwest edge of downtown Raleigh on a southwest-to-northeast trajectory, passing through miles of suburbs surrounding the city. It eventually crossed three interstate highways and narrowly missed striking a nuclear power plant, but did significantly impact the Shaw University campus in downtown Raleigh so severely that classes were suspended for the remainder of the semester.[1] The high EF-3 tornado ultimately generated an estimated $115 million in damages to the Raleigh area with more than 2,500 homes and businesses impacted.[2] To visualize this damage in relationship to the path and in the context of debris management and damage assessment, the City of Raleigh created a map through Google Maps that reflected city inspector reports of affected areas and surveyed damaged buildings. Each assessed property was divided into gray, yellow, red, and purple dots that corresponded to isolated, minor, major, and destroyed damage classification, respectively.[2] This use of geospatial technology is a phenomenal application of Web 2.0 technologies that undoubtedly is a valuable response and recovery tool not only for professional responders but also for private insurers and citizens alike.

Figure 13.1 Damage from April 16, 2011, North Carolina F3 tornado. (From FEMA, David Fine.)

Location-Based Social Networking

Geospatial technologies are a powerful tool for emergency preparedness, response, and recovery. One of the fastest growing subcategories of geospatial technologies is location-based social networking from sites such as Foursquare, Gowalla, Loopt, and Google Latitude. (See Figure 12.2.) These sites allow for individuals to check in or register within these systems at a particular location and be placed on a map in

Figure 13.2 FourSquare on mobile device. (From Adam Crowe.)

the corresponding location. These geographic locations are not preset; instead, they are created by the users of the system. Although most of the users mark geographic locations of commonly identifiable places (e.g., local library), some individuals have established locations like "Tom's House" or "Best Pizza in Town." This type of connectivity allows for social networking based not only on relationships but also on geographic proximity. For example, if a person has checked in at the local airport, he or she might notice via a location-based social network that a friend, family member, or co-worker had also checked in at that same location. Much like traditional social networks such as Facebook and MySpace, location-based social networks facilitate relationship coordination and collaboration with a particular focus on the geospatial connectivity that might not otherwise naturally exist via social networks specifically or social media in general.

Moreover, most of these location-based social networking systems maintain incentive programs to encourage active participation within the systems and to create third-party marketing and advertising possibilities for the facilities, businesses, and organizations in geographic proximity to those who check in on the system. For instance, on Foursquare there are three incentive programs. First, users are given badges that are stored on their profiles for reaching certain systematic milestones such as checking in to the same location numerous times, checking in to numerous different locations, or other geographic specific considerations.[3] Secondarily, local businesses or organizations are allowed to create special offers that are generated when a person checks in within the geographic vicinity of the location. In essence, this type of special offer becomes a virtual coupon where local users of the system can show their check-in to the local business and receive the corresponding offer. Lastly, users are deemed a "mayor" of the particular location when they check in more than anyone else during a particular period of time. Similar functionality and incentive programs exist on all other major location-based social network systems with some slight variations based on user counts and system dedication to location-based services.

Because these systems are inherently only available via mobile devices, which have lower usage saturation, and because they are relatively new forms of social media, location-based social networking has a relatively low number of users in comparison to other social media systems. However, these systems have some of the largest growth rates of any type of social media. For instance, Foursquare has a reported 10 million users and grew 3,400% in 2010.[4,5,33] Likewise, Google Latitude maintains 3 million to 9 million active users depending on who is reporting the numbers.[7] On the other end of the spectrum, Gowalla has fewer than 1 million users but has strategic marketing relationships with organizations such as Disney.[6] In almost all cases, location-based social networking is utilized via mobile devices or apps, including smart phones and tablet devices. Each system has created mobile applications to access its system via all major mobile providers (e.g., Google Latitude offered on all Google Android phones). Because some mobile phone providers are also providing location-based social networking, the continued growth of these systems may be skewed by embedded software on mobile devices.

The one major concern for location-based social networking is user privacy. The privacy concerns are based on both physical and technological concerns. At the most basic level, users utilizing location-based social networking to check in at a geographic location are by default also publicly declaring where they are not. Public websites like www.PleaseRobMe.com were developed to list location-based social networking reports of people not being at their home. Although ostensibly created to improve public awareness about these risks, it clearly created vulnerability for the user's safety and home security.[8] This particular site has since closed down, but this type of outward risk still exists in the personal use of these systems. Additionally, there are technological security risks that exist in that these individual systems as well as the mobile devices they are engaged on often store the sites and times of check-ins over long periods of time. For instance, in April 2011 it became public knowledge that iPhones were tracking user locations over time based on Wi-Fi utilization and cellular tower pings. Without a doubt, if hacked by external parties, this type of long-term storage would create significant personal vulnerability for individuals and property.

Potential Emergency Management Uses of Location-Based Social Networking

Like all social media systems discussed in this book, the application of location-based social networking to emergency management and all its related disciplines is critical to the future of the profession. However, as location-based social networking systems are relatively new even by social media standards, emergency management professionals have yet to widely adopt systematic usage of these systems. As a matter of fact, based on general research and communication with emergency management professionals active in social media, there are few, if any, location-based social networking applications being currently utilized at any level of government in the field of emergency management. However, this absence does not mean there are no potential applications. Emergency managers across all disciplines should consider the use of location-based social networking systems for debris management, damage assessment, search and rescue, and personnel accountability.

For instance, the location-based social networking incentives mentioned earlier are not limited to local businesses for marketing purposes. Governmental application, including emergency management, is definitely possible but poorly utilized by most agencies. For instance, local emergency managers could utilize advanced programming interfaces (APIs) within these systems to use the special-offer feature of location-based social networking to make emergency public notifications such as severe weather advisories like a tornado warning or hurricane evacuation. These special offers would be tied to government buildings or commonly known public locations (e.g., local park). This type of alert would provide a secondary means of alerting the general public in the geographic vicinity of those landmarks.

Figure 13.3 **Highly complex restoration and recovery activities like debris management could be enhanced through the use of location-based social networking systems. (From FEMA, Leif Skoogfors.)**

Additionally, debris management is a common activity in short- and long-term recovery activities after a disaster. (See Figure 13.3.) Regardless of whether local, regional, or statewide agencies are involved in the process, debris management is a critical component of community restoration that impacts both citizens and local businesses. Proper debris management activities also have long-term environmental effects on historical landmarks, landfill utilization, water quality, and total costs to responding governments. Because of the inherent size and scope of debris management activities, most communities require private contractors to facilitate the majority of operations. Unfortunately, due to the third-party involvement and high cost to support debris management activities, contracted activities can sometimes be impacted by fraud and operational deception. For example, contractors may deviate from assigned pickup routes, add artificial weight (or lack thereof), or create voids in the storage space in their trucks. While much of this potential abuse is addressed through accountability processes commonly utilized by emergency managers, this process also lends itself to the use of location-based social networking sites like Google Latitude. Specifically, contractors could be required via self-provided (or government provided) smartphones to document their location via a "check-in" process at periodic intervals to create a documentation of location and activity at minimal to no additional cost to the process.

Similarly, location-based social networking could also potentially be utilized during damage assessment after localized emergencies or disasters. (See Figure 13.4.) Much like the debris management process described above, damage assessment teams are sent into disaster areas immediately after the hazard impacts the community to assess physical damages in the area via classifications such as minor, moderate, significant, and/or complete damage. This process occurs in two stages.

Figure 13.4 Location-based social networking could be used as a tool to aid individual assistance teams like this one traveling by boat to assess damage to homes caused by Missouri River flooding. (From FEMA, Jeannie Mooney.)

The first of these stages is a so-called window or drive-by assessment, while the second is a more thorough process that creates a deeper analysis of the damage or destruction. Part of this duplication is due to the time it takes to transfer information from the initial survey back to incident management at the Emergency Operations Center (EOC) or Incident Command. Location-based social networking would allow for real-time damage assessment data to be available to command staff as the assessor is reporting it rather than delayed. Although there are some commercial systems available that perform a collective function during damage assessment, the utilization of location-based social networking creates a cost-effective and potentially equally efficient option for smaller communities or areas that have not yet implemented any technologies to use during damage assessment.

A location-based social network is also a suitable tool for search and rescue activities. Oftentimes when first responders and law enforcement personnel are conducting time-sensitive searches for lost individuals or for clues to suspected criminal activity, they conduct the search in set patterns creating a measurable grid in the inspected geographic area. Because there is an inherent geographic nature to search and rescue activities, the location-based social networks could be utilized in a similar fashion as the debris management activities. Specifically, searchers could report findings (or lack thereof) in real-time through the location-based systems and have the aggregation of those findings be presented on a map for those in command and management. Moreover, if multiple findings are found, incident commanders would have a visual depiction of any pattern the evidence was indicating far faster than traditional reporting mechanisms would allow.

Lastly, there are numerous emergency management activities that place volunteers and/or workers into field operations where safety and accountability must be maintained. For instance, in "Tornado Alley" many local emergency management offices deploy volunteer amateur radio volunteers to serve as weather spotters during escalating severe weather events. These volunteers are typically utilizing their own equipment and vehicles to come and go from their assigned deployment spot and primarily communicate through amateur radios only. Although the use of radios is an effective means of communication, most emergency managers are totally dependent on such verbal reporting to access current field accountability. Much like the debris management, damage assessment, and search and rescue operations already discussed, these types of volunteer and staff deployments are inherently geographic in nature and would lend themselves to the support of location-based social networking. Having these volunteers plot themselves as they move from location to location would be a valuable visual aid for most emergency managers in a variety of operational settings. This type of utilization could also be accompanied by mobile streaming-video applications (as discussed in Chapter 12) to continue to improve the real-time situational awareness of the event.

Although rarely utilized within emergency management, location-based systems show strong possibilities for use in a variety of areas. Not unexpectedly, emergency managers of all levels of governments and types of implementation are cautious of location-based social networking for a variety of reasons, but perhaps most importantly the security of these systems. Admittedly, location-based social networking is built like all social media on the concept of building relationships and networking. However, again like most social media systems, many of the location-based systems also allow for limited and controlled access to these systems to predetermined groups of individuals. Moreover, all of these systems allow for opt-out participation, which means participants in no way would be forced to utilize the systems even if the government was implementing them. This type of control helps limit perceptions about "Big Brother" in regard to movement and geography.

Impact of Geospatial Programming

In addition to the location-based social networking possibilities, there are significant emergency management activities already being utilized in various geospatial and mapping programs that exist on the internet and via social media and Web 2.0 portals. Various major mapping providers such as Google, Ushahidi, StreetMaps,

ESRI, and Virtual USA provide dynamic mapping interfaces to plot aggregated content, measure incident progression, and establish interactive presentations of emergency and disaster-related information. Unlike the location-based social networking, mapping and geospatial systems are not intended to be built around common or shared networks but rather are open to anyone with an interest and engagement to the scenario or incident being mapped.

The first of these systems is the U.S. Department of Homeland Security (DHS) supported Virtual USA platform. According to the corresponding DHS website, the Virtual USA platform is "an end-user driven…initiative focusing on cross-jurisdictional information sharing and collaboration among the homeland security and emergency management community."[9] Moreover, they state that the system will help meet the end user's "unique needs to save lives, protect property and realize operational efficiencies through improved situational awareness." The website does not stress the mapping and geospatial capabilities of the system even though that is the primary foundation of the information utilized for situational awareness. Several states have utilized these systems, such as the Alabama Department of Homeland Security who created Virtual Alabama, which utilizes a three-dimensional (3D) mapping interface to retrieve geographic information system (GIS) images and data that can be accessed by both technical and nontechnical users. According to the Virtual Alabama site, the tool "reduces technology gaps in economically challenged areas and levels the information 'playing field' throughout the state."[10] For instance, the tool was utilized by National Aeronautics and Space Administration (NASA) engineers in the Huntsville area after the April 2011 tornado outbreaks to establish an accurate path for damage assessment flyovers by the regional Civil Air Patrol.[32] By late 2010, the Virtual Alabama system had over 28,000 registered users representing 1,500 agencies throughout Alabama.[10] Additional applications of the Virtual USA concept include the Florida Geospatial Assessment Tool for Operation and Response (GATOR), Oregon Geospatial Enterprise Office (GEO), Virginia Interoperability Picture for Emergency Response (VIPER), and Virtual Lousiana.[9]

A similar geospatial and mapping interface tool is Google Earth. This system shows a map of the Earth created by the superimposition of images obtained from satellite imagery, aerial photography, and public GIS data.[11] This combined imagery creates an extremely detailed mapping view of areas of the globe. This software is currently available on computers running Windows, Mac OS, and

---

IN A NUTSHELL

Geospatial technologies provide functions that are in support of a user's "unique needs to save lives, protect property and realize operational efficiencies through improved situational awareness."

—Virtual USA website[9]

Linux as well as iPhone and Android-based phones. Moreover, the inputted data is available in 37 different languages thanks to Google's translation protocols. Moreover, since Google Earth's initial release in 2005, the utilization of mapping figures and diagrams by traditional media to add to traditional storytelling has increased tenfold.[12]

Because of the various sources of data layers that comprise the Google Earth output mechanism, there are significant types of disaster reporting that can exist through this system. For instance, after the 2011 Japan earthquake, Google Earth was utilized to show the damage and impact of the earthquake and related tsunami.[13] Additionally, Google Earth allows for mapping output in files that can be used and manipulated by other geospatial programs. For instance, the Federal Emergency Management Agency (FEMA) utilizes Google Earth to output flood-mapping data that can be utilized by local and state governments for preparedness efforts.[14] This type of reporting and data manipulation would be extremely valuable to emergency managers maintaining local or regional situational awareness. (See Figure 13.5.) Likewise, public awareness is vastly improved as both the general public and traditional media seek out visual aids to understand and comprehend the complexity and scope of disasters that impact not only their communities but also other areas throughout the world. This access to information can ultimately lead to greater response to requests for donations and volunteerism as well as political implications related to the disaster. This type of visual aid is invaluable particularly with minimal user engagement and at nearly no cost to emergency managers.

Figure 13.5 Geospatial technologies can benefit mapping efforts in flooded areas and other disaster zones by participants throughout the impacted areas. (From FEMA, David Valdez.)

Figure 13.6   Geospatial technologies can be utilized to visually display the spread of contagious health conditions like seasonal flu. (From CDC, James Gathany.)

In addition to Google Earth, there are several third-party geospatial systems that allow for user-generated and -manipulated disaster-related data. For instance, OpenStreetMap was used to map various components of disaster response and recovery during the 2010 Haiti earthquake.[15] Likewise, ESRI, one of the early pioneers in GIS technologies, provides dedicated personnel and hardware to support the software and internet interface that can be utilized during emergencies and disasters. Specifically, ESRI Disaster Response supports global mapping of disasters with a specific focus on earthquakes, flooding, severe weather, hurricanes, hazardous material spills, volcanoes, and wildfires.[16] Over the past several years, ESRI Disaster Response has provided support for most major disasters, including the Deepwater Horizon oil spill in 2010 and the Japan earthquake and tsunami in 2011.[17]

The use of geospatial technologies is not limited to strictly mapping damages. In some cases, the capability to identify patterns and correlations quickly across limited or broad geographic ranges can be a powerful preparedness and response tool. For instance, Google has developed its Flu Trend application that utilizes the Google internet searches of users around the world who are searching for health-related information online to create algorithms that provide strong patterns related to actual physical conditions in those areas. (See Figure 13.6.) At the most basic level, this process is based on the (often) accurate assumption that only people who are sick would search for information about the flu. Therefore, during flu season, this type of assessment provides extremely valuable data to healthcare providers and responders to try and reduce or mitigate the spread in certain areas.[18] This type of trend data was particularly valuable during the H1N1 influenza pandemic and will be for future outbreaks of disease to ensure proper response is coordinated.[19]

Enhanced Information via Physical Interface

In addition to the location-based social networking and geospatial programming previously discussed, social media and Web 2.0 systems also allow for the enhanced information availability based on the location or area of interest. This enhanced capability to receive information primarily occurs through the utilization of quick response (QR) codes and augmented reality. In both cases, information providers (e.g., local governmental entities) can create and/or utilize systems that have extra information embedded or incorporated into secondary mechanisms to receive that information. Utilizing current mechanisms to receive information is extremely valuable, particularly during emergencies and disasters due to the need to maximize benefits of systems used without significant additional work or cost given the time and financial constraints that will exist in such a condition.

Quick response (QR) codes are two-dimensional bar codes that are readable by dedicated QR readers that are available on most smartphones as a downloadable application. The code generally consists of black and white variable shapes in a square pattern on a white background. This unique combination of shapes and colors allows for hyperlinks, videos, photos, text, and other multimedia forms to be embedded and read by an end user using the bar code. Although originally utilized for material tracking in vehicle manufacturing, they have a much broader purpose now and are widely utilized in parts of Asia and especially Japan, but have been only slowly adopted in the United States; however, the use increased tremendously in 2011 due to increased awareness and certain large-scale campaigning related to QR codes.[20] Various QR code standards have existed since 1997 with the most commonly used formats being settled on in 2006.[20]

In the United States, the most common application for QR codes is for marketing and guerrilla advertising. Specifically, many vendors have begun to place QR codes on commercial packaging or promotional materials that include a variety of pieces of information such as nutritional information, locations of stores, and environmental impact (or lack thereof) of the manufacturing of the product. Although primarily utilized for marketing, there is a growing trend for the use of QR codes in government with particular consideration for emergencies and disasters. Perhaps the most well-known use of QR codes by a local municipality is the small town of Manor, Texas. Through the leadership of Dustin Haisler, the City of Manor began to place QR codes throughout the community to allow local citizens to bring up supplementary information about construction projects, maintenance schedules, and availability of some basic municipal services.[21]

Haisler has also suggested that QR codes distributed within a municipality could also be embedded with content that would be critical during emergency response. (See Figure 13.7.) For example, if a local fire department was responding to a local community fire, they could scan the closest QR code (perhaps attached to the local fire hydrant) that would contain embedded information about local utility cutoffs, property ownership, and other valuable response information that might

Figure 13.7   QR code sample with embedded text. (From Adam Crowe.)

supplement and/or be redundant to localized mobile data terminals (MDTs) in their equipment.[22] Other emergency managers have suggested utilizing QR codes for emergency preparedness activities. For instance, community-posted QR codes (e.g., hotel room information) might contain links to local, state, or federal emergency preparedness websites that could provide emergency content during response and recovery activities such as evacuation routes, debris management activities, or local shelters.[23] (See Figure 13.8.)

In addition to QR codes, augmented reality is another type of technology that supports enhanced information through physical interfaces. Augmented reality is a generic technology term to describe live views of a real physical environment that are augmented by computer-generated multimedia. This multimedia can be in the format of sounds, videos, graphics, or links. Augmented reality contrasts with virtual reality, which replaces the real world with a simulated one.[24] It is believed that the term *augmented reality* was first used as early as the late 1960s[25]; however, a commonly agreed-upon definition for augmented reality was established in 1997. This definition defined augmented reality as combining real and virtual environments, interactive in real time, along with three-dimensional presentation.[26] Augmented reality is similar to other emerging technologies in that its progress and development is quickly pushing the limits of any boundaries of definition.

Much like QR codes and the location-based social networking, augmented reality is just beginning to be applied for emergency management in the various phases and disciplines. For instance, U.S. Army field paramedics are beginning to consider virtual augmented "goggles" that would include medical protocols and patient

Figure 13.8 Potential emergency services usage of QR codes is wide and varied. (From Adam Crowe.)

information, which would allow for medical engagement without the distraction and delay of checking secondary sources.[27] Likewise, it has been suggested by some public health professionals to allow end users to utilize augmented reality to visualize local health providers in their actual physical vicinity.[28] This type of application would also be extremely valuable for emergency managers and local response professionals to utilize for local mass care shelters or volunteer reception centers or at the federal level for disaster recovery centers. Organizations like the University of Washington's Pacific Rim Visualization and Analytics Center (PARVAC) and the Human Interface Technology (HIT) Laboratory in New Zealand are exploring various applications for augmented reality within governmental and disaster response sectors.[29]

Additionally, some augmented reality systems allow for the recognition of landmarks, topography, architecture, and objects within the physical environment.[30] A common example of this type of augmented reality technology is Google Goggles, which allows for landmarks and other well-known areas to be recognized and associated with background information and content already available from public sources such as governmental websites or Wikipedia.[31] This type of application would be extremely valuable to emergency managers and related disciplines at various stages of disaster activities. For instance, since the Great Flood of 1993, many emergency managers and residents in the midwestern United States have been concerned about how current flooding risks might compare to the 1993 benchmark; however, this type of activity is often only available on two-dimensional mapping projections provided by floodplain managers in the area. However, to utilize augmented reality to stand in specific locations and visualize the flooding estimates and how they compare to the benchmark floods would be valuable to better ascertain what local properties and infrastructure might be at risk from current conditions or the conditions created after projected response or mitigation activities.

Practitioner Profile: Cheryl Bledsoe, Clark Regional Emergency Services

As the director of the Clark (Washington) Regional Emergency Services Agency and an avid user and proponent of social media, Cheryl Bledsoe (Figure 13.9) is in a unique position to speak to the current and future potential uses of social media by emergency managers. Ms. Bledsoe's understanding and influence of social media implementation is further reflected in her numerous national speaking engagements, membership on the U.S. Department of Homeland Security's Virtual Social Media Working Group, and establishment of the Social Media for Emergency Management website (www.sm4em.org). When asked why it is important for the

Figure 13.9   Cheryl Bledsoe.

emergency management community to implement social media, Ms. Bledsoe stated that "Social media allows the emergency response community to actively listen to better collaborate and engage with their communities," which allows for "quicker response and recovery from disasters because they can tap into resources and creative solutions that might not originally be seen by emergency responders." However, she stressed that "Emergency response planning still requires much face-to-face collaboration to build relationships…[but] webinars, wikis and collaborative technologies can replace some meetings…but will never be fully replaced by technology." Regarding the future, Ms. Bledsoe stated that SMS technologies continue to show strong resiliency, but "specific technologies change so quickly that it's hard to know what will be popular in 10 years…[as] collaboration-based technologies like Skype and Yammer allow for voice, chat, and archiving capabilities." In closing, Ms. Bledsoe stated that the single biggest impact of utilizing social media for her organization has been "better dialogue and direction relationships with our community… [where] people ask questions more directly about emergency preparedness…[which] has specifically impacted volunteer recruitment efforts, especially when there are short-term needs."

Chapter Terms

Augmented reality: Generic technology term to describe live views of a real physical environment that is augmented by computer-generated multimedia formats, including sounds, videos, or graphics.

QR codes: Two-dimensional square bar code that can be user generated and that includes embedded content such as links to websites, text, photos, or videos and read by mobile application readers.

Location-based social networking: Social networking based on connectivity between geospatial relationships such as local buildings, shops, governmental buildings, or user-named sites.

Geospatial programming: User-controlled public presentation of combined public geospatial layers on a publicly accessible internet map.

Chapter Questions

General Questions

1. Which of the following is not a location-based social networking system?
   a. Google Latitude
   b. Foursquare
   c. Gowalla
   d. Google Earth

2. Which is not a geospatial technology system?
    a. Virtual USA
    b. VIPER
    c. GATOR
    d. TIGER
3. True/False: QR codes are widely utilized by emergency management.

Essay Questions

1. Discuss security concerns versus benefits of utilizing location-based social networking for emergency management activities.
2. Discuss the possible uses of QR codes and augmented reality for emergency management activities.
3. Consider the impact on traditional disaster response from the utilization of location-based social networking, QR codes, and augmented reality.

Works Cited

1. "April 15–16, 2011 Tornado Outbreak." *Wikipedia*. http://en.wikipedia.org/wiki/April_14%E2%80%9316,_2011_tornado_outbreak (accessed March 3, 2011).
2. Pardon, Charles C. Duncan. "Mapping Raleigh Tornado Damage." *Raleigh Public Record*, April 22, 2011. http://www.raleighpublicrecord.org/news/2011/04/22/mapping-raleigh-tornado-damage/ (accessed March 3, 2011).
3. "4Square Badges List." *4Square Badges List*, 2011. http://www.4squarebadges.com/foursquare-badge-list/
4. "Foursquare." *Wikipedia*. http://en.wikipedia.org/wiki/Foursquare_(social_network)#cite_note-3 (accessed March 3, 2011).
5. "...So We Grew 3400% Last Year." *Foursquare Blog*, January 24, 2010. http://blog.foursquare.com/2011/01/24/2010infographic/ (accessed March 3, 2011).
6. Swartz, Jon. "The Latest from Gowalla Is Worth Checking Out." *USAToday*, December 2, 2010. http://content.usatoday.com/communities/technologylive/post/2010/12/the-latest-from-gowalla-is-worth-checking-out/1 (accessed March 3, 2011).
7. Siegler, M. G. "Where Is Google Hiding the 9 Million Active Users?" *TechCrunch*, December 14, 2010. http://techcrunch.com/2010/12/14/google-latitude/ (accessed March 3, 2011).
8. Siegler, M. G. "Please Rob Me Makes Foursquare Useful for Burglars." *TechCrunch*, February 17, 2010. http://techcrunch.com/2010/02/17/please-rob-me-makes-foursquare-super-useful-for-burglars/ (accessed March 3, 2011).
9. "Pages—Virtual USA." *DHS First Responders*. http://www.firstresponder.gov/Pages/VirtualUSA.aspx (accessed March 3, 2011).
10. "Welcome to Virtual Alabama." *Alabama Department of Homeland Security*, 2011. https://www.virtual.alabama.gov/ (accessed March 3, 2011).
11. "Google Earth." Wikipedia. http://en.wikipedia.org/wiki/Google_Earth (accessed March 3, 2011).

12. "Media Coverage of Geospatial Platforms." *Geospatial Web*, 2007. http://www.geospatialweb.com/figure 4 (accessed March 3, 2011).
13. "Resources Related to the 2011 Japan Crisis." *Google Crisis Response*, 2011. http://www.google.com/crisisresponse/japanquake2011.html (accessed March 3, 2011).
14. "Using the National Flood Hazard Layer Web Map Service (WMS) in Google Earth™." *FEMA Mapping Information Platform*. https://hazards.fema.gov/femaportal/wps/portal/NFHLWMSkmzdownload (accessed March 3, 2011).
15. "Haiti Earthquake 2010." *OpenStreetMap*. http://haiti.openstreetmap.nl/ (accessed March 3, 2011).
16. "ESRI Disaster Response." *ESRI*. http://www.esri.com/services/disaster-response/index.html (accessed March 3, 2011).
17. "Public Safety: ESRI's Response Program. *ESRI Blog*, May 31, 2011. http://blogs.esri.com/Dev/blogs/publicsafety/archive/2011/05/31/Esri_1920_s-Disaster-Response-Program.aspx (accessed July 3, 2011).
18. "How Does This Work?" *Google Flu Trends*, 2009. http://www.google.org/flutrends/about/how.html (accessed March 3, 2011).
19. Westly, Erica. "Tracking H1N1: Google Trends Go Global." *FastCompany*, October 8, 2009. http://www.fastcompany.com/blog/erica-westly/science-inc/google-flu-trends-gets-global (accessed March 3, 2011).
20. "QR Code." *Wikipedia*. http://en.wikipedia.org/wiki/QR_codes (accessed March 3, 2011).
21. Haisler, Dustin. "Redefining Government Communications with QR Codes." *City of Manor*, September 2009. http://www.scribd.com/doc/23990715/QR-code-Whitepaper (accessed March 3, 2011).
22. "QR Codes in Emergency Management." Dustin Haisler presentation at Midwest Disasters Social Media Workshop, 2011.
23. "Japan's Earthquake and Tsunami: How QR Codes Could Have Helped." *BeQRious*, 2011. http://www.beqrious.com/show/japan-s-earthquake-and-tsunami-how-qr-codes-could-ve-helped (accessed March 3, 2011).
24. "Augmented Reality." Wikipedia. http://en.wikipedia.org/wiki/Augmented_reality (accessed March 3, 2011).
25. "History of Mobile Augmented Reality." *ISMAR Society*. https://www.icg.tugraz.at/~daniel/HistoryOfMobileAR/ (accessed March 3, 2011).
26. Azuma, Ronald T. "A Survey of Augmented Reality." *In Presence: Teleoperators and Virtual Environments*, August 1997. http://www.cs.unc.edu/~azuma/ARpresence.pdf (accessed March 3, 2011).
27. "Augmented Reality for Army Medics in New Plan." *Wired*, May 17, 2011. http://www.wired.com/dangerroom/2011/05/augmented-reality-for-army-medics-in-new-plan/ (accessed March 3, 2011).
28. Rees, Dianne. "QR Codes, Augmented Reality, and Health Learning." *Instructional Design Fusions Blog*, September 30, 2010. http://instructionaldesignfusions.wordpress.com/2010/09/30/qr-codes-augmented-reality-and-learning-for-health/ (accessed March 3, 2011).
29. Haselkorn, Mark. "Just-In-Time Command and Control Center (JITC3)." *Pacific Rim Visualization and Analytics Center, University of Washington*. http://parvac.washington.edu/projects/view.php?shortname=jitc3 (accessed March 3, 2011).
30. Parr, Ben. "Top 6 Augmented Reality Mobile Apps." *Mashable*, August 19, 2009. http://mashable.com/2009/08/19/augmented-reality-apps/ (accessed March 3, 2011).

31. "Google Goggles." Wikipedia. http://en.wikipedia.org/wiki/Google_Goggles (accessed March 3, 2011).
32. Do, Trang. "Software Developed in Huntsville Helped in Tornado Response." *WAFF 48 News*, June 1, 2011. http://www.waff.com/story/14820404/software-developed-in-huntsville-helped-in-tornado-response?clienttype=printable (accessed March 3, 2011).
33. "Foursquare Surpasses 10 Million Users." *Mashable*, June 20, 2011. http://mashable.com/2011/06/20/foursquare-10-million/ (accessed March 3, 2011).

Chapter 14

Get Your Head into the Cloud: Available Tools and Systems to Improve Emergency Management Functions

Privacy is dead, and social media holds the smoking gun.

—Pete Cashmore, Mashable CEO[1a]

Chapter Objectives

- To evaluate the characteristics of the open government movement
- To consider the impact of "gamification" on the use of Web 2.0 systems for emergency and disaster management activities
- To evaluate potential social media and Web 2.0 solutions to functional and accessible needs challenges
- To identify social media and Web 2.0 improvements to emergency management operational efficiency
- To identify the potential utilization of collaborative and contributory systems

DISASTER FOCUS—JAPAN EARTHQUAKE AND TSUNAMI (2011)

On Friday, March 11, 2011, an undersea earthquake occurred off the coast of Japan that registered a magnitude 9.0 (Mw). The so-called 2011 Tōhoku earthquake or Great East Japan earthquake was the most powerful earthquake known to have hit Japan and one of the five most powerful earthquakes ever recorded in the world. (See Figure 14.1.) The earthquake triggered a destructive tsunami with waves up to 120 feet high that traveled in some cases up to six miles inland. There were more than 900 aftershocks, with approximately 60 registering over magnitude 6.0 Mw and 3 over 7.0 Mw. The Japanese National Police Agency confirmed more than 15,000 deaths, 5,000 additional injuries, and 125,000 buildings damaged across 18 prefectures (local jurisdictions). Approximately 4.4 million households in northeastern Japan were left without electricity and 1.5 million without water immediately after the incident. Additionally, the earthquake and subsequent tsunami caused a number of nuclear accidents, including the meltdown of three reactors in the Fukushima I Nuclear Power Plan complex. Specifically, the nuclear reactors in question suffered explosions due to hydrogen gas that built up after internal cooling system failures. Residents within a 10-kilometer radius of the nuclear power plant were evacuated. Local emergency management and government officials estimated that the disaster costs were more than US$300 billion. Additionally, geologists confirmed that the earthquake moved Honshu (Japan's main island) 8 feet east and shifted the Earth on its axis by 4–10 inches.[1] This disaster was catastrophic and far beyond the scope experienced by Japan or any other country in the world. Consequently, the use and utilization of social media was also unmatched by other previous disasters or emergencies. For instance, there were approximately 1,200 tweets per minute immediately after the disaster, which is an astronomical rate of information exchange and strongly indicates both the intense distribution of information in and out of Japan for various reasons.[2] A similar level of activity was found on Facebook, where there were 4.5 million status updates from 3.8 million users across the world on March 11 that mentioned keywords such as "Japan" or "earthquake."[5] A Ushahidi Crowdmap was also created for the event that accepted more than 3,000 postings.[3] Additionally, a partnership between Facebook, Save the Children, and the online social gaming company Zynga allowed users to donate money to disaster relief and recovery through the purchase of virtual goods on Zynga games (e.g., FarmVille). The impact of social media and Web 2.0 technologies on this event was so great that the U.S. embassy in Tokyo sent a letter to Americans in Japan stating, "We encourage you to continue to be in contact with your loved one(s) using SMS texting and other social media (e.g., Facebook, MySpace, Twitter, etc.) that your loved one(s) may use."[4] This letter also included a social media tool called Google Person Finder that allowed people to post messages about their whereabouts and status or seek information about a missing person. Within three days of the event, there were more than 158,000 records for the Japan event, which were 140,000 more records than had been posted for the previous international disaster one month earlier.[5] While Google Person Finder is similar to a system utilized by the American Red Cross, it is a strong indicator along with the plethora of other social media and Web 2.0 applications utilized during the Japan earthquake and tsunami that social media tools and systems are here to stay and need to be utilized and/or leveraged by emergency managers at all levels to optimize preparedness, response, and recovery activities.

Figure 14.1 View of Japan from a U.S. Navy SH-60B helicopter after the 9.0 magnitude earthquake and related tsunami struck the area. (From U.S. Navy.)

Open Government and Gamification

The cloud has long been a representative word, phrase, or context to describe something that is out of reach and unattainable to the perceiver. For instance, if a local high school baseball pitcher dreams of playing baseball as a professional but can't throw strikes during a game, he might be told to get his "head out of the clouds." The detractors might tell the pitcher that his dream is unachievable because he lacks the skills, resources, ability, resourcefulness, and so forth to accomplish the required task. In most cases, people who dream "in the clouds" eventually give up on those dreams and heed the recommendations of others that they have heard repetitiously over an extended period of time.

Emergency managers of all disciplines and types are often no different than the aforementioned baseball pitcher. Foundational and systematic structures about how, when, why, and where various emergency management activities and functions operate and are effective is often repetitiously and routinely shared from one emergency manager (or government official) to another. This pattern often creates a rigid system that is slow and possibly incapable of embracing modification and change. Similar to the baseball pitcher, the reasons for these systematic behaviors include lack of skills, resources, ability, and resourcefulness in budgetary application, training availability, and technological knowledge and comfort. Fortunately, social media and Web 2.0 technologies potentially shatter this paradigm due to the inherent and fundamental structure based on openness, robustness, flexibility, growth, and dynamic utilization at minimal to no cost. There are many social media systems that are already being utilized and/or impacting emergency and disaster response. Emergency managers can no longer wait for social media to blend with traditional functionality but rather should get their heads "in the cloud" by embracing change through the adaptation and adoption of social media systems that improve efficiency and effectiveness at a variety of levels.

In some governmental sectors and limited emergency management offices, this adaptation of social media and Web 2.0 concepts has led to a movement that is generally referred to as open government or government 2.0. Henry Chesbrough, executive director of the Center for Open Innovation at the University of California in Berkeley, was the first person to use the term *open innovation* in his book *Open Innovation: The New Imperative for Creating and Profiting from Technology* in 2003.[6] He defined open innovation as "the use of purposive inflows and outflows of knowledge to accelerate internal innovation, and expand the markets for external use of innovation, respectively."[7] This definition is expanded by well-known government 2.0 advocate and utilizer Dustin Haisler, who defined open innovation "as the ability to tap the collective knowledge of employees and/or constituents to drive agency innovation."[7] Regardless of the definition, you can begin to see the incorporation of a new style of thinking that better incorporates social media, Web 2.0, and other emerging technologies.

A prime example of open innovation for emergency and disaster management is the Sahana Software Foundation. Sahana is a nonprofit organization that focuses on the development of free and open source software to "provide services that help solve concrete problems and bring efficiencies to disaster response coordination between governments, aid organizations, civil society, and the victims themselves."[8] Since 2004, Sahana has been utilized by local and state governments for survivor reunification, shelter mapping, and tracking of volunteering organizations active in disaster response, including the Southeast Asia tsunami, Pakistan earthquake, Haiti earthquake, Joplin tornado, and Japan earthquake and tsunami.[8] (See Figure 14.2.) No longer are emergency managers or local governments required to purchase and utilize commercial products to perform these types of functions, due to the creativity, altruism, and open innovation that is being utilized by systems like Sahana.

In addition to the open equipment systems supplementing response processes, there are additional characteristics to open innovation and government 2.0 that are

Figure 14.2 Open innovation systems like Sahana were used in response and recovery to the 2011 Joplin (Missouri) tornado. (From FEMA, Steven Zumwalt.)

beginning to become more prevalent. For example, more than 200 million people play social games online each month, but what does this mean to emergency managers?[29] According to Gabe Zichermann, author of *Game-Based Marketing*, "syncing government with the governed is challenging from a systems perspective…with so many moving parts, money, competing interests and lives at stake, it's no wonder that sometimes the only way to fix things is to do a complete wipe and reinstall."[9] Consequently, some governmental agencies are beginning to implement components of a phenomenon known as "gamification." Zichermann defines gamification as "the use of game-thinking and game mechanics to solve problems and engage audiences…[that can] transform organizations and systems…to understand what drives [citizens] to succeed and what 'journey' they are on."[9] Most experts agree that fundamentally the gamification concept is the incorporation of any concept, systematic tool, or structure device that builds in gaming structures such as short- and long-term objectives, timelines, and challenges that facilitate competition.

This gamification concept was present in incentivized programs through the XPrize Foundation and the 2010 America COMPETES Act that specifically allowed and encouraged U.S. government agencies the authority to use prizes and challenges to solve problems of national importance.[9] Within the emergency management community, gamification has yet to be widely embraced; however, there are some areas that have successfully implemented the strategy. Many emergency management organizations across all disciplines have long utilized games for educational opportunities, but gamification is much more complex than that. For example, the Clark Regional Emergency Services Agency (CRESA) in Washington state has implemented several emergency preparedness games, including the "12 Days Prepared" and "30 Days, 30 Ways" challenges that were used during 2010 and 2011. CRESA utilized Facebook, Twitter, and a local blog as well as daily objectives and an ultimate financial reward to encourage, provide incentive, and gamify the preparedness process. Likewise, the Great Hurricane Blowout created by the Federal Alliance for Safe Homes (FLASH) utilized achievable objectives over various stages to increase preparedness efforts for hurricanes. They also combined public and private funding and activities to allow people to collect goods for emergency preparedness kits that could be publicly reported via social media and then donated to economically challenged families. These types of creative gamifications have shown excellent results at improving emergency preparedness and improving the overall public perception about when, why, and where to be prepared.

Functional and Accessibility Challenges

Emergency managers across all public safety disciplines must also strive to find ways to strategically utilize emerging technologies for applications that go beyond the straightforward uses of social media that have already been discussed in this book. Specifically, there are a variety of social media and Web 2.0 systems that can supplement and/or replace operational and planning components or systems during all phases of emergency management in a more effective and efficient way. As open government opportunities increase, so will the applications of these systems to address needs and considerations currently administratively or financially challenging to emergency managers.

For instance, emergency managers have long been challenged by the need to communicate with all citizens within their community regardless of any social, economic, or physical characteristics. Citizens or groups of citizens within a given community often have functional or access needs that are exacerbated during an emergency or disaster that must be addressed in planning and preparedness. Although no single definition exists, these functional and access needs are often broken down into five categories: economic disadvantage, language proficiency, physical disabilities, age vulnerability, and cultural or geographical isolation. There are significant challenges for many individuals with functional needs to utilize social media in the traditional way because many of these systems are not built to embrace this unique consideration. For instance, many social networking and microblogging sites require the use of a visual verification system (e.g., Completely Automatic Public Turing Test to Tell Computers and Humans Apart, CAPTCHA) in an attempt to minimize bots and other malicious computer systems from logging into these systems artificially. Unfortunately, these types of visual verification systems are not easily interpreted by those with vision impairment, dyslexia, or other learning difficulties.[13] Although some systems have begun to utilize audio verification systems, these systems still systematically challenge some functional needs.[27] Likewise, a 2011 Pew Internet study found that persons with disabilities access the internet 23% less often than those without disabilities.[14] Consequently, much like traditional communication strategies, once emergency managers begin to implement social media strategies, they must consider how to ensure it is effectively used for the whole community.

However, there are some positive examples where social media and Web 2.0 systems are helping create tools for emergency managers to use to address these functional and accessible needs considerations. For instance, social media systems like EasyChirp provide alternatives to mainline systems like Twitter that are designed to be easier to use and be optimized for disabled users.[11] EasyChirp was even the recipient of the American Foundation for the Blind's 2011 Access Award due to its efficiency and effectiveness at addressing this particular functional need.[11] Similarly, YouTube has had the capability since 2009 to add closed captioning to all posted YouTube videos to improve the experience for people who are deaf or hard of hearing. Although YouTube can only add video captions in English, the Google translation capability can convert the captions into any one of 51 languages.[12] Due to federal laws, systematic components like video captioning are required for social media and Web 2.0 systems used by federal government agencies, but that application is not uniformly applied across state and local governments.

Hackers, Zombies, and Second Life: Potential Improvements to Operational Efficiency

Emergency managers across all disciplines must also consider applying Web 2.0 and emerging technologies against functional and systematic processes that could be improved by its use. This improvement could potentially produce more effective processes or provide cheaper and more cost-effective options to technologies only currently available or applied via commercial means. For instance, law enforcement and public safety officials utilize commercial applications for facial recognition if the investigation warrants such action and it is available for use by the particular department. However, since Facebook and Google Photos added the capability of facial recognition within their systems, this is an extremely valuable application for law enforcement to consider in replacement of or in addition to commercial systems. Moreover, with Facebook reportedly adding more than 100

IN A NUTSHELL

The web is at a really important turning point right now. Up until recently, the default on the web has been that most things aren't social and most things don't use your real identity. We're building toward a web where the default is social.

—Mark Zuckerberg, Facebook co-founder

million photos and photo tags per day, the database of photos is not a trivial database of potential matches.[15]

In addition to the potential improvements to operational efficiency, there are a growing number of opportunities for emergency management professionals to consider Web 2.0 and emerging technologies as real and conceivable alternatives to current models of operation. For instance, the modernization of materials has quickly pushed computers, monitors, mobile devices, and personal interfaces to be thinner, lighter, and faster. These types of physical changes often outpace application changes considered by emergency managers. Unfortunately, that process must change to be more inclusive of emerging technologies, particularly in light of tough economic times that are limiting procurement of expensive commercial systems. For example, third-party developers have hacked the capability of the Xbox Kinect technology to mimic the control and engagement of a traditional computer mouse.[16] Consequently, although this example is not legally condonable, the application of these seemingly unrelated technologies might have significant application in Emergency Operations Centers (EOCs), Incident Command Posts (ICPs), Joint Information Centers (JICs), or other technology-intensive environments where visual displays are critical to the exchange of information.

In addition to response applications, there are numerous social media and Web 2.0 systems that have emergency preparedness applications as well. For instance, creatively applying social media and Web 2.0 systems to improve emergency preparedness activities has been a calling card of the U.S. Centers for Disease Control and Prevention (CDC). The CDC was one of the first national response agencies to implement an organized and strategic implementation of social media systems. For instance, in August 2006 the CDC set up a virtual community within Second Life to offer health information to system users that paralleled real-world information.[17] Second Life creates a three-dimensional world that has predefined ownership areas (called islands), communities, and person-to-person engagement for more than 3 million users. Although a fringe social media system when compared to the likes of Facebook, Twitter, and YouTube, the use of Second Life is an interesting and cost-effective method of improving upon emergency preparedness activities. For example, the CDC in conjunction with the University of Illinois at the Chicago School of Public Health has built virtual islands in Second Life to simulate public points of mass prophylaxis dispensing in response to various bioterrorism events.[18] These islands are detailed, virtual representations of real sites, layouts, and characteristics that impact the efficiency and effectiveness of response. In addition to being inherently interesting, utilizing Second Life for training and exercise evaluations is extraordinarily cost effective. For instance, utilizing this format would eliminate the need to pay extra personnel for overtime or backfill and would eliminate the actual procurement and use of expendable materials without significant reduction to operational takeaways or conclusions.

Another phenomenally creative application of social media was the 2011 CDC "Zombie Apocalypse." (See Figure 14.3.) While seemingly totally unrelated to

Figure 14.3 The zombie preparedness widget released by the Centers for Disease Control and Prevention (CDC) as part of their public preparedness campaign. (From CDC.)

emergency preparedness efforts that are ordinarily pushed by emergency management and preparedness officials, the CDC found a unique way to leverage the significant subculture throughout the world interested in all things related to zombies. Hollywood has produced a string of zombie-related movies, including "Night of the Living Dead," "Dawn of the Dead," "28 Days Later," "Resident Evil," "Shaun of the Dead," and "Zombieland," to name a few.[19] To tap into this strong interest in zombies, the CDC posted to the Public Health Matters Blog in May 2011 an entry written by Assistant Surgeon General Ali Khan that feigned the need for basic emergency preparedness in case of a zombie invasion.[20] This creative social media campaign was so popular that by the end of the first day of the campaign the CDC had received more than 60,000 hits to the page, which was six times greater than any previous blog entry. This level of internet demand was so great that the CDC servers supporting the page actually crashed in the process.[21] This type of proverbial "out of the box" thinking is a phenomenal example of utilizing social media and Web 2.0 systems to maximize the impact of emergency preparedness functions across all disciplines and operational phases.

Additional Web 2.0 and Social Media Tools

There are numerous additional tools that are available to emergency managers that are currently underutilized and have the strong potential to improve not only operational challenges but day-to-day tasks and activities as well. For instance, there are various challenges that emergency managers face within their own organizations, including issues related to office productivity, collaboration, system enhancement, and resource allocation. In each case, one or more social media systems exist that can improve upon these challenges and/or create a bridge between commercial systems commonly deployed and new social media systems that are robust.

The first and perhaps most pervasive of these common issues is related to office productivity. While there are numerous robust commercially available systems such as Microsoft Office and IBM Lotus Notes that handle administrative and productivity functions including email, calendar, contacts, tasks, and peer-to-peer communications as well as internal websites, these systems can sometimes be challenging for usability and interoperability. However, these functions are replicated via social media and Web 2.0 systems in ways that are often more integrated with other communication systems and as robust as commercial products. For instance, Google maintains a suite of applications that are designed to allow the end user to have functionality that is similar in look and fully compatible with the structure and extensions available through the commercial systems already mentioned. Specifically, Google Docs is a suite of apps that allow documents, spreadsheets, and presentations to be stored within the Google system and modified on demand while maintaining controlled levels of public access to these materials. Likewise, because of Google's strong connectedness between its various systems, Google Docs also interfaces with Gmail (Google's email system), which in turn allows for calendar, contacts, and tasks functionality.

Individual users have access to this spectrum of Web 2.0 office productivity systems for free as long as it is in association with a Google account that has been created. However, the suite of Google products has also been collected and provided to small, medium, and large businesses as an enterprise-wide option for office and administration productivity. According to Google, over 3 million companies have adopted their suite of products across their organizations and saved money without any loss of system reliability or robustness.[22] For example, in 2009 the City of Los Angeles adopted a contract with Google to provide systemwide application of its products in replacement of a commercial system widely used. This change was projected to save the city $13.8 million over the course of the contract.[23] Additionally, Google's office productivity apps also include programs specifically designed to ensure electronic record retention, e-discovery, and other complex compliance issues that organizations of all sizes must be aware of and that are often considered hindrances to Web 2.0 implementations.[24] Although not free when applied by businesses, these Google apps are evidence of the potential for radical impacts from Web 2.0 applications on traditional systems.

Google is not the only provider of office productivity systems within the Web 2.0 sphere. For instance, OpenOffice is a third-party provider of open and free software that will create and edit documents, spreadsheets, and presentations that are compatible with commercial systems and widely acceptable.[25] Other productivity systems such as TimeBridge and Doodle allow users to allow for group feedback about calendared events such as meetings, presentations, and vacations to

Figure 14.4 The difficulty of scheduling complex meetings with representatives from various organizations can often be remedied by the use of social media and Web 2.0 tools like Doodle. (From FEMA, George Armstrong.)

efficiently select the most agreeable condition. This type of functionality is much more efficient than traditional processes that require paper trails or strings of emails to suggest, counterpropose, and confirm dates, especially when multiple people across different organizations are involved. (See Figure 14.4.) Lastly, address books and contacts are often dispersed across a variety of platforms, including written address books, email programs, mobile devices, and various personal and social networking sites. Consequently, social media systems like Plaxo allow for all of these address sites to be synced automatically to ensure accuracy and redundancy of this critical personal and business information.

Web 2.0 and social media applications are not limited to office productivity products such as spreadsheets and word processing. Emergency managers and office professionals throughout the world are also impacted by the type of web browser they use on a variety of levels. Certain webpages or support systems operate only on certain web browsers while others are considered more robust or efficient at uploading pages and content. In all browser systems, users are given the capability to place bookmarks in the browser that link to certain websites that may be of interest or operational applicability in the future. Unfortunately, these links are inherently attached to that specific browser on that particular computer, which means that an emergency manager working in his office will be unable to utilize those bookmarks while utilizing another computer in response to an incident. This type of disconnection can lead to a delay in information retrieval as system addresses must be recalled manually. However, social media and Web 2.0 systems can address this challenge through social bookmarking.

Social bookmarking sites allow users to access and potentially share their internet bookmarks via any computer that has internet access because the links are stored on third-party servers and retained until they are needed. Furthermore, these links can be categorically tagged to allow for natural groupings that are independent of file and folder hierarchy, unlike most traditional browser bookmarking. These sites also allow for sharing of some or all of the bookmarked sites, which indicates the possibility of a powerful tool for emergency managers across all disciplines that may not always be working in the same location or may need access to stored links in various response conditions. Sites such as Delicious, Diigo, Evernote, and Google Bookmarks are commonly utilized social bookmarking systems. Each is structured differently and maintains slightly modified functionality, but the basic concept is applicable across these systems.

In addition to social bookmarking, there are other social media and Web 2.0 sites that allow for the collection and distribution of large files such as presentations. These bulk sending and sharing sites again allow for these large files to be stored on third-party servers operated by the social media system and accessed via generated web links that are typically available for a short period of time (e.g., no more than 14 days). This allows the third-party servers to only have to store the content for a relatively short period of time before it is replaced by another file from a different user. Common examples of this type of system include YouSendIt, MegaUpload, and DropSend. However, these systems seem to be constantly in flux as technology changes and as major internet mail carriers buy out the company and integrate its benefits into primary email systems. Other systems like SlideShare allow presentations and large files to be uploaded to a user's site and shared through an embedded player on the site. In all cases, the capability to share large files such as presentations not only minimizes the impact to email systems on both ends but also allows long-term accessibility and easy storage of a variety of content that could include important training documents or educational materials.

Another powerful social media tool that can be utilized by emergency managers to optimize office productivity and ensure mobile access to files is online file storage systems. Sites such as MyOtherDrive, DropBox, Carbonite, Amazon Cloud, and Google Docs allow for the upload of files of nearly any type to third-party servers, much like localized servers utilized by emergency managers within their own organizations. While localized servers have a much larger capacity, online storage sites currently maintain up to 5 GB of storage per user for free with additional capacity available for small fees.[26] These online storage sites are backed up and are as much or more redundant than localized systems because of the size and resources dedicated to the network itself. Additionally, much like the social bookmarking, these online storage sites often have access levels that allow the original user to control which files are available for download for specific individuals or to the general public. This type of capacity is extremely valuable not only as a form of inexpensive redundancy but for emergency managers across all disciplines to utilize these types of storage sites for quick file storage and transfer as well as the creation of user-controlled networks that are not usually controlled or limited by localized information technology filters.

Collaborative and Contributory Systems

Emergency management during all phases and across all disciplines is inherently collaborative. Because of the overwhelming characteristics of emergencies and disasters, individual agencies or responders are often incapable of handling the situation themselves and therefore must establish strong partnerships with other agencies and responders to ensure preparedness, response, or recovery activities are efficiently and effectively managed to address the most pressing issues. Fortunately, social media and Web 2.0 systems also add significant collaborative capabilities to the spectrum of tools available to emergency managers. The needed collaboration must go beyond simply working together to include nearly simultaneous creation and editing of information and materials to reduce the time it takes for review and approval of activities related to the operation.

For instance, per national response models, any internal working documents, situation reports, or press releases must be created by individual sections and then reviewed by the chain of command within the organization with ultimate approval by the incident commander or Emergency Operations Center management. As already discussed in Chapter 10, this process takes time that can adversely impact the distribution and reception of information during a disaster. The need to reduce this review and approval time as well as other real-world needs for quick and clear collaboration is a strong indicator of why real-time collaborative editing systems are becoming extremely useful to emergency managers across all disciplines.

Real-time collaborative editing systems allow for multiple users to edit and review a created document simultaneously within an online interface. Many of these systems support chat functionality as well as change tracking protocols to allow group dynamics to naturally progress in a similar fashion to traditional review and approval processes that are defined by group creation. Some real-time collaborative editing systems are based on wiki-sourcing where material is added by an individual and saved but is always editable by other individuals or groups of individuals with access to the information. From a commercial standpoint, Microsoft SharePoint is being widely utilized using this style for internal communications and collaborations because of its availability, ease of use, and integration with other Microsoft Office products like Excel and Access. However, wikis are only one component of collaborating editing and are not always supported within an individual agency or response structure. Consequently, real-time collaborating creation systems like Zoho Writer, PiratePad, TypeWith.Me, and the all-encompassing Google Docs allow for selected users to simultaneously edit and change documents. Utilizing these tools to improve the pace and efficiency is extremely

Figure 14.5 Emergency managers must be cautious when utilizing photos available from the internet that support their needs because the rights to the photo like this one are potentially owned by someone else. (From Mike Hall, Olathe [Kansas] Fire Department.)

powerful. For example, a press release is much more likely to get command and control approval if it has already been edited and reviewed by personnel in the various response sections.

Emergency managers are also often in need of pictures, videos, and graphics to support various education and outreach efforts in support of preparedness, response, recovery, and mitigation activities. While some emergency managers are active photographers and videographers, the vast majority of emergency managers will simply seek out pictures, videos, and graphics from websites that support the information they are trying to present. Unfortunately, there is some legal liability in this action that is often overlooked by emergency managers. (See Figure 14.5.) In all cases, photos that are available on the internet are owned by the original photographer or the publisher who maintains the rights of when and where their photos and videos can be reused or republished. Consequently, it is technically illegal for emergency managers to download and utilize photos available from Google Images or Flickr Photos unless permission is stated. However, there is a nonprofit organization and movement called Creative Commons that according to its website "develops, supports, and stewards legal and technical infrastructure that maximizes digital creativity, sharing, and innovation."[28] Ultimately, Creative Commons has helped established a set of copyright licenses and tools that help create fair user-generation rights while allowing a standardized way for certain uses of the created work to be used in selected ways. According to Creative Commons leaders, this type of functionality is a fair and effective way to further maximize the potential of the internet without loss of creator rights. This type of pre-established sharing policy is occasionally provided by a larger agency such as the Federal Emergency

Table 14.1 Social Media and Web 2.0 Productivity Systems

	Documents	Spreadsheets	Presentations	Record Retention	Calendar	Contacts	Scheduling	Bookmarking	Bulk Sending	Online Storage	Collaborative Edits
Amazon Cloud										X	
Carbonite										X	
Delicious								X			
Diigo								X			
Doodle							X				
DropBox										X	
Evernote								X			
Gmail					X	X					
Google Bookmarks								X			
Google Docs	X	X	X	X						X	X
MyOtherDrive										X	
OpenOffice	X	X	X								
PiratePad											X
Plaxo						X					
SlideShare									X		
TimeBridge							X				
TypeWith.Me											X
YouSendIt									X		
Zoho Writer											X

Management Agency (FEMA) to allow emergency managers at all levels to use high-quality and professional photography.

Practitioner Profile: Kim Stephens, Emergency Management Researcher, Practitioner, and Blogger

Kim Stephens (Figure 14.6) has over a decade of emergency management (EM) experience as a researcher and practitioner at all levels of government. As of 2010, Ms. Stephens became the lead blogger for the iDisaster 2.0 blog and a national advocate for the use of social media by emergency management professionals. Ms. Stephens quickly identified that most emergency managers are not thoroughly utilizing social media systems primarily because of issues related to policy, training, staffing, and desire. When asked how emergency managers can begin to address this issue and utilize social media, Ms. Stephens stated that "Participation is key, even before a crisis, because it helps organizations understand the 'culture' and language of the medium, [and] increase the chance that their information will be shared with the broadest possible audience." Assessing success is another complex

Figure 14.6 Kim Stephens.

issue that was addressed by Ms. Stephens. Specifically, she stated, "It should be noted that goals for social media do differ based on the phase of emergency management…[for example] during the mitigation/preparedness phase a goal…might be to engage citizens with emergency preparedness information, but how can you measure success of such a mushy concept as engagement?" She went on to say that this type of return on investment (ROI) evaluation is no different from traditional preparedness strategies that can only really measure how many flyers were handed out or how many people attended an event rather than how many took action and implemented the preparedness directive. Ms. Stephens goes on to state that mobile communications, gamification, and geospatial technologies will define the next generation of challenges for emergency mangers. For instance, she states that gamification is the "process based on rewarding behavior change, not necessarily with tangible rewards, such as cash or 'stuff,'…[but] intangible items including status," which is completely foreign to the common emergency manager. She concludes by stating, "These three items really just represent the tip of the iceberg…[and] that it will be important for the EM community to stay abreast of changing technologies that can help and improve the application of emergency management."

Chapter Terms

Open government: Process of utilizing the knowledge, skills, and abilities of employees, constituents, and other stakeholders to encourage and facilitate innovation within governmental organizations. This is sometimes called government 2.0.

Gamification: Concept of utilizing gaming principles like competitive behaviors, achievable goals, and timelines into the application of social media and Web 2.0 outreach systems.

Visual verification systems: Social media and Web 2.0 systems that utilize third-party systems for verification when inputting certain information that could otherwise be mimicked by malicious computer systems to gain access to the original system.

Social bookmarking: Capability to bookmark and categorize web links to a third-party Web 2.0 system, eliminating dependency on individual web browsers.

Bulk sending and storage: Utilization of third-party Web 2.0 systems that allow for the storage and distribution of large files via web-based interfaces.

Real-time collaborative editing: Third-party Web 2.0 systems that allow for multiple users to simultaneously edit and collaborate on documents.

Creative Commons: Nonprofit movement that promotes the utilization of produced media by others through the creation of various levels of licenses that allow for third-party uses based on the predetermined circumstance.

Chapter Questions

General Questions

1. Which of the following Web 2.0 systems allows for website links to be stored on a third-party site that is not limited to an individual browser on an individual computer?
   a. Bulk storage
   b. Bulk sending
   c. Social bookmarking
   d. Creative Commons
2. True/False: Emergency managers can use any picture they find on the internet as long as it is for educational purposes.
3. Which of the following is not a reason for emergency managers to consider using social media and Web 2.0 systems?
   a. Improved efficiency and effectiveness
   b. Improved collaboration
   c. Systematic redundancy
   d. Access to all available online content

Essay Questions

1. Describe the collaborative and engagement benefit to emergency managers for using the social media and Web 2.0 systems discussed in this chapter.
2. Consider how gamification concepts may positively impact emergency management practices.
3. Discuss the challenges and potential benefit of emergency managers embracing open government concepts.

Works Cited

1a. Cashmore, Pete. (2009). "Privacy is dead and social media holds the smoking gun." CNN. http://articles.cnn.com/2009-10-28/opinion/cashmore.online.privacy_1_twitter-followers-sharing-smoking-gun?_s=PM:OPINION (accessed January 9, 2012).

1. Biello, David. "Details of Japan Earthquake Explain Its Extraordinary Strength and Unexpectedness." *Scientific American*, May 19, 2011. http://www.scientificamerican.com/article.cfm?id=details-of-japan-earthquake (accessed October 30, 2011).

2. Taylor, Chris. "Twitter Reacts to Massive Quake, Tsunami in Japan." *Mashable*, March 11, 2011. http://mashable.com/2011/03/11/japan-tsunami/ (accessed April 15, 2011).

3. "Crisis Mapping Japan's Earthquake and How You Can Help." *Ushahidi Blog*, March 16, 2011. http://blog.ushahidi.com/index.php/2011/03/16/crisis-mapping-japans-earthquake-and-how-you-can-help/ (accessed April 15, 2011).

4. "Tokyo Earthquake US Embassy Message." *Mashable*, March 14, 2011, via U.S. Embassy. https://docs.google.com/a/mashable.com/leaf?id=1R7BFxeLLLELgtmG 1Sr87GX0m10eJXZZa28BjtfS4Rsw&sort=name&layout=list&num=50 (accessed April 15, 2011).

5. Kessler, Sarah. "How Facebook Users Reacted to the Japan Earthquake and Tsunami." *Mashable*, March 14, 2011. http://mashable.com/2011/03/14/how-facebook-users-reacted-to-the-japan-earthquake-tsunami-animated-graphic/ (accessed April 15, 2011).

6. "Henry Chesbrough: Open Innovation Community." *Open Innovation*, November 21, 2011. http://www.openinnovation.net/category/henry-chesbrough (accessed October 30, 2011).

7. Haisler, Dustin. "Blogging Series: 10 Ways Open Innovation Can Transform Your Agency." *GovLoop.com*, January 5, 2011. http://www.govloop.com/profiles/blogs/blogging-series-10-ways-open?xg_source=activity (accessed April 15, 2011).

8. "Products: Sahana Software Foundation." *Sahana Foundation*, 2011. http://sahanafoundation.org/products/ (accessed April 15, 2011).

9. Zichermann, Gabe. "Can Games and Gamification Fix Washington?" *Huffington Post*, February 4, 2011. http://www.huffingtonpost.com/gabe-zichermann/can-games-and-gamificatio_b_817872.html (accessed April 15, 2011).

10. "Great Hurricane Blowout: How to Breathe Easy." *Federal Alliance for Safe Homes*, 2011. http://greathurricaneblowout.org/breathe_easy.php (accessed April 15, 2011).

11. "Easy Chirp." *EasyChirp*, 2011. http://www.easychirp.com/ (accessed April 15, 2011).

12. Helft, Miguel. "Google to Caption YouTube Videos." *New York Times*, November 19, 2009. http://www.nytimes.com/2009/11/20/technology/internet/20google.html (accessed April 15, 2011).

13. "Social Networking Sites Lock Out Disabled Users." *AbilityNet.org*, January 18, 2008. http://www.abilitynet.org.uk/enation85 (accessed April 15, 2011).

14. Watters, Audrey. "Pew Internet Study Points to Challenges Americans with Disabilities Have with Internet Access." *ReadWriteWeb.com*, January 23, 2011. http://www.readwriteweb.com/archives/pew_internet_study_points_to_challenges_americans.php (accessed April 15, 2011).

15. McCarthy, Caroline. "Facial Recognition Comes to Facebook Photo Tags." *CNET News*, December 15, 2010. http://news.cnet.com/8301-13577_3-20025818-36.html (accessed April 15, 2011).

16. "Use a Hacked Kinect as a Mouse in Windows 7." *Softpedia*, November 29, 2010. http://news.softpedia.com/news/Use-a-Hacked-Kinect-as-a-Mouse-in-Windows-7-169339.shtml (accessed April 15, 2011).

17. "Second Life Lets CDC Be Everywhere—All at Once." *Air University.* http://www.au.af.mil/au/awc/awcgate/cdc/state-of-cdc-2006-2d-life.pdf (accessed April 15, 2011).

18. Hoffman, Liz, and Chris Kelly. "First Responders Meet Second Life: Public Health Enters the Virtual World." *Medill Reports Chicago*, February 4, 2009. http://news.medill.northwestern.edu/chicago/news.aspx?id=114473 (accessed April 15, 2011).

19. Franko, Kantele. "Ohio Mock Zombie Outbreak Inspired by CDC Message." *MSNBC*, 2011. http://today.msnbc.msn.com/id/45087497/ns/health/#.Tq4VTlJifNQ (accessed October 30, 2011).

20. Khan, Ali S. "Social Media: Preparedness 101: Zombie Apocalypse." *CDC Emergency Blog*, 2011. http://www.bt.cdc.gov/socialmedia/zombies_blog.asp (accessed April 15, 2011).

21. Marsh, Wendell. "CDC Zombie Apocalypse Disaster Campaign Crashes Website." *Reuters*, May 19, 2011. http://www.reuters.com/article/2011/05/19/us-zombies-idUS-TRE74I7H420110519 (accessed April 15, 2011).

22. "Businesses Share Their Stories—Google Apps." *Google*.com, 2011 http://www.google.com/apps/intl/en/customers/index.html (accessed April 15, 2011).

23. Mills, Elinor. "Los Angeles Gets Its Google Apps Groove." *CNET*, August 20, 2009. http://news.cnet.com/8301-27080_3-10313846-245.html (accessed April 15, 2011).

24. "Message Security for Google Apps, Powered by Postini." *Google*, 2011. http://www.google.com/apps/intl/en/business/security_discovery.html (accessed April 15, 2011).

25. "Why OpenOffice?" *OpenOffice*, 2011. http://why.openoffice.org/ (accessed April 15, 2011).

26. "Amazon Cloud Drive: Learn More." *Amazon*, 2011. https://www.amazon.com/cloud-drive/learnmore (accessed April 15, 2011).

27. "Usable Audio CAPTCHA." *University of Washington*. http://webinsight.cs.washington.edu/projects/audiocaptchas/ (accessed April 15, 2011).

28. "About—Creative Commons." *Creative Commons*. http://creativecommons.org/about (accessed April 15, 2011).

29. Angel, Mark. "Gamification and Customer Service—How Virtual Reality Is Changing Business." *KANA*, June 6, 2011. http://blog.kana.com/service-experience-management/gamification-and-customer-service-how-virtual-reality-is-changing-business-processes/ (accessed April 15, 2011).

Appendix A: Disasters Referenced by Chapter

	1	2	3	4	5	6	7	8	9	10	11	12	13	14
Atlanta councilman					X									
Brazil floods and landslides							X							
Chile earthquake							X		X		X			
Christchurch earthquake									X		X			
Connecticut biker	X	X												
Cyclone Nargis							X							
Deepwater Horizon oil spill		X		X			X				X	X	X	
Eau Clair (Wisconsin) mother					X									
Fargo flooding									X	X				
Fort Hood (Texas) shooting							X							
H1N1 pandemic influenza		X											X	

	1	2	3	4	5	6	7	8	9	10	11	12	13	14
Haiti earthquake							X		X		X	X	X	X
Hurricane Gustav							X							
Hurricane Ike							X							
Hurricane Katrina	X							X	X	X		X		
Icelandic volcanic eruption											X	X		
Indian Gulch (Colorado) wildfire										X				
Japan earthquake and tsunami									X		X	X	X	X
Joplin tornado														X
L'Aquila earthquake							X							
London bombings		X						X		X				
Minneapolis I-35 bridge collapse										X				
Miracle on the Hudson		X												
Mumbai financial district terrorism		X	X		X					X				
Nashville flooding											X			
North Carolina tornado outbreak											X		X	

	1	2	3	4	5	6	7	8	9	10	11	12	13	14
Pakistan earthquake														X
Pakistan floods and landslides							X				X			
Queensland floods							X				X			
Red River floods							X							
San Diego wildfires										X				
Santa Cruz wildfires							X							
Seven Signs of Terrorism video					X									
Sichuan earthquake							X							
Southeast Asian tsunami	X		X		X						X			X
Southwest Airline incident												X		
TVA's Kingston Fossil Plant leak							X							
Tuscaloosa tornado									X		X	X	X	
Typhoon Morakot							X							
Virginia Tech shooting				X						X				
Washington, DC winter storms		X									X			
Vancouver riots												X		

Appendix B: Answer Key

Chapter 1

1. True
2. False
3. Short messaging

Chapter 2

1. Twitter
2. True
3. False

Chapter 3

1. Citizen journalism
2. False
3. False

Chapter 4

1. False
2. True
3. None of the above

Chapter 5

1. False
2. All of the above
3. True

Chapter 6

1. False
2. Hashtag
3. Facebook

Chapter 7

1. True
2. False
3. All of the above

Chapter 8

1. False
2. Outdoor warning sirens
3. False

Chapter 9

1. Checkins-for-Charity
2. False
3. All of the above

Chapter 10

1. True
2. All of the above
3. Yammer

Chapter 11

1. False
2. True
3. CrisisCamp

Chapter 12

1. True
2. Streaming video
3. BlogTalkRadio

Chapter 13

1. Google Earth
2. TIGER
3. False

Chapter 14

1. Social bookmarking
2. False
3. Access to all available online content

Index